SAA
IBM's Systems
Application Architecture

Larry Press, VNR Computer Library Editor-at-Large

Larry Press is a consulting editor for the VNR Computer Library. His books are on the leading edge of computer technology, ranging over a wide area of his special interests—artificial intelligence, computer-human interaction, graphics, and new systems and architectures from major hardware companies.

Dr. Press is a Professor at California State University at Dominguez Hills and is a Contributing Editor for ACM Communications.

His titles for the VNR Library include:

Beach/INTRODUCTION TO CURVES AND SURFACES OF COMPUTER DESIGN
Burkan/EXECUTIVE INFORMATION SYSTEMS
Helgerson/CD ROM: FACILITATING ELECTRONIC PUBLISHING
Kehoe/NEWWAVE AND WINDOWS
Randesi and Czubek/SAA: IBM'S SYSTEMS APPLICATION ARCHITECTURE
Randesi and Czubek/SNA: IBM'S SYSTEMS NETWORK ARCHITECTURE
Steinhardt/WINDOW MANAGEMENT SYSTEMS

SAA
IBM's Systems
Application Architecture

Stephen J. Randesi
Donald H. Czubek

VNR VAN NOSTRAND REINHOLD
New York

Copyright © 1991 by Van Nostrand Reinhold

Library of Congress Catalog Number 91-18857
ISBN 0-442-00468-0

Manufactured in the United States of America

Published by Van Nostrand Reinhold
115 Fifth Avenue
New York, New York 10003

Chapman and Hall
2-6 Boundary Row
London, SE 1 8HN, England

Thomas Nelson Australia
102 Dodds Street
South Melbourne 3205
Victoria, Australia

Nelson Canada
1120 Birchmount Road
Scarborough, Ontario M1K 5G4, Canada

16 15 14 13 12 11 10 9 8 7 6 5 4 3 2 1

Library of Congress Cataloging in Publication Data

Randesi, Stephen J., 1947–
    SAA: IBM's Systems Application Architecture / Stephen J. Randesi,
Donald H. Czubek.
        p. cm.
    Includes index.
    ISBN 0-442-00468-0
    1. IBM Systems Application Architecture. I. Czubek, Donald H.,
1947– . II. Title
QA76.9.A73R36   1991
004.2'2—dc20

91-18857
CIP

To Diane, Karen, Jeff, and Joey—
all the inspiration I ever need.
S.J.R.

To my parents for all of their support
over the years.
D.H.C.

CONTENTS

PREFACE

When Systems Application Architecture (SAA) was introduced in March 1987, it was IBM's most significant announcement since the introduction of Systems Network Architecture (SNA) in 1974. Whereas SNA was designed to bring consistency in the communications area, SAA was designed to bring consistency to applications and the software environments available on different IBM systems. The primary focus of SAA is to support cooperative processing across IBM's major application platforms.

Like SNA, SAA is a long-term, evolutionary strategy. Indeed, since its introduction, SAA has already evolved quite significantly with several major new components added and changes to many of the original components. IBM has even evolved its strategy in various areas addressed by SAA.

SAA has received a great deal of publicity and criticism, not unlike when SNA was first introduced. Despite its slow start, SNA has become a de facto networking standard, used by a large majority of IBM's largest customers. Similarly, SAA, which is off to a slow start, should follow the same scenario.

SAA is the framework upon which applications and cooperative processing will be based in the 1990s. It will continue to evolve as IBM will shape it to meet customer and market demands and broaden it to address evolving issues. Its impact will be felt throughout the industry. Few systems, applications, or products will be unaffected by SAA.

This book is intended to provide a sound, conceptual basis and understanding of SAA. It will benefit users who may be using SAA products or contemplating whether to adopt SAA or not. It will benefit those building SAA products and those trying to compete with IBM in the SAA arena.

Part 1 of the book provides introductory material on IBM's SAA strategy, key SAA concepts, and the major elements and components of SAA. The first chapter provides important background information on SAA and why IBM developed the SAA strategy. It looks at the impact SAA will have on IBM, IBM's customers, and IBM's competitors. Chapter 2 provides a basic overview of the concepts and elements of SAA. It covers the major SAA elements, the goals of each element, and the components included in each element.

Part 2 focuses in more detail on each of the major elements of SAA. Chapter 3 provides a detailed analysis of SAA's Common User Access (CUA) element which addresses the user-interface alternatives that may be used by SAA applications.

Chapter 4 focuses on SAA's Common Programming Interface (CPI) element by looking at the programming languages and CPI services and programming interfaces that can be used in the development of SAA applications.

Chapter 5 describes the SNA and Open Systems Interconnection (OSI) components included in SAA's Common Communications Support (CCS) element. These are the components that are used to support interoperability and cooperative processing across SAA environments.

Chapter 6 looks at the characteristics of SAA Common Applications and shows how Common Applications are developed using components of the CUA, CPI, and CCS elements. Also described is IBM's first SAA Common Application, OfficeVision, and their AD/Cycle strategy for developing SAA applications.

Part 3 of the book then looks more closely at SAA's distributed services which support cooperative processing among SAA enviroments. The major SAA components used to support cooperative processing are examined. Chapter 7 examines Advanced Program-to-Program Communications (APPC)/Logical Unit 6.2 and its role and usage by SAA's Application Services architectures. Chapter 8 looks at Node Type 2.1 and its support for Low Entry Networking (LEN) peer-to-peer connectivity. It also discusses the relationship of Node Type 2.1 and LU 6.2 as well as covers Advanced Peer-to-Peer Networking (APPN). Chapter 9 examines the architectures included in CCS's Application Services category which provide the basis for SAA distributed services. Included are architectures such as Distributed Data Management (DDM), Document Interchange Architecture (DIA), SNA/Distribution Services (SNA/DS), and Distributed Relational Database Architecture (DRDA).

Chapter 10 discusses the network management requirements of SAA environments. It describes the SNA/Management Services (SNA/MS) architecture and SystemView, IBM's structure for enterprise-wide systems management.

Part 4 concludes the book with a discussion of what the future might hold in store for SAA.

part 1

INTRODUCTION

1

Introduction to Systems Application Architecture

Systems Application Architecture (SAA) is a set of guidelines that IBM has established primarily to support the development of cooperative processing applications. Cooperative processing provides the ability to distribute application programs and data across a networking environment. The design and implementation of distributed applications used in a cooperative processing environment involves not only communications and networking issues, but also many aspects of the application development process itself. SAA creates a standard environment across several otherwise incompatible IBM product lines in order to support cooperative processing among these products.

The driving force behind the trend toward cooperative processing is the migration of application processing power from large, centralized mainframe computers to distributed departmental and desktop processors. The single most important element in this migration has been the widespread use of personal computers and workstations in large enterprises.

The distribution of computing power and data across networks leads to a requirement for new levels of standardization in the computer industry. Standards must be set not only for communications between systems, but also for the structure of the application programs that will be distributed across the networks.

SAA is a single-vendor architecture which is IBM's standard for supporting cooperative processing across its major application platforms. Despite the fact that SAA is a single-vendor architecture, its impact is likely to reach far beyond IBM and its product lines because of IBM's market position in the computer industry. The greatest impact is likely to be in the large enterprises which have traditionally been major users of IBM's mainframe computers.

Other vendors in the computer industry are already adopting elements of SAA within their product lines to achieve compatibility with IBM's SAA products. This trend is likely to continue because coexistence with IBM products and architectures is important to many competitors in the computer industry and it is often a requirement of IBM's mainframe customers.

EVOLUTION OF IBM'S NETWORKING ARCHITECTURES

IBM's networking architectures have always reflected IBM's installed base of products. In order to protect its customers' investments in IBM products, an evolutionary approach is almost always IBM's strategy. IBM's first networking architecture, Systems Network Architecture (SNA), reflects this. SNA was originally announced by IBM in 1974 to set standards for the design of the networks that IBM was marketing at that time.

These networks supported a strictly hierarchical network topology for connecting nonprogrammable terminals to large mainframe computers. The end users of these networks used the nonprogrammable terminals to access the mainframe-based applications. IBM's standard interactive terminals for use with its mainframe processors were, and continue to be, the 3270 product line. Likewise, the IBM 3770 product line was the standard for batch communications with mainframes.

In addition to its mainframe terminals, another line of IBM nonprogrammable, interactive display stations and printers, called the IBM 5250 product line, is widely used by IBM customers who are users of the midrange IBM AS/400, System/36, and System/38 product lines. Similarly to 3270 terminals, which are used to access System/370 host applications, 5250 terminals are used to access application programs that reside on System/3X and AS/400 hosts.

The networking requirements imposed by nonprogrammable terminals such as these are very simple. The network only needs to be concerned with the reliable transfer of data to and from the terminal. Since the terminals were nonprogrammable, that is, essentially nonintelligent (dumb), there was little or no processing that they could perform. The nonprogrammable terminal is, in essence, little more than an input/output device that is geographically separated from its mainframe or midrange host processor.

Since dumb terminals performed no processing, the main compatibility issues were focused on the communications protocols used to interconnect these terminals to their host systems and to allow data to be exchanged between them. These are exactly the compatibility issues that SNA was designed to address.

INTELLIGENT SYSTEMS EMULATING DUMB TERMINALS

The introduction of personal computers and other intelligent workstations changed all this. These were systems that had their own application processing capability. They were no longer "dumb" devices. Users could run applications locally on these personal computers and workstations and data could be stored locally on them. They, of course, became very popular and were often desired over nonprogrammable terminals.

A problem, though, was how to move from terminals to intelligent systems without totally upsetting the apple cart. In fact, the migration from nonprogrammable terminals to intelligent workstations has been an incremental process.

Even as personal computers, workstations, and multi-user systems began to replace the old nonprogrammable terminals in SNA networks, most users continued to network the programmable systems as if they were still dumb terminals. This was accomplished by making the programmable workstations emulate the protocols and capabilities of the older 3270, 3770, and 5250 terminals.

This obviously did not make the maximum use of the workstation's computing power since the workstation was still treated as a dumb terminal. But, it made the new devices easy to integrate into the networks that were designed to support nonprogrammable terminals.

In addition to accessing host-based applications, users of personal computers and intelligent workstations also needed a method for sharing data between their systems and the host computers where most of the corporate databases reside. In response to these requirements, IBM added file transfer capabilities to the basic 3270 and 5250 communications protocols. The strengths of file transfer protocols are that they are based on existing terminal communication protocols and their use does not require modifications to the application programs that use and create the files. The latter characteristic is due to the fact that file transfer operations are decoupled from the applications. There is no real-time interaction between applications that communicate via file transfer.

This lack of coupling between applications and file transfer communications has some drawbacks, though. File transfer does not provide real-time access to remote resources. For example, if an application needs to access a record in a remote file, that file must be transferred from the remote system to the local system before access can occur. Another drawback is that the entire file must be transferred, even if only one record needs to be accessed. Finally, there is no coordination between applications running on distributed platforms; they are only coupled by the data file that is transferred.

Many new applications require a tighter coupling between the distributed applications running on host computers and intelligent distributed systems. One way this kind of interaction has been achieved is through the addition of application programming interfaces (APIs) which are designed to link distributed applications. The IBM communications API that has been most widely used in the 3270 environment is the Enhanced High-Level Language Application Programming Interface (EHLLAPI).

The EHLLAPI interface is deeply rooted in 3270 terminal emulation technology. Application programs which use this interface must actually take on the role of a terminal operator by sending 3270 keystrokes across the API. While the EHLLAPI interface does allow some real-time interaction between distributed applications, it still has limited capability. EHLLAPI is not a generalized application programming interface; it is designed to act as a front-end to existing 3270-based applications which run on IBM mainframes. It does not address the issue of peer-to-peer communications among a wide variety of intelligent systems in a network.

What was really needed was a means for two programs to communicate with one another as actual programs, in real-time as opposed to a terminal communicating with a program (or a program emulating a terminal communicating with a host program). The programs could be distributed, one running on a host system and the other running on another remote system.

SNA PROGRAM-TO-PROGRAM COMMUNICATIONS

In the early 1980s, IBM addressed the networking requirements of distributed applications by defining a set of SNA communications protocols that were specifically targeted at program-to-program communications rather than terminal-to-host connections. This set of SNA protocols is called Logical Unit Type 6.2 (LU 6.2) and is also known as Advanced Program-to-Program Communications (APPC).

LU 6.2 is specifically designed to support applications that are distributed across communications networks. Applications that use LU 6.2 can operate peer-to-peer, that is, any LU 6.2 product can communicate directly with any other LU 6.2 product in a network. Unlike the older SNA terminal emulation protocols (e.g., 3270), LU 6.2 is not limited to communications with SNA mainframe-based applications.

Another important difference between LU 6.2 and other SNA LU types is the fact that LU 6.2 provides more than just communications capabilities. LU 6.2 includes some of the capabilities provided by multi-tasking operating systems. These include the ability to initiate the execution of application programs on remote systems and to synchronize processing between distributed applications. These features create a distributed application operating environment and not just a set of protocols for exchanging data between systems. LU 6.2 is a key SAA component used to support cooperative processing and is explained in more detail in Chapter 7.

However, program-to-program communications is not the entire solution. LU 6.2 is the vehicle used for communications between distributed programs, but other issues must be addressed as well in order to provide full-scale cooperative processing.

The role of modern data communications networks is to provide not only connectivity among users of computer systems, but also to promote the sharing of an organization's information resources. In order to achieve these goals, standards must be established for both communications and application services. SNA and LU 6.2 define communications environments while SAA sets standards, not only for communications, but also for the distribution of application resources across a network.

SAA includes SNA and adds the additional standards needed to support cooperative processing. For example, distributed services such as electronic mail, document and program distribution, remote file access, remote database access, and network management are all addressed by SAA. These services are described in more detail in Chapter 9.

NETWORK COMPUTING MODELS

The migration of computing power across communications networks has led to the development of several different network computing models. These network computing models are only loosely defined within the industry, but they provide some guidelines for discussion.

The model that has become very widely used, particularly among PC users, is the client-server computing model. This model creates a hierarchy between a client system which requests services on behalf of a user, and a server which provides the service to the user. The client-server model is typically used to provide generic network services like electronic mail, remote file access, and database access, or print services.

Distributed processing is another common model. This term is generally applied to situations where a single application program runs on several different platforms that are geographically dispersed. Each of these systems provides application services to a group of users and these systems may or may not be networked. This model is characterized by the presence of a single application program at several geographic locations. Often when these distributed systems are networked, they rely on simple batch communications (like file transfer) between systems, rather than on a more interactive style of communications.

Cooperative processing is a term that is generally applied to applications that are designed to support the flexible distribution of application resources such as files, databases, and the application software itself. Cooperative processing is the network computing model that IBM has targeted with its SAA applications. The particular cooperative processing configuration that IBM focuses on is the case where part of a cooperative application resides on an SAA host and the other part runs on intelligent workstations. It should be noted that SAA's focus on workstation-host connections does not preclude its use to implement other network computing models.

FOCUS ON HOST-WORKSTATION CONNECTIVITY

While, in general, cooperative processing applications can be developed on any combination of application platforms, most of SAA's current impact has been focused on tying together host computers with user workstations such as personal computers. There are two main reasons for this focus.

One reason has to do with the current state of the computer industry and the other a function of history. The widespread use of powerful low-cost workstations, particularly personal computers, is a powerful driving force. Low-cost computing power is now available on the desktops of most enterprises. The challenge in many of these organizations is to apply that new computing power to enhance the capabilities of the old host-based application programs that have been predominant at most IBM customer sites. The host computers are mainly large IBM mainframes and, to a lesser extent, IBM midrange systems like the System/36, System/38, or AS/400 system.

The tremendous investment in these existing applications must be preserved. Other critical resources that exist on these host computers are huge corporate databases. SAA can provide the link between these host-based resources and the desktop power of personal computers and workstations. Because SAA sets standards for developing and linking distributed application programs, IBM's customers can write workstation-based applications that add value to existing host-based applications.

HOST VS. DESKTOP TRADE-OFFS

While there is clearly a trend toward locating both application software and data nearer to the end users of the network, there are a number of trade-offs that need to be considered. The level of distribution chosen for a given application might depend on a number of factors including:

> Processing power of the user workstation
> Security requirements
> Constraints on existing applications
> Size of databases and user access activity
> Response time requirements
> User interface requirements
> Data sharing requirements

The bottom line is that each application will have its own requirements which will influence the decision-making process. Within SAA, IBM has identified three basic cooperative processing configurations which, in combination, can accommodate almost any desired distribution of application processing power and/or data. These basic cooperative processing configurations are the distributed dialog model, the distributed data model, and the distributed function model. Each of these will be discussed later.

REQUIREMENTS FOR A COOPERATIVE PROCESSING ENVIRONMENT

An environment designed to support the development of cooperative processing applications must address several issues. First, these applications require a networking environment that will allow connectivity among all the resources that applications will access. This implies a decentralized networking scheme that supports peer-to-peer communications. It also means that the communications protocols must be suitable for tightly coupling application programs across a network. There is also a requirement to standardize the networking protocols used to implement generic cross-system services such as electronic mail and remote database access.

A second requirement is for a consistent application development environment across platforms. This is important because a consistent environment allows application program developers to use the same languages, programming interfaces, and development tools regardless of which platform the particular piece of software will ultimately run on. It also makes it relatively easy to migrate pieces of the application from platform to platform over time. As technologies evolve, the optimal location of network resources is sure to change.

The third major requirement for establishing a cooperative processing environment is to standardize the user interfaces of application programs that might be executing on different types of processors and supporting various types of workstations and terminals. Furthermore, these user workstations and terminals are very likely to have very different levels of processing power available to support the user interface.

These requirements are addressed as the major goals of SAA, which are to standardize user interfaces, programming environments, and communications. These goals must be satisfied in order to support cooperative processing. The result is that SAA defines standard interfaces to users, programs, and other systems in the network. These interfaces are system-independent and consistently supported on all SAA platforms.

OBJECTIVE IS MOBILITY OF APPLICATION RESOURCES

In a cooperative processing environment, one of the key objectives is to provide for the mobility of resources that are used by applications. These resources include both the functions of the application programs themselves as well as the data that is required to support these applications.

At any given point in time there is an optimal location in the network for each resource including application programs, databases and files, hardware such as printers, and the users of these systems. The application designer determines the best location for each application resource based on current economic and technical considerations. This kind of optimization is difficult to achieve, even at a single point in time. It becomes even more challenging in the real world of computing where the economics and available computing power change almost daily.

In order to minimize the cost of relocating resources within the network, the availability of consistent computing environments is essential. SAA attempts to create this consistency by standardizing the application programming environment, communications protocols for accessing remote resources, and user interfaces to applications.

The standardized application programming environment promotes the mobility of applications software. The communications protocols provide connectivity between applications as well as between applications and resources such as remote files and databases. The standard user interface allows the users of applications to move more freely from system to system. The user interface becomes the window into the network. It makes transparent to the user the location of resources that are being accessed.

IBM'S COOPERATIVE PROCESSING MODELS

Cooperative processing provides for the distribution of application resources across two or more application platforms in a network. The application designer must determine the appropriate distribution of these resources. The designer must further consider the fact that the optimal distribution will change over time.

As we indicated earlier, IBM has focused on three basic models which describe the location of resources in a cooperative processing application. These models are based on the fact that any application will be made up of three major elements that are shown in Figure 1-1.

The dialog element is the software that controls the interactions between the user and the application program. The application processing element is the software that provides the application's functionality. The data element is the software that is used to access data in files and databases.

The Standalone Model

Not all applications are based on cooperative processing. Some applications reside entirely on a single application platform. This is represented by the standalone model which is shown in Figure 1-1. While applications that conform to the standalone model are not distributed across hardware platforms, they can be structured so that they can be migrated to one of the distributed application models in the future. The standalone model is important because this is the starting point for host-based applications that use nonprogrammable terminals or intelligent workstations that emulate nonprogrammable terminals.

The Distributed Dialog Model

The distributed dialog model uses the power of intelligent workstations to implement a high-performance user interface. This model, which is shown in Figure 1-2, does not necessarily require a restructuring of the application's main func-

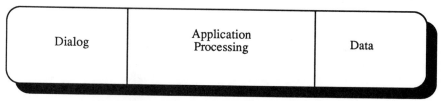

Figure 1-1. SAA standalone application model.

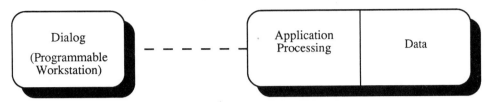

Figure 1-2. *SAA distributed dialog model.*

tional software. One of the benefits of the distributed dialog model is that it allows designers to add a new user interface to existing applications.

In the distributed dialog model, the intelligent workstation contains the software which directly interfaces to the user's display station. These workstations almost always have graphics capability which can be used to create a powerful and easy-to-use interface. The workstation will also contain the software that allows the user to navigate through the application and select functions within the application.

The distributed dialog model can also be used to provide an integrated user interface to multiple independent applications. This approach can make these separate applications appear to the user as a single, integrated application. IBM has used this strategy within its OfficeVision family of software products.

The benefits of the distributed dialog include a user interface with much higher performance and functionality than could be achieved in standalone configurations using nonprogrammable terminals. The distribution of the user interface into an intelligent workstation can also be used as the first evolutionary step in migrating mainframe-based applications into a cooperative processing environment. Since this approach to cooperative processing does not necessarily require major restructuring of the application, it can be used to preserve investments in existing host-based application software while offering at least some of the benefits of intelligent workstations to application users.

The Distributed Data Model

Access to remote files and databases is provided by the distributed data model for cooperative processing. This model allows application software running on one platform to access data which resides on one or more remote platforms.

The implementation of this model, which is shown in Figure 1-3, can be greatly simplified by the use of application-enabling software which makes

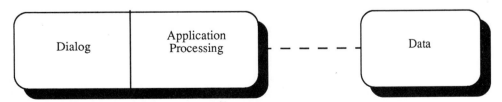

Figure 1-3. *SAA distributed data model.*

Figure 1-4. SAA distributed function model.

remote data access transparent to the application software. These enablers allow the application software to treat all files and databases as if they were local resources, while transparently accessing the requested data from any location in the network.

Examples of these application enablers would include distributed database managers and extensions to the file input/output subsystems of operating systems. These are representative of the client-server computing environments that are in widespread use, particularly on local area networks. This demonstrates that client-server computing can be accommodated within SAA.

The Distributed Function Model

The most complex cooperative processing model to implement is the distributed function model. This model, which is shown in Figure 1-4, splits the functional processing of the application program across two or more application platforms in a network. Unlike the other cooperative processing models that we have discussed, the distributed function model requires that the functional processing logic of the application be designed to be split across a network. It is very difficult to retrofit this design model into existing applications.

The distributed function model can make maximum use of distributed processing power in a network. This model is particularly effective in applications that require different kinds of processing to implement a function. For example, part of the function might be a number-crunching operation that is best implemented on a high-performance RISC (Reduced Instruction-Set Computer) processor while the rest of the function could be implemented on a small-scale personal computer.

In addition to the individual cooperative processing models that we have discussed, it is possible to combine the models into more complex arrangements. For example, the distributed function and distributed data models might be used in combination across three different SAA platforms.

HOW SAA HELPS TO IMPLEMENT COOPERATIVE PROCESSING

The cooperative processing models that we have discussed provide some guidelines for structuring cooperative processing applications across platforms. SAA defines the specific elements that designers can use to implement these applications. By providing a consistent set of programming elements on all of the SAA platforms, the applications can evolve more easily to change the distribution of application resources over time.

The three major categories of programming elements that are standardized by SAA are:

> Programming languages and interfaces
> User interface design and implementation
> Protocols for system-to-system interoperability

The standardization of programming languages and interfaces across platforms promotes the migration of application software from system to system. The user interface standards allow users to move more easily from one application platform to another with minimal retraining. The communications protocols provide a consistent level of system-to-system communications capability to tie all these systems together and to share resources.

All these SAA standards are covered in more detail in other chapters of this book. The SAA user interface design is described in detail in Chapter 3; SAA programming languages and interfaces are described in Chapter 4; SAA communications protocols that support interoperability between SAA platforms are described in Chapter 5.

SAA VS. OPEN SYSTEMS

SAA is not the only way to standardize network computing environments. There are several major industry standards, in addition to SAA, whose objective is to provide application consistency across dissimilar hardware platforms. The international effort to standardize the UNIX operating system environment is the best example of a strategy that is, in many respects, an alternative to SAA. The standards organizations such as X/Open and the Open Software Foundation (OSF) are (as IBM is doing with SAA) dealing with the standardization of the application programming environment, communications and networking, and user interfaces.

Despite the similarities, there are two major differences between IBM's SAA and these open-systems standards. The first, and probably the most obvious difference, is that SAA is a proprietary IBM architecture while the open-systems organizations are made up of many different computer manufacturers. The objective of SAA is consistency among a group of IBM systems while the objective of open-systems standards is consistency among systems from different vendors— an attempt to achieve vendor independence.

The other unique feature of SAA is that it is designed to provide consistency with IBM's existing mainframe computing environment. In fact, many of the major elements of SAA are derived from mainframe-based software products that existed before SAA was developed. SAA specifications are not identical to those of the products from which SAA is derived, though.

IBM refined the SAA specification to create an architecture that could reasonably be implemented not only on mainframes, but on a wide range of systems all the way down to desktop workstations. SAA's mainframe roots make it easier for IBM's mainframe customers to migrate computing power from the traditional host environment to midrange and desktop systems. SAA is clearly targeted at IBM's largest mainframe customers. In fact, it has been driven largely by these customers.

SAA'S IMPACT ON IBM

SAA has both an internal and an external impact on IBM. Internally, IBM is using SAA as a management tool to improve IBM's own application development productivity. IBM has a wide range of product lines that have incompatible architectures. These products include the System/370 and System/390 (System 370/390) processors, the AS/400, the Series/1 minicomputer, the RISC-based RS/6000, and the Intel-based PC and PS/2 products. These product lines are all incompatible with one another. Furthermore, each of these product lines also has one or more operating systems that are also incompatible with one another. This situation led to unnecessarily high application software development and maintenance costs for IBM.

SAA will not totally solve this problem, though, since not all of these dissimilar IBM product lines are addressed by SAA. SAA is designed to provide a high level of consistency across IBM's major general-purpose application platforms. These platforms include the System/370/390 processors, the AS/400, and the PS/2. One of the benefits of this consistency should be reduced software development costs for IBM as more of IBM's software becomes reusable across these SAA platforms. The other non-SAA platforms will still exist. While some non-SAA platforms have been made obsolete, others will remain outside the realm of SAA. How IBM will deal with these platforms which include their AIX-based offerings will be discussed in Chapter 2. SAA should also reduce IBM's ongoing maintenance and support costs for all these different systems.

SAA also has an external benefit for IBM as a marketing tool. SAA makes IBM's key application platforms appear to be a more cohesive product line. This can give IBM a competitive advantage in selling its key application platforms to customers who need a wide range of systems from personal computers to mainframes, but who require compatibility with existing mainframe applications.

SAA'S IMPACT ON IBM'S CUSTOMERS

IBM's customers have had to deal with IBM's wide range of hardware and software product offerings for many years. SAA offers some guidelines to these customers to help them identify the products and technologies that IBM considers to be strategically important. By focusing on the technologies that are part of the

SAA architecture, customers can exploit the consistent application environments across systems to minimize development costs and training requirements.

SAA is particularly attractive to IBM's base of mainframe computer customers. This is due to the fact that most of the SAA technologies are derived from software products that have existed on IBM's System/370 processors for many years. Since the mainframe customers are already familiar with these technologies, training requirements are reduced and most of these customers have software development groups who are already familiar with many of the SAA technologies.

SAA does not, in the short run, offer customers any independence from IBM application systems. This is in contrast to the industry's open-systems movement whose objective is vendor independence. As competing vendors begin to implement the SAA environment on their product lines, SAA may also provide consistency across multi-vendor product lines. This is similar to the situation in the early days of IBM's Systems Network Architecture (SNA). SNA support was originally limited to IBM products, but today virtually all of IBM's competitors also provide SNA-compatible products and almost all SNA networks contain products from multiple vendors. Many vendors in the computer industry have already announced support for at least some of the major elements of SAA.

SAA'S IMPACT ON HARDWARE AND SOFTWARE VENDORS

The impact of SAA is very different depending on the types of products that a vendor is supplying. For independent software vendors (ISVs), SAA creates a very attractive marketing opportunity. Since one of the goals of SAA is to create a standardized application development environment across IBM's otherwise incompatible product lines, ISVs can more easily build applications that will run on each of IBM's key application platforms. This potentially expands the target markets for applications that otherwise would be written to run on just one of IBM's application platforms. While expanding the market, software development costs should be reduced by allowing reuse of application elements across multiple IBM platforms.

SAA will have a very different impact on vendors of computer systems (application platforms) who compete with IBM. These vendors must decide whether they will offer some degree of SAA compatibility in their products or if they will pursue other alternative industry standards, or even a combination of these strategies.

It will be difficult for competitors to replicate the entire SAA environment, but selective strategies could be employed to provide more specific types of SAA compatibility. For example, some vendors might focus on SAA communications compatibility to allow coexistence in networks with IBM's SAA platforms. Another area of compatibility that many vendors are focusing on is the SAA user interface. An SAA-compatible user interface makes products appear, from a user's point-of-view, to be SAA compliant.

SUMMARY

SAA addresses the major issues involved in the design and implementation of cooperative processing applications. The consistency of the SAA environment across application platforms results in greater mobility of application resources. This is accomplished through the standardization of application programming environments, user interfaces, and networking technologies across the SAA application platforms.

Like most of IBM's key architectures and products, SAA will have an impact not only on IBM and its customers, but across much of the computer industry. Compatibility and coexistence with SAA will be important to independent software vendors and manufacturers of computers and networking equipment. SAA, along with the evolving industry open systems standards, will play a key role in the cooperative processing networks of the 1990s.

2

SAA Concepts and Elements

Before looking more closely at the elements of SAA, additional background information on the issues addressed by SAA, some of which were raised in Chapter 1, would be helpful. This will aid in understanding why various elements have been made a part of SAA and why IBM has structured SAA in such a manner. Let's start by looking at a typical IBM corporate customer—the traditional IBM mainframe user at whom SAA is targeted.

A typical IBM corporate customer has a network of interconnected computer systems. The systems in the network range from large mainframe computers to midrange, departmental systems down to personal computers and terminals as shown in Figure 2-1. Each of these systems and devices plays a different role in the network.

The mainframe system is typically where a corporation's major data processing applications execute, where the major files and databases reside, and where network management is performed. Terminals in the network are used to access applications, files, and databases that reside on host mainframes or midrange systems. Personal computers provide their own local application processing and are also used to access mainframe and midrange system resources. Midrange systems can provide departmental level processing, function as file servers, and provide access to mainframes and other systems in the network.

Many corporations view their network as a corporate asset. The network can provide the corporation's employees and customers with valuable services which can generate revenues as well as give the corporation a strategic advantage over its competitors.

What is needed to accomplish this and, indeed, turn the network into a

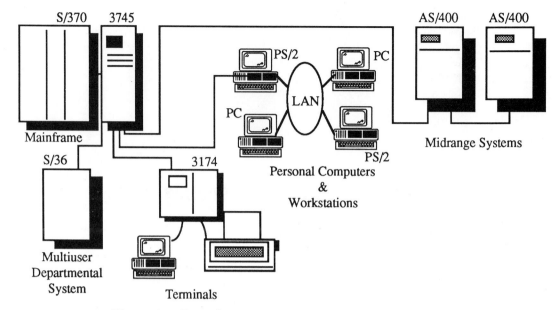

Figure 2-1. *Typical corporate network includes mainframes, multi-user midrange systems, personal computers, workstations, and terminals.*

valuable corporate asset, is the flexible placement of people, programs, and data across the systems in the network. This is desirable for a number of reasons. For one, people often move from one location to another or from one department to another within a business. Often the move entails using a different computer system. If massive retraining were required whenever individuals moved to different systems, productivity and operations would be negatively affected, which is often the case.

A second example involves moving application programs. There may be a desire to off-load some of the application processing being done on a mainframe. Applications could be distributed to midrange or personal computer systems or workstations. This not only frees up the mainframe to reduce its load, but also allows applications to take advantage of local workstation facilities such as highly graphical user interfaces.

The ability to move applications off mainframes can result in significant cost savings. It may mean that the company will not have to purchase another mainframe priced at millions of dollars. The trend towards downsizing reflects this.

In addition, this gives users direct local control over application processing. No longer do they have to wait for access to a mainframe or wait for the mainframe to process their job. They can run their applications when they want to or need to with immediate results. The result is often improved productivity.

Another example is the movement of files or databases from one system to another in the network. While most corporate files are stored on mainframes, it may be desirable to distribute some of these files to the sites where they are often used. This not only can improve performance but also gives users more control over their own data. Data can be placed where it makes the most sense. This allows companies the potential to operate more efficiently and to provide better and different services to their customers.

THE PROBLEM

The problem with moving people, programs, and data across different IBM systems is that the various computer systems are fundamentally incompatible with one another. They are incompatible in a number of ways. They have their own, unique:

> Hardware architectures
> Operating systems
> File systems
> Database management systems
> Programming tools
> Application programming interfaces
> Communications
> User interfaces
> Applications

When systems are used in a standalone manner, independent of other systems, the lack of compatibility is not much of a problem. The incompatibilities cause a lot of problems, though, when systems are networked together and are expected to interoperate with one another.

User-training problems are caused when users move from one system to another. How do users learn to use all these different systems and applications?

Programmer productivity problems result when programmers try to develop distributed applications that will span dissimilar systems or to develop programs for more than one system. How do the programmers learn to use all the different tools, services, and programming interfaces on different systems?

Problems also arise in trying to distribute data across systems and provide easy access to and sharing of the data. How is access provided to data on different systems that have incompatible file systems? Or, how are distributed programs able to talk to one another when different systems use different communications protocols?

What it boils down to is this: What is the corporation going to do about all these users, all these programmers, and all these systems?

The goal is to place people, programs, and data where they make most sense; where they are most appropriate to optimize operations. What is needed is the flexibility to easily move people, programs, and data across different systems in the network without major disruptions in operations and without major training requirements.

Let's look at some specific examples of these problems. In the case of users, an individual may be faced with using either a new system or new applications. For example, the individual may have been using a PS/2 but is now using an AS/400 system. Although a different system is in use, the individual may be using an application on the AS/400 similar to one used on the PS/2 (e.g., a word processing application). It would be nice if the word processing application on the AS/400 had the same look and feel as the word processing package that was used on the PS/2. If so, no retraining would be required.

Likewise, individuals often use more than one application on their system. For example, they may use word processing, spreadsheet, and electronic mail packages. When different applications have totally different user interfaces, it is more difficult to learn how to use them. A more consistent user interface across applications can make them easier to learn and use.

In the case of programmers, there may be a requirement to develop an application to off-load processing from the mainframe. The application, which previously executed only on the mainframe, will have some of its processing logic distributed to a PS/2. This will allow users to take advantage of the graphical, windows-based OS/2 Presentation Manager interface, rather than having to use a text-based 3270 terminal interface. It also allows local editing and some application functional processing to be performed right at the PS/2, thereby improving response time.

It would be convenient if the same programming language could be used for developing the PS/2 part of the application as well as the mainframe part. It would also be beneficial if the same system services and programming interfaces could be used for both systems. This would not only make it easier to program but should significantly decrease development time and programmer training requirements.

Lastly, let's look at data distribution. In order to give users more control over their own files and better response time in accessing these files, it may be desirable to distribute the files to the departmental and desktop systems. It would still be necessary to access centralized, host-based files and files on other systems in the network. It would be beneficial to be able to have access to data anywhere in the network without having to know or care where the data is actually located.

ALTERNATIVE APPROACHES

There are a few ways in which consistency across a range of systems could be provided that would solve many of the problems just discussed. Let's review three basic approaches:

Use a single hardware/software platform.
Use the same operating system on all systems.
Use different systems but provide standardized environments to mask differences.

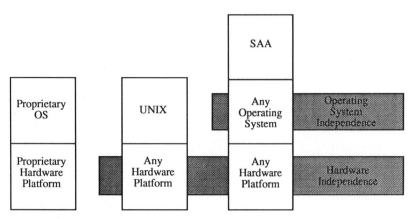

Figure 2-2. *Three approaches to consistency across a range of systems.*

These alternatives are illustrated in Figure 2-2. Can you guess the approach that IBM took? We will get to it shortly.

A Single Platform

The first approach, standardizing on one type of system throughout the corporation, is not practical. Small businesses, with few or no computers, could decide to standardize on a system such as the PS/2 or a UNIX-based system for all their data processing needs. Any company with a sizable installed base of systems has a problem in doing this, however. What do you do with the existing systems? Just throw them out? What about the investment that has already been made in all these systems and the applications that have been developed for them? The majority of IBM's largest customers face these problems with their installed base of mainframe systems and applications.

A better strategy for such a corporation would be one that allowed use of the installed systems. Also, the broader the data processing needs of an organization, the less likely that a single system will suffice. Most large corporations need a wide span of systems that provide a range of processing power and capacity with appropriate price/performance ratios. Different applications and different uses will require different systems at different price points. Not all users need mainframes. Low-cost PCs might suffice for many of the uses. On the other hand, low-cost PCs cannot support the massive databases or high-volume transaction processing requirements of most large organizations.

No single system can be optimized for all the tasks required. Price/performance trade-offs will have to be made. For these reasons, and many others, most corporations will continue to use many different kinds of systems. The key will be to integrate these systems together in networks in order to optimize the business's operations. The bottom line is that any approach must address the installed base of computer systems. Users must be provided with a migration path.

A Single Operating System

Having quickly rejected the single system approach, let's explore the single operating system approach. With this approach, a company could standardize on one operating system that could be used on their different computer systems. This is what has been done with UNIX. UNIX is a relatively portable operating system that runs on many different hardware platforms.

The beauty of this approach is that it provides a relatively high degree of program portability. Programs that were written to run under UNIX, using UNIX interfaces, will naturally port to systems on which UNIX runs. Wherever UNIX moves, the applications can move.

This actually sounds better than it really is. This approach would be better if there were a single UNIX standard. Unfortunately, there are still a lot of different versions of UNIX in place. Which version do you standardize on? And, will all vendors standardize on this same version?

Portability of UNIX applications is not always automatic either. Very often applications have to be modified when they are ported from one version of UNIX on one system to another version of UNIX supported on another system. The degree of portability across UNIX platforms is relatively high, though, and it is certainly better than rewriting applications from scratch for a new environment.

More good news about this approach is that there is a good level of vendor independence. Almost all major computer vendors offer UNIX on their systems. You are not locked into any particular hardware, since UNIX runs on different platforms, and you are not locked into any vendor.

What you are locked into, however, is the UNIX operating system. You have a degree of hardware independence, but not operating system independence. How bad is this? Good question. Let's look at some of the negatives.

There are areas in which UNIX is still lacking. These include high-performance transaction processing, fault-tolerance, and security, to name a few. There are UNIX vendors who do provide support in these areas in their versions of UNIX. But, this support is not available across the board from all vendors as a standard UNIX offering. The Open Software Foundation (OSF) and UNIX International (UI) are working to solve this problem but it is still a problem.

Although there are many commercial applications available for UNIX, there is still the problem of existing applications that run under other operating systems. For example, IBM's mainframe customers have developed many custom applications for the MVS (Multiple Virtual Storage) and VM (Virtual Machine) operating systems. What do these customers do with all these applications? Rewrite them or port them to UNIX? This is unlikely to happen. Most MVS and VM customers will stick with these operating systems, at least for the foreseeable future. They are too locked into these environments and the related subsystems and applications. Again, they must be provided with a migration path that allows them to get from where they are to where they would like to be.

Another important consideration is the impact on programmers. What do you do with all the MVS and VM system programmers and application programmers coding in COBOL and PL/I? Do you train all these people on UNIX and C? The reality is that these mainframe systems will remain firmly entrenched for some time. The existing operating systems, such as MVS and VM, will also continue to be predominant for many years.

UNIX could make inroads into new system purchases. These could include high-end PCs, engineering workstations, local area network (LAN) servers, midrange systems. Even IBM is going after these markets with a UNIX-based (AIX) offering, the RISC System/6000. UNIX offerings should do quite well in many of these selected markets and should continue to penetrate commercial data processing markets as well. But, not to the exclusion of non-UNIX systems. Again, the likely scenario is a mixture of different system types and different operating systems.

There are also current technical drawbacks to a UNIX-only approach. It is difficult to imagine that any operating system could be optimized for the wide range of systems that will be used in large corporations. We are talking about everything from very-high-end mainframes, through supercomputers, down to midrange offerings and PCs. It is possible to get one operating system to run on all these types of systems, as UNIX does across this range of platforms, but it probably will not be the best solution in all cases.

Standardization Across Different Systems

This brings us to the last alternative. Keep the same hardware platforms and operating systems in place (at least the more strategic ones), but mask their underlying differences from users and programs. This is the IBM SAA approach.

IBM has both marketing and technical reasons for doing this. First, the marketing reasons. As we said earlier, IBM cannot abandon its existing mainframe customer base. These customers have invested too much time, money, and effort in IBM systems and software as well as customized software that they have developed for these systems. There is too large an installed base of MVS and VM users for this to go away. Any strategy must deal with these systems. IBM's largest mainframe customers have been a driving force behind SAA.

On the technical side, IBM's reasoning is along the lines of what we discussed regarding the UNIX approach. IBM's position is that no one system is "best" across the board. Some systems are optimized for ease of use at low cost, others are optimized for data-storage capacity and transaction processing, others are optimized for scientific and engineering usage. This position may be somewhat self-serving since IBM created the problem of incompatible systems in the first place and they naturally argue this point. However, it does have merit especially when looked at from a longer perspective. What may be best today may not necessarily be best tomorrow. Any strategy should consider how new technologies will be incorporated in the future. A key is not to be constrained by a particular hardware architecture or operating system.

So, what is the solution? It is not to standardize on any one hardware platform or operating system. Rather, it is to build on existing and future environments in a system-independent manner. It is to provide consistency across dissimilar environments and to support interoperability between environments.

The SAA solution is to provide IBM's major customers with a migration path of least resistance while allowing them to take advantage of new technologies as well as future technologies. Part of this strategy is to allow customers to continue to use their existing systems. But here is where IBM had a dilemma. How do you allow customers to continue to use old systems while continuing to sell them new systems? After all, IBM needs to continue to generate revenue. Actually, IBM followed a two-pronged strategy here.

The approach is to let their customers continue to use their existing mainframe systems—the System/370 processors and the MVS and VM operating systems. Then, propagate many of the technologies being used on the mainframe to selected midrange and workstation platforms. These technologies include relational database managers, dialog managers, communications protocols, and applications.

This approach assumes that there will be a mixture of dissimilar systems in the network. It allows users to select which systems and operating environments are most appropriate for various functions. It focuses on the interoperability of different systems in order to allow programs and data to be distributed easily.

While allowing existing mainframes to be used, IBM came out with new midrange and personal computer offerings. They did this for a few reasons. In the midrange area, one reason was to clear up the confusion caused by the multiple, overlapping midrange system offerings being sold. The solution was to come out with a new midrange offering, the AS/400, and provide a migration path for the System/3X customer base to move to the AS/400.

In the personal computer area, the strategy was to come out with a new, proprietary offering that would allow IBM to recapture control of the personal computer marketplace that they lost to the PC clone manufacturers. This strategy included incompatible hardware (the PS/2 MicroChannel) and a new, incompatible operating system (OS/2). IBM has not succeeded in this strategy to the extent that they would like, however. The large installed base of DOS users will not easily migrate to OS/2.

The difficulty of moving customers off their existing platforms holds true for PCs as well as for mainframes. IBM seems to have ignored this reality. While this fact has worked to IBM's advantage in the larger systems arena, it has worked to their disadvantage in the PC arena. Part of IBM's solution will be to allow DOS workstations to be used with SAA applications. They need to provide their DOS users with a good migration path into SAA. One way they are doing this is with products such as EASEL from Interactive Images which allows users to build SAA-compliant interfaces for DOS which can then front-end existing host applications.

The major issues facing IBM's largest customers, to whom SAA is directed, are these: They have invested enormous amounts of money and effort in System/370-based mainframes and applications that cannot be abandoned. In the past, mainframe applications were accessed by dumb terminals but personal computers have proliferated throughout the organization. Rather than limit the PCs to acting like terminals, users want to exploit the full range of PC capability. This includes running local applications as well as providing graphical, icon-based user interfaces.

Midrange systems are being deployed in departments and locations where the cost of a mainframe is prohibitive but individual PCs are not the solution. In some cases, midrange sytems serve as file servers on PC-based LANs. The large installed base of midrange system applications need to continue to be used.

All these dissimilar systems need to be tied seamlessly together in a network. The same pools of programmers must continue to be used and be productive in developing new applications. These include both standalone applications on various systems as well as distributed processing or cooperative processing applications that will span multiple systems. Retraining must be minimized for both programmers and users. At the same time, productivity must be improved.

A very important requirement is to allow data to be distributed and shared by users and programs in the network. Data access must be transparent. That is, users or programs should be able to access data as if it were local on their system. They should not have to be concerned with the actual physical location of data or the type of system on which it resides.

The realities for these customers, then, is that their networks will consist of a mixture of dissimilar systems. The existing System/370-based (and System/390-based) systems will continue to play major roles in the network. These will include serving as a centralized repository for large volumes of data, as a centralized network management host, and running major data processing applications.

The workstation of choice will become a personal computer. New applications will distribute processing across systems. Data will be distributed throughout the network to locations where it makes most sense for it to reside. In a nutshell, the flexible placement of people, programs, and data is required to allow corporations to match their data processing needs to the business needs of the organization.

These large corporations, IBM's major mainframe customers, have driven IBM to come up with a solution to their problems. How do they seamlessly integrate the many dissimilar systems in their networks; protect their investments in existing systems, applications, and people; move from where they are to the next generation of systems and applications; leverage their existing personnel; improve productivity; minimize training requirements; and speed up application development? And, how do they do so in a way that does not lock them into environments that may become obsolete over time and in a way that allows them to incorporate new systems and technologies that may come along in the future? This is no small task.

THE SAA SOLUTION

SAA goes about doing this by standardizing the interfaces to users, programs, and systems. This allows applications to be developed that are not dependent on any particular type of system. It allows applications to be distributed or moved across systems, data to be distributed across systems, and users to move from system to system with minimal training required.

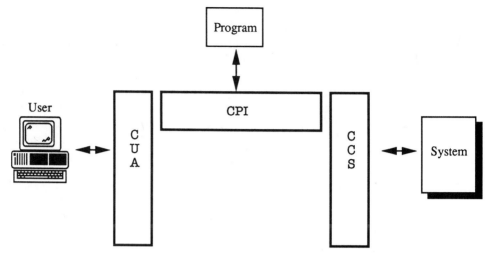

Figure 2-3. *SAA's three major elements standardize the interfaces to us-*
ers, programs, and systems.

Consequently, SAA is structured into corresponding elements that address
the interfaces to users, programs, and systems as shown in Figure 2-3. These
major SAA elements are:

> Common User Access (CUA)—user interface
> Common Programming Interface (CPI)—program interface
> Common Communications Support (CCS)—system interface

Each of these elements consists of a set of specifications or components that can
be used to support the particular type of interface. These components will be
supported consistently in each of the SAA operating environments on various
platforms.

Another SAA element is called Common Applications. This element itself
does not contain specifications or individual SAA components. Rather, Common
Applications are application programs that were developed using components
from the CUA, CPI, and CCS elements. An SAA Common Application, therefore,
will provide an SAA CUA-compliant user interface, use SAA programming
interfaces and services, and, if required, use SAA CCS components for communicating with other systems. SAA Common Applications are discussed more
completely in Chapter 6.

The specific SAA platforms and operating environments will be explored
next, followed by a more in-depth description of these major SAA elements and
the role of each.

SAA PLATFORMS

As we indicated earlier, a major goal of SAA is to bring greater consistency to
IBM's dissimilar computer systems. One problem with trying to do this is that
IBM has so many different kinds of computer systems, all of which are basically
incompatible with one another. The problem exists across the board for all of

IBM's different systems, from low-end personal computers up through very-high-end mainframes.

Look at the extent of this problem. Here is a list of some of IBM's different hardware and corresponding operating systems that have been offered over the years.

Hardware	Operating System
System/370	MVS, VM, VSE, AIX/370
(303X, 308X, 3090, 43XX, 9370)	
System/390 (ES/9000)	MVS/ESA, VM/ESA, VSE/ESA
System/36	SSP
System/38	EDX, RPS
Series/1	CPF
8100	DPCX, DPPX
System/88	CPF
AS/400	OS/400
PC	DOS
PS/2	OS/2, AIX
RT	AIX
RISC System/6000	AIX Version 3

Let's take a look at some of the different categories within which these systems fall. A word of caution: Although we are going to discuss categories of systems that are often used throughout the industry, the lines are blurred between them. As an example, System/370-type processors are typically described as mainframe systems. However, the lower end of the line are more appropriately midrange systems. On the other hand, the upper end of IBM's AS/400 family, which is typically referred to as a midrange systems offering, has greater power and capacity than many of the mainframe systems. And, of course, many of the higher-end PS/2 workstations are more powerful than many of IBM's midrange systems and even more powerful than some of the lower-end mainframe offerings.

We will discuss the general categories of mainframe, midrange, and workstation systems because this is how IBM viewed the world and positioned these systems relative to SAA. Just remember that there is significant overlap in the capabilities of the machines that will be discussed in each of these areas.

Mainframe Systems

What are typically considered traditional IBM mainframe systems are a wide range of processors based on the System/370 architecture. Processors which support the System/370 architecture include the 303X, 308X, 3090, 43XX, and 9370 families. All come in a variety of models. The 3090 series forms the top of the System/370 mainframe line while the lower-end 43XX and 9370 systems are often used at distributed sites functioning more like midrange systems.

Different levels of hardware architecture are supported on some or all the models within a particular processor family. For example, there are standard System/370 architecture models, Extended Architecture (XA) models, and Enterprise Systems Architecture (ESA) models. The different architectural levels support different hardware features. Different versions of operating system software are required to support the different hardware features.

Although there are multiple architectural levels within the System/370 family, IBM has done a very good job of providing a migration path up through the System/370 line. Upward compatibility of software on these various architectures is supported through the various versions of their operating systems. For example, software written to run on one level (e.g., MVS/XA, which supports processors that support extended architecture features) can also run on a higher-level system (e.g., MVS/ESA, which supports the architectural features supported by ESA processors). However, software written to take advantage of extended ESA/370 hardware features supported by MVS/ESA will not run under MVS/SP or MVS/XA on processors that do not support ESA/370. So, the situation still exists that applications could be tied indirectly to a particular hardware platform.

IBM's System/390 architecture is the successor to the System/370 architecture. Enterprise Systems/9000 (ES/9000) is the current family of processors based on System/390 architecture. ES/9000 processors are upward compatible from the System/370 and ESA/370 series of processors. The ES/9000 family of compatible processors spans the entire range of System/370-compatible processors from low-end 9370s to high-end 3090s. This provides a migration path from System/370 to System/390 machines. The ES/9000 processors include additional architectural features that are part of the new Enterprise Systems Architecture/390 (ESA/390). All ES/9000 models are supported by IBM's MVS/ESA, VM/ESA, and VSE/ESA operating systems. Software that takes advantage of new ESA/390 features will not run on processors that do not support these features.

Midrange Systems

In the midrange systems area, the problem is even worse. There has been a proliferation of different IBM midrange system offerings over the years. Examples are the System/34, System/36, System/38, AS/400, Series/1, System/88, 5520, 3790, 8100, RISC System/6000, and others. And, as we indicated above, the lower end of the System/370 family (e.g., 9370 and 4361) and the lower-end ES/9000 models can be considered midrange systems as well.

Each of these families of systems is based on a different hardware architecture. Each has its own operating system (multiple operating systems in some cases) that is tied into the hardware. Consequently, applications developed for any of these operating systems and platforms are tied to that system. For example, applications written to run on the AS/400 will not run on System/370-based or System/390-based machines.

Workstations

The problem is not so bad in the workstation area, but it still exists with the different PC, PS/2, RT, and RISC System/6000 systems and the different operating systems that run on these platforms. Again, applications developed for a particular system and environment are tied to it. Applications developed to run under OS/2 will not run under DOS. Although DOS applications can run under OS/2, they cannot take full advantage of OS/2's advanced features.

Unfortunately (for the problem, that is, but not for IBM revenues), most of IBM's systems sold relatively well. Each hardware platform and its corresponding operating system(s) and related software were developed to exploit various markets. They were developed independently of one another with little regard for consistency of any kind. The result is that there are sizable installed bases of many of these incompatible systems. What do you do with the installed bases of customers?

Clearly, it is not very efficient to try to maintain, support, and enhance all these different systems over time. Their power and capacity, usage, and marketplaces overlap in many cases. The resources needed to keep all these systems going is too much for even IBM to bear.

One goal of IBM's, then, is to focus on a smaller number of system types. This, in fact, is what IBM did in selecting SAA platforms. They had to pare down the list of systems to a manageable few. For each of the major categories of systems (mainframe, midrange, and workstation), IBM selected a family of systems on which SAA support will be provided. These families of systems, shown in Figure 2-4, are the designated SAA hardware platforms:

System Category	Designated SAA Hardware Platform
Mainframe	ESA/370 processors (ESA/3090, ESA/4381, ESA/9370) ESA/390 processors (ES/9000)
Midrange	AS/400
Workstation	PS/2

The choice of these systems is not too surprising. IBM, of course, had to include their mainframes since this is what the bulk of their major customers use—and where IBM makes most of its money.

The AS/400 system, though, did not even exist at the time of the original SAA announcement. At this time, IBM referred to a future System/3X offering as the strategic SAA midrange platform. The AS/400 has since assumed this role. IBM has been very successful in selling this system as it is the successor to its popular System/36 and System/38 machines.

IBM's goal with the AS/400 was to merge the System/36 and System/38 platforms in order to focus on a single strategic offering. The AS/400 is based primarily on the System/38's architecture and includes many of the ease-of-use facilities of the System/36. A migration path is provided by allowing System/36 and System/38 application programs to run on the AS/400.

The degree of modifications needed to allow these programs to execute on the AS/400 varies. Some System/38 programs can execute without any changes, other programs need minor modifications and recompilations, while others may require more substantial changes.

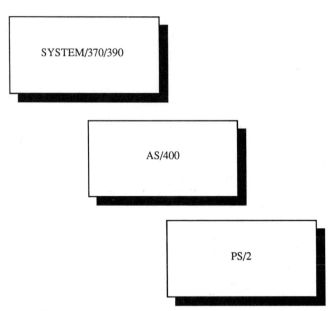

Figure 2-4. *The major SAA hardware platforms.*

In the workstation area, the PS/2 has now replaced the original PC as the personal computer of choice in most cases. This is the system that is being widely installed by many of IBM's largest mainframe customers. While PCs can still be used, the real target workstation platform is the PS/2.

SAA, however, is not about hardware platforms. More important is the software that runs on each of these platforms. This software includes the operating systems, file and database management systems, communications subsystems, compilers, and other program products. Together, all this software forms a particular operating environment for a given hardware platform.

IBM has an even greater problem in the software area than they do in the hardware area. Unlike the early days of computing when applications directly interfaced to hardware, most operating systems today mask the underlying hardware from users and application programs. The different hardware architectures are not usually directly a problem for users or programs, but users and programs are directly affected by the operating system and related software provided on a particular system. Users and programs directly interact with the operating system and are therefore much more exposed to operating system differences than they are to hardware differences.

With SAA, IBM is attempting to standardize the software operating environments that will be provided on their System/370/390 mainframe, AS/400 mid-range, and PS/2 workstation platforms. They are attempting a level of standardization across operating environments in order to make them more consistent with one another.

Some of the areas in which IBM is attempting to achieve greater consistency across their different systems is in the user interface, programming languages and tools, file and database management systems, communications support, and other areas.

INCOMPATIBLE OPERATING ENVIRONMENTS

As we have said, a major problem IBM has in achieving greater consistency across their different systems is the many different, incompatible operating environments that they support across the range of hardware platforms. For example, on System/370-type processors, IBM provides MVS, VM, and VSE operating systems (as well as AIX and DPPX operating systems). These are all different, all incompatible, and all have their own different file systems, database management systems, utilities, programming tools, programming interfaces, communications support, subsystems, and so on.

For non-System/370 processors, each different system has its own (multiple in some cases) operating system(s) and related software. They are all incompatible with one another.

Each of the operating systems has its own different file systems, database systems, communications systems, programming languages, programming tools, etc. Applications developed for any of these environments will execute only in that environment.

In the personal computer and workstation area, IBM sells or sold PCs, PS/2s, RT, and RISC System/6000 systems. PC DOS, OS/2 (Standard and Extended Editions), AIX (UNIX), and other operating systems are supported on one or more of these platforms. Again, all these operating systems are incompatible with one another as well as being incompatible with the operating environments supported on the System/370-based and non-System/370 processors.

There is clearly a problem in trying to support, maintain, and continue to enhance so many different operating environments for so many different platforms. The solution is similar to the hardware platform solution. That is, select just a few of these operating environments as the strategic environments and designate them as the SAA operating environments and commit to provide full SAA support in these designated environments only.

This is what IBM has done with SAA. Rather than trying to bring SAA to all their existing system environments, they have selected a small subset of environments to be SAA environments. Much of this selection was done by default when IBM decided to focus on the hardware platforms—ESA/370, AS/400, and PS/2. This naturally eliminated those operating systems for other platforms (e.g., SSP for System/36).

However, in the case where multiple operating systems were supported, IBM had to make a decision as to which ones would be the SAA operating environments. IBM did select one or more operating environments on each of the platforms discussed above. IBM will provide SAA software within these designated SAA environments that will bring greater consistency to them. As indicated in Figure 2-5, IBM has designated the following operating systems and subsystems as SAA operating environments:

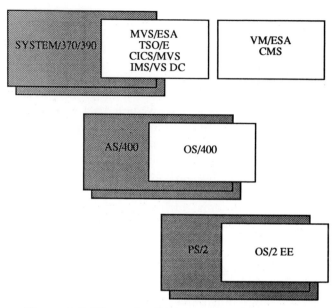

Figure 2-5. *The major SAA operating environments.*

Hardware Platform	SAA Operating Environment
System/370/390	MVS/ESA TSO/E CICS/ESA* IMS/VS DC* VM/ESA CMS
AS/400	OS/400
PS/2	OS/2 Extended Edition

*Limited operating environments

For each of these SAA operating environments, IBM will provide support for all the SAA components where appropriate. Note that the CICS/ESA and IMS/VS Data Communications subsystems for the MVS/ESA environment are not full SAA operating environments. That is, IBM will not be providing the full range of SAA components in these subsystems. Rather, IBM will provide a limited subset of SAA support for these subsystems.

The limited SAA support will allow these environments to be accessed from intelligent workstations (i.e., PS/2 workstations running OS/2 EE) using SAA's LU 6.2 protocols. In addition, support for the SAA Common Programming Interface for Communications (CPIC) will be provided so that LU 6.2–based applications can be developed for these subsystems that can use the CPIC for communications with remote programs.

One reason for this limited support in CICS and IMS is that these are old subsystems that were designed long before SAA. IBM cannot do away with them because of the large installed base of users. Indeed, IBM has reemphasized the roles of CICS/ESA and IMS/ESA Transaction Manager as their key SAA host transaction processing environments. The fact remains, however, that IBM would like to migrate their customers to newer, more strategic SAA environments such as DB2. The CICS and IMS environments will get tied more closely to DB2 over time.

When discussing SAA, we are talking about facilities that will span these operating system environments on the designated hardware platforms. This means that SAA will span IBM's ESA/370 mainframe processors, AS/400 mid-range systems, and PS/2 workstations. In particular, consistent SAA support will be provided in selected operating environments on these systems. These SAA environments are MVS/ESA TSO/E, VM/ESA CMS environments for ESA/370 and ESA/390 processors; OS/400 for AS/400 systems; and OS/2 EE on PS/2 systems (and PCs supported by OS/2 EE). Let's look at each of the SAA environments in a little more depth.

SAA Mainframe Environments

IBM has designated multiple SAA operating environments for their traditional mainframe systems. First let's look at the hardware platforms upon which SAA software support will be provided. The Enterprise System Architecture/370 (ESA/370) and ESA/390 processors are the target hardware platforms. These are the higher-end processor models that support extensions to the System/370 standard and extended architectures and the entire line of ES/9000 processors.

The implication of this is that IBM will provide SAA software for the ESA/370 and ESA/390 processors in order to take advantage of the specialized hardware features. Such software will not run on non-ESA processors. This is one way in which IBM will attempt to motivate their mainframe customers to upgrade to ESA-level machines. If they want the new SAA applications, they must upgrade to ESA/370 or ESA/390 models. Software sells hardware.

On the software side, IBM has designated particular versions of both their MVS and VM operating systems (which are the most widely used System/370 and System/390 operating systems) as SAA environments. For MVS, it is the MVS/ESA version of the operating system that is the designated SAA environment. MVS/ESA supports the ESA extended hardware features.

Again, there are implications in the designation of MVS/ESA, to the exclusion of MVS/SP and/or MVS/XA, as the SAA operating environment. Of course, MVS/ESA is required to support the ESA/370 and ESA/390 extended architecture features. These features are not supported by the MVS/SP or MVS/XA versions of the operating system. This is another indication that IBM will provide SAA software to run under MVS/ESA, exploiting its advanced features, that will not run under MVS/SP or MVS/XA. This will tie SAA mainframe software to MVS/ESA and, indirectly, to ESA/370 and ESA/390 processors.

In the VM area, the VM/SP and VM/XA versions of the operating system were originally referred to as SAA environments. These have now been superceded by VM/ESA which, like MVS/ESA, will be the strategic SAA operating environment in which IBM will build future SAA support.

In addition to designating particular operating systems, IBM has further qualified where SAA support will be provided by designating particular sub-systems with MVS and VM that will receive SAA support. For MVS/ESA, the TSO/E subsystem is a full SAA environment while CICS/ESA and IMS/Data Communications (IMS/DC) are limited SAA environments. For VM/ESA, CMS is a full SAA environment.

SAA Midrange Environment

The SAA midrange hardware platform is the Application System/400 (AS/400). This means that none of IBM's other midrange system offerings (e.g., System/36, System/38, Series/1, System/88, etc.) are SAA platforms. Remember that the 9370 and some ES/9000 processors, which support VM, are also midrange systems. Here we are talking about non-System/370/390 machines.

The AS/400 is the successor to IBM's highly successful System/36 and System/38 systems. It combines the ease-of-use features of the System/36 with the powerful architecture and system facilities of the System/38. Programs written to run on the System/36 and System/38 can be ported (sometimes with no change) to run on the AS/400.

The SAA operating environment for the AS/400 is the OS/400 operating system. Support for all SAA components (where appropriate) will be provided within OS/400.

SAA Workstation Environment

The PS/2 is the target SAA workstation platform. Support is also provided for 80286-based and above PCs. One of the distinguishing hardware features of the PS/2 is its MicroChannel Architecture. SAA applications will be developed that exploit the capabilities of the MicroChannel. These applications will not run on PCs that do not support the MicroChannel.

The designated SAA operating environment of the PS/2 is the OS/2 Extended Edition (OS/2 EE) operating system. Although OS/2 Standard Edition (OS/2 SE) does contain some SAA support, it is not a full SAA operating environment.

WHAT ABOUT NON-SAA SYSTEMS?

A natural question to ask is: What about those operating systems that have not been designated as SAA environments—are they obsolete? The answer is yes and no. Several of the non-SAA environments have, in fact, been made obsolete by IBM's decision to exclude them as strategic SAA environments. This would be the case for operating systems such as SSP for the System/36, CPF for the System/38, and EDX for the Series/1.

This is not too surprising since the systems on which these OSs run have been superceded by other IBM systems such as the AS/400, and, one of IBM's goals with SAA is to reduce the number of "strategic" systems on which SAA support will be provided.

For other environments, however, the fact that they have not been included under SAA does not necessarily mean that they are obsolete or not important. Remember that SAA addresses IBM's major commercial data processing offerings, their major general-purpose application platforms. Included in SAA are components that are commonly needed in all the commercial systems such as System/370/390-based mainframes, AS/400 systems, and PS/2s.

Some systems that may require specialized hardware or software to support the applications for which they are targeted are not SAA systems precisely because of this specialized need. This would be the case with IBM's banking systems and retail Point-Of-Sale (POS) systems. These are systems supporting hardware and software that is specialized for their usage and is not needed across the board for other systems used primarily for general-purpose data processing. These kinds of systems are targeted at various niche markets or vertical markets that in many cases are extremely important for IBM. IBM will not abandon these systems. It is just that they do not meet the SAA criteria or address the same set of goals as SAA, which are targeted at promoting commonality rather than uniqueness.

SAA and UNIX

Another example of a non-SAA environment that is very strategic to IBM is the UNIX environment. Hence, IBM's version of UNIX, which is named AIX, is very important to IBM, and the markets at which AIX is targeted are very important for IBM. IBM has targeted AIX as the solution of choice in selected marketplaces where UNIX is a requirement or a de facto standard. These markets include engineering workstations, universities, government, and others.

AIX, as with UNIX in general, will continue to gain ground in general-purpose commercial application marketplaces as well. For now, however, IBM has elected to keep AIX out of the SAA fold. In fact, IBM is following a parallel strategy with SAA and AIX. This parallel SAA and AIX strategy will be discussed further below.

Other Non-SAA Systems

It can also be expected that IBM will introduce new systems and operating environments in the future that will be targeted at new markets or might incorporate new technologies. These systems might very well be important and strategic to IBM, but they might not be designated SAA environments because of all the issues discussed above.

The moral is do not assume something is not important just because it is not SAA. Also, do not expect that everything that IBM comes out with in the future will automatically be SAA. SAA and non-SAA environments both have their roles. SAA will ensure consistency across a selected set of environments. Interoperability and the ability to access and share resources distributed across SAA and non-SAA environments will be provided by IBM.

In summary, a major goal of SAA is to provide greater consistency across dissimilar IBM systems. Rather than try to do this for every IBM system, IBM has designated a major family of systems in the mainframe, midrange, and workstation categories on which SAA support will be provided. These hardware platforms are ESA/370 and ESA/390 mainframes, AS/400 midrange, and PS/2 workstations. More important, however, is the operating software that will include SAA support on these platforms. For each of these hardware platforms, IBM has designated one or more operating systems as SAA operating environments. These SAA operating environments are:

Hardware Platform	Operating Environment
ESA/370, ESA/390	MVS/ESA TSO/E (CICS/ESA, IMS/DC) VM/ESA CMS
AS/400	OS/400
PS/2	OS/2 EE

SAA support will span these operating environments. This will bring greater consistency to these environments in the user interface area, in programming tools and services, and in communications support.

Let's now discuss the major elements of SAA and the components included in each of these elements.

SAA ELEMENTS

Remember there are four major SAA elements:

        Common User Access (CUA)
        Common Programming Interface (CPI)
        Common Communications Support (CCS)
        Common Applications

The first three of these elements consist of individual components which are used to standardize on user interfaces (CUA), programming interfaces (CPI), and the interfaces to other systems (CCS).

These elements match the goals of SAA, which are to provide consistent user interfaces, consistent programming environments, and cooperative processing across IBM's major computing environments. Common Applications are developed using components from these three elements.

SAA CONCEPTUAL MODEL

The three SAA elements are built on top of a conceptual operating environment model, shown in Figure 2-6, which describes major pieces of software that will exist on SAA systems. The model includes:

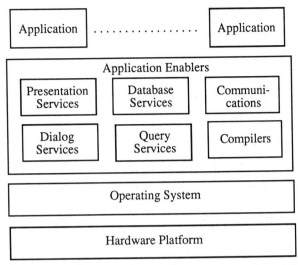

Figure 2-6. *Conceptual operating environment model.*

Operating systems (system control programs)
Communications software
Application enablers
Applications

The operating systems (OSs), or system control programs as IBM sometimes refers to them, directly interface to the hardware of a particular system. The OS isolates other system and application software from the underlying hardware architecture. The OS also provides numerous services to application programs and users. These include program execution services, memory management services, program and data protection services, and others.

As discussed earlier, IBM has selected various OSs as SAA operating environments. In fact, SAA implies the existence of different operating systems. If there were only a single OS involved, there would not be a need for SAA. A goal of SAA is to make the different operating systems transparent to users and application programs by providing consistent services and programming interfaces within each SAA operating environment.

Communications software provides the support to connect systems and allow interoperability between them. This support includes data link protocols, network interfaces, higher-level session protocols, distributed transaction services, and network management facilities. This is all the support required for different systems to exchange information and thus allow programs on different systems to communicate and to cooperate with one another in carrying out distributed services such as remote file and database access, electronic mail, and others.

Application enablers are software that support application programs by providing various types of programming services. They "enable" the use of such services as database and query services, program compilation services, dialog services, and others. With the availability of such enabling software in an operating environment, applications do not directly have to implement these services themselves. The applications can use the enablers via programming interfaces. The enablers, in turn, will provide support for the particular service requested. This not only makes it easier to write application programs but it also isolates the application from the underlying operating system in many cases.

Applications are the programs developed to run in the operating system environments. These might be office applications, banking applications, insurance applications, manufacturing applications, or any other kinds of applications. A goal of SAA is to make the applications independent of the underlying environment so that applications can be moved across different environments.

This conceptual model can be mapped onto the SAA operating environments—MVS/ESA, VM/ESA, OS/400, and OS/2 EE. These form the base operating systems (system control programs) for the ESA/370 and ESA/390, AS/400, and PS/2 platforms.

Each environment also supports a set of communications software which provides connectivity to other systems. For the MVS/ESA and VM/ESA environments, this software is the Advanced Communications Function/Virtual Telecommunications Access Method (ACF/VTAM or VTAM for short). For OS/400, this software is its integrated communications subsystem. OS/2 EE includes an integrated Communications Manager that provides this support as well.

Each SAA operating environment also supports various application enabling products. We will discuss these in more detail in Chapter 4—Common Programming Interface (CPI). An example of a system enabler is a database management system. DB2 is the SAA relational database management system for MVS/ESA. SQL/DS provides the same services for the VM/ESA environment. Both OS/400 and OS/2 EE have integrated relational database management systems.

All SAA operating environments also support applications. An example of a common application that runs in all environments is the OfficeVision family. The family consists of OfficeVision/MVS, OfficeVision/VM, OfficeVision/400, and OfficeVision/2, which is discussed in more detail in Chapter 6.

THE SAA SHELL

The three SAA elements (CUA, CPI, CCS) form a "shell" around the major pieces of software defined by the conceptual model, as shown in Figure 2-7, and are implemented in every SAA environment. The shell isolates users, programs, and other systems from the underlying software and hardware of a particular system.

This brings us to another issue that is important to understand about SAA. The various pieces of software within each SAA environment are unique to that environment. That is, each SAA environment includes its own system software or program products that act as the communications software or system enablers for that environment. For example, VTAM is the software that implements SAA

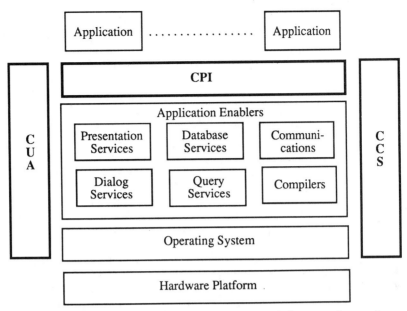

Figure 2-7. *SAA interfaces form a "shell" around the operating environment.*

communications support for the MVS/ESA and VM environments while OS/400 and OS/2 EE have their own communications software.

The different pieces of software in each environment have their own implementations that are tied to that environment. VTAM runs only under the mainframe operating systems and not in OS/400 or OS/2 Extended Edition. These pieces of software are not SAA Common Applications. They will not be ported (moved) across SAA environments. For example, do not expect to see VTAM ported from MVS to OS/2. Rather, IBM refers to them as SAA "product participants." They implement support for one or more SAA components within a particular SAA environment. Each SAA environment has its own SAA products, its own implementation of SAA that is different from the implementations of similar products in other SAA environments.

Consistency across systems is achieved because these individual products, while having different implementations, produce consistent results as far as what users, programs, or other systems see.

Let's briefly summarize the role of the SAA elements.

Common User Access (CUA)

The Common User Access (CUA) element deals with the user interface. CUA is a set of specifications, rules, and guidelines that application programs should follow in developing their end-user interface. The intent is for all SAA applications to present consistent user interfaces. Doing so will make these applications easier to learn and use.

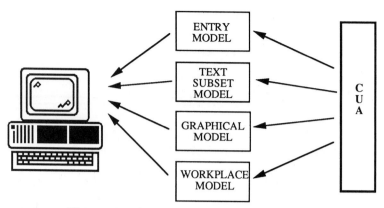

Figure 2-8. *SAA CUA user-interface models.*

There are many aspects of the user interface addressed by CUA. These include the layouts of panels that are displayed, keyboard assignments, dialog interactions between the user and program, use of windows, use of color and highlighting, and others.

As shown in Figure 2-8, CUA describes four different user-interface models that applications can use as a basis for their user interface. These user-interface models are:

> Entry
> Text Subset
> Graphical
> Workplace

These user-interface models are grouped into two major classes of interface: Basic Interface and Advanced Interface.The Basic Interface models are primarily for use with nonprogrammable terminals and include the Entry and Text Subset models. The Advanced Interface models are for use with programmable workstations and include the Graphical and Workplace models.

The Entry and Text Subset models are text-based interfaces that can be used with nonprogrammable terminals (e.g., 3270s) while the Graphical and Workplace models are windows-based, graphical models for use with programmable workstations such as PS/2s running OS/2. SAA's CUA and these different user-interface models will be discussed in more detail in Chapter 3.

Common Programming Interface (CPI)

The CPI element consists of two categories of components as indicated in Figure 2-9 and listed below:

> Programming languages
> C
> COBOL
> FORTRAN

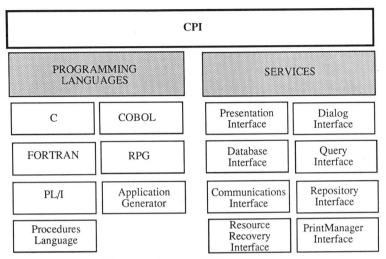

Figure 2-9. SAA CPI components.

    RPG
    PL/I
    Procedures Language
    Application Generator
Services
    Presentation Interface
    Dialog Interface
    Database Interface
    Query Interface
    Communications Interface
    Repository Interface
    Resource Recovery Interface
    PrintManager Interface

The intent is to provide consistent language support and consistent services and programming interfaces across SAA environments. This will make it possible to develop cooperative processing applications and to distribute applications across SAA environments. It also promotes portability of applications across SAA environments. The components of the CPI element will be discussed in more detail in Chapter 4.

Common Communications Support (CCS)

The CCS element consists of the standard components that are used for communications between SAA environments. These components will be used to provide cooperative processing among SAA environments and interoperability of these environments. SAA includes support for both SNA and OSI-based communications. The SNA-based CCS components, as indicated in Figure 2-10, are grouped into the following categories:

Objects
  Presentation Text Object Content Architecture (**PTOCA**)
  Image Object Content Architecture (**IOCA**)
  Graphics Object Content Architecture (**GOCA**)
  Font Object Content Architecture (**FOCA**)
  Formatted Data Object Content Architecture (**FDOCA**)

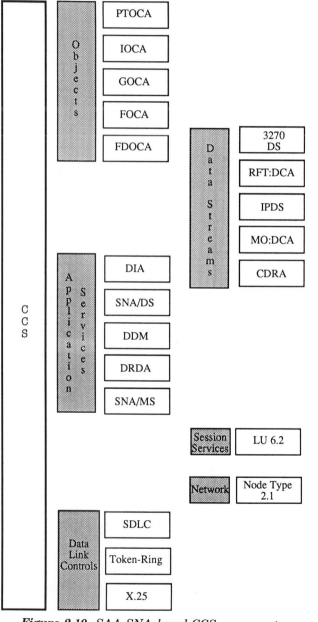

Figure 2-10. *SAA SNA-based CCS components.*

Data Streams
  3270 Data Stream
  Revisable Form Text: Document Content Architecture (RFT:DCA)
  Intelligent Printer Data Stream (IPDS)
  Mixed Object: Document Content Architecture (MO:DCA)
  Character Data Representation Architecture (CDRA)
Application Services
  Document Interchange Architecture (DIA)
  SNA/Distribution Services (SNA/DS)
  Distributed Data Management (DDM)
  Distributed Relational Database Architecture (DRDA)
  SNA/Management Services (SNA/MS)
Session Services
  LU 6.2
Network
  Node Type 2.1
Data Link Controls
  Synchronous Data Link Control (SDLC)
  Token-Ring
  X.25

Each CCS category addresses a different aspect of communications between SAA platforms. The Objects category consists of Object Content Architectures (OCAs) that are used to describe the structure and layout of various types of objects that can be exchanged between platforms.

Data streams are used to carry objects between systems. The Data Streams category includes those data streams that can be used to carry objects between SAA environments.

The Application Services category consists of architectures that define how different types of distributed services are carried out across SAA environments. This includes architectures defining electronic mail services, remote file and database access services, and distributed network management services.

The Session Services category consists of components that provide session-level protocols used to support communications between distributed Application Services programs. LU 6.2 is the only SNA-based component included in this category.

The Network category addresses the level of network connectivity required of SAA platforms. SNA Node Type 2.1 capability is specified in this category.

The Data Link Controls category includes those data link interfaces that will be supported on all SAA platforms. The data link protocols support the exchange of information across a data link between two adjacent nodes.

Consistent support for all these components will be provided in all the SAA operating environments. This will allow interoperability among SAA environments. As we said above, SAA also includes OSI components such as FTAM and X.400. These are described, along with the SNA-based CCS components, in Chapter 5.

COMMON APPLICATIONS

Common Applications are those that span SAA environments, provide an SAA-compliant user interface, and/or support SAA cooperative processing. Common Applications are built using components from SAA's CUA, CPI, and CCS elements. OfficeVision is an example of an SAA Common Application. The characteristics of SAA Common Applications are discussed in detail in Chapter 6.

The SAA elements promote consistency across and interoperability between SAA platforms, which makes cooperative processing among SAA platforms possible. But, what about other important, non-SAA platforms which support non-SAA environments such as AIX, IBM's implementation of the UNIX operating system? Let's look at IBM's AIX strategy and see how it relates to SAA.

AIX FAMILY DEFINITION

We indicated earlier that IBM is also following a strategy that parallels SAA with its Advanced Interactive Executive (AIX) UNIX-based operating system. This parallel AIX approach is embodied in IBM's AIX Family Definition which was announced by IBM in March 1988. Like SAA, the AIX Family Definition is a collection of specifications and components that IBM will support in a consistent manner in each of their AIX environments. These components include programming interfaces, user interfaces, communications protocols, database interfaces, and others.

Whereas SAA is based primarily on IBM proprietary standards, the AIX Family Definition is based on UNIX and other related industry standards. The goal of the AIX Family Definition, also a primary goal of SAA, is to provide a consistent environment across platforms—AIX platforms in this case—in order to aid in program development, system interoperability, program portability, and ease of use. The AIX Family Definition, then, will form the framework for developing applications that are consistent across AIX platforms or that may be portable across these platforms.

The platforms on which IBM will provide support for AIX Family Definition elements are AIX/370 for System/370 processors, AIX Version 3 for the RISC System/6000, and AIX PS/2 for the PS/2.

The AIX Family Definition consists of the following elements:

AIX Base System
AIX Programming Interface
AIX User Interfaces
AIX Communications Support
AIX Distributed Processing
AIX Applications

The AIX Base System element defines the level of UNIX which IBM will support on their strategic AIX platforms. It specifies, therefore, the base AIX operating system which will be provided on these platforms. This base operating system includes the operating system calls, libraries, commands, and utilities that IBM will support in their various versions of AIX.

Currently, the AIX Base System definition provides compatibility with UNIX System V Release 2 and Release 3 and Berkeley Software Distribution Release 4.3 (4.3 BSD). IBM's AIX systems will support most of the commands and routines included within these environments as well as IBM-added enhancements. (IBM always adds their own enhancements.) It also conforms to the POSIX IEEE Standard 1003.1–1988. IBM has also stated that it will comply with the X/OPEN Portability Guide, Issue 3 (XPG3) and the OSF Application Environment Specification Level 0.

The AIX Programming Interface element includes the programming languages that IBM will support in its AIX environments. The languages included under this element today are C, FORTRAN, and COBOL. Originally, C and FORTRAN were the only languages included in the AIX Family Definition. IBM added COBOL in February 1990. The definition for each language has been upgraded to provide compatibility with the corresponding SAA language specifications. This means that the C language definition will conform to the ANSI C definition when that standard (Draft X3J11/88-159, dated December 1988) is approved and it will conform to the SAA C language Common Programming Interface (CPI) specification as well. The FORTRAN language definition conforms to the ANSI FORTRAN standard and SAA FORTRAN CPI specifications. And, the COBOL definition conforms to the ANSI COBOL standard and SAA COBOL CPI specifications.

The intent of this element is to promote application source code portability between AIX environments. Supposedly, source code written in one of the above languages can be compiled in any of the AIX environments. This is similar to one of the goals of SAA's Common Programming Interface (CPI) element.

The SAA CPI element includes a language category which also includes C, COBOL, and FORTRAN along with a number of other programming languages. C, COBOL, and FORTRAN compilers that support the SAA CPI elements for these languages will be available in both the SAA and AIX environments, thereby promoting source code portability between these environments.

The AIX User Interfaces element of the AIX Family Definition addresses, as its name implies, user interfaces that will be supported in various AIX environments. This element includes the following:

> AIXwindows
> X Window System
> C Shell
> Bourne Shell
> GKS and graPHIGS Graphics Routine Libraries
> XGSL

AIXwindows provides a graphical user interface and toolkit that is based on the Open Software Foundation's OSF/Motif interface and is built on the X Window System. The X Window System is based on MIT's Version 11, Release 3 X Window System.

The popular C and Bourne command shells are included as part of this element. Graphics support includes GKS and graPHIGS Graphics Routine Libraries and XGSL. Not all AIX environments will have full support for all of the above user-interface services, however. For example, X Window server and graphics library routines will be provided on AIX workstations only.

The OSF/Motif support via AIXwindows was a later addition to the AIX Family Definition. With the AIXwindows and other presentation services support, multiple end-user interfaces are supported and can be used under AIX. Users will choose the interface that is most appropriate for their systems or applications.

IBM is taking a similar approach here as they have done with SAA's Common User Access (CUA) specifications. Rather than try to standardize on just a single user interface, multiple user interfaces will be supported. While consistency of the user interface across systems may vary, users are not locked into a user interface that is the lowest common denominator. Rather, they can build user interfaces optimized for particular applications.

The inclusion of OSF/Motif (AIXwindows), the X Window System, and the graphics support reflects the trend toward icon-based, graphical user interfaces, especially on personal computers and workstations.

The AIX Communications element includes components that will be used for communications between different AIX systems. The goal of this element is to define a standard set of communications protocols that will be supported in each environment in order to facilitate interoperability between these environments.

This element of the AIX Family Definition has been extended to include OSI and SNA LU 6.2 support. Following is a list of the components included as of this writing:

> Local Area Network (LAN) interface support:
>   Ethernet and IEEE 802.3
>   Token-Ring and IEEE 802.5
> Wide Area Network interface support:
>   X.25
>   ANSI 3.64
>   UUCP
> Protocol Support:
>   TCP/IP
>   SNA LU 6.2
>   OSI

AIX systems will be able to connect across either Ethernet LANs or Token-Ring LANs. Wide area network interfaces include standard X.25 support, ANSI 3.64 async ASCII terminal support, and support for the UNIX-to-UNIX Copy program, UUCP.

TCP/IP and SNA LU 6.2 protocols will be supported over either Ethernet or Token-Ring LANs as well as over X.25 networks. These protocols, and OSI protocols, will be supported in SAA as well as in AIX environments. In fact, IBM has committed to supporting interoperability between SAA and AIX environments using these sets of protocols.

The AIX Family Definition also includes a similar level of OSI communications support as is included in SAA. This includes support for FTAM, X.400, and similar levels of OSI layers 3–6 support.

This element parallels SAA's Common Communications Support (CCS) element in that it includes the communications and networking related interfaces and protocols that will be supported across platforms in order to facilitate interconnectivity and interoperability. In the case of the AIX Family Definition, it is to facilitate communications between AIX platforms, while in the case of SAA, it is to facilitate communications between SAA platforms.

The AIX Distributed Processing element includes facilities to be provided under AIX to support access to programs, files, and databases that are distributed across AIX systems in a network. Originally, this element included Distributed Services (DS) and SUN's Network File System (NFS). Now, however, DS support has been dropped from the AIX Family Definition.

Familiar remote functions such as rlogin, rwho, rcmd, and rexec are included as part of the AIX Family Definition. While IBM has settled on NFS for now, this could change in the future. IBM has indicated that they are looking at industry standards for distributed processing and distributed file access that are currently under development. These standards, when adopted, could either replace NFS or be added to the AIX Family Definition.

IBM has also committed to providing support for distributed relational database access as part of the AIX Family Definition. This will include support for SAA's DRDA and will allow distributed access between SAA and AIX relational databases.

AIX applications will be available across the AIX environments. By conforming to the AIX Family Definition, applications may be portable across the AIX environments. This element corresponds to SAA's Common Applications element. These elements themselves do not define any interfaces, conventions, etc. Rather, applications that conform to the interfaces, conventions, etc. (the components of the other elements) will be common applications. This means that such applications may be portable to other conforming environments, or may provide a consistent user interface with other conforming applications, or may interoperate with applications running in other environments.

These AIX Family Definition elements will be consistently supported on IBM System/370/390, RISC System/6000, and PS/2 platforms.

Figure 2-11 shows the parallel between AIX Family Definition elements and SAA elements. The goals are the same—consistency across a range of systems. For SAA, this means primarily IBM's commercial systems interconnected in SNA-based networks. For AIX, this means UNIX-based systems interconnected via industry standard protocols.

THE POSITIONING OF SAA AND AIX

IBM views SAA and AIX as two complementary operating system environments, each positioned to address particular market segments. SAA is targeted at IBM's traditional, mainframe-based customers. It defines system elements that will

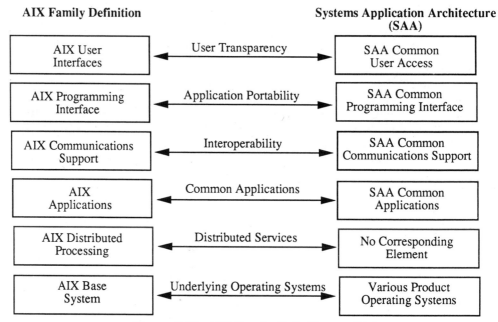

AIX Family Definition   **Systems Application Architecture (SAA)**

AIX User Interfaces	User Transparency	SAA Common User Access
AIX Programming Interface	Application Portability	SAA Common Programming Interface
AIX Communications Support	Interoperability	SAA Common Communications Support
AIX Applications	Common Applications	SAA Common Applications
AIX Distributed Processing	Distributed Services	No Corresponding Element
AIX Base System	Underlying Operating Systems	Various Product Operating Systems

Figure 2-11. *AIX Family Definition vs. SAA.*

consistently be supported across IBM's major commercial data processing platforms. These include System/370/390-compatible processors, AS/400 systems, and PS/2s.

SAA includes components that are commonly used by IBM's largest customers on these different systems. IBM is maintaining the status quo, in a sense, while providing these users a migration path to the next generation of applications. SAA provides the path of least resistance for this migration.

AIX, on the other hand, is targeted at markets where UNIX is already entrenched and is a requirement. IBM's AIX platforms are System/370/390-compatible processors, RISC System/6000 systems, and PS/2 workstations. As you can see in Figure 2-12, there is an overlap in the SAA and AIX platforms. Both SAA and AIX environments are provided on System/370/390 processors and PS/2s. However, only AIX is provided on the RISC System/6000 and only SAA is provided on the AS/400. This is positioning the AS/400 as the general-purpose commercial midrange system of choice while the RISC System/6000 is positioned as the UNIX box of choice. The RISC System/6000 will probably penetrate the AS/400 marketplace over time.

While SAA and AIX environments are available on System/370/390 mainframes, it is unlikely that the majority of MVS and VM customers will migrate to AIX. Likewise, moving from AIX to MVS or VM is not likely to occur. This is one reason why AIX is not included as an SAA operating environment. IBM is keeping SAA and AIX separate to address different markets, the installed bases of users and systems, and the needs of customers in each area. Designating AIX as another SAA operating environment would commit IBM to providing

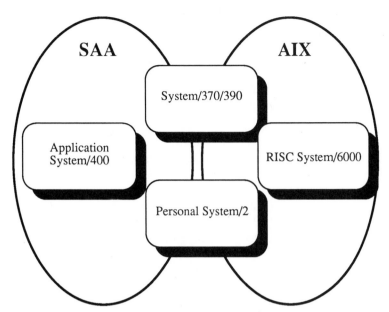

Figure 2-12. *IBM's SAA and AIX platforms overlap.*

support for *all* the SAA components under AIX. This would require major development and support efforts, and would be an ongoing commitment as SAA evolves.

IBM has taken the alternative approach of keeping SAA and AIX separate but tying them together in a number of ways. AIX to SAA interoperability will be provided so users can mix and match SAA and AIX systems. IBM will continue to add SAA support to AIX to make it more consistent with the SAA environments over time. Since AIX is not an SAA environment, though, IBM does not have to provide support for all SAA components in AIX. This is a luxury that IBM hopes to enjoy for a while.

SAA AND AIX CONVERGENCE

There are a number of areas in which IBM either is or will be providing convergence between their SAA and AIX environments. These areas include communications and connectivity, network management, distributed databases and files, presentation services, electronic mail, and common programming languages. We will take a brief look at each of these areas.

Communications/Connectivity

IBM will focus on three sets of communications components that may be used for interconnecting and communicating between SAA and AIX systems. These are:

Protocols:
  SNA LU 6.2
  TCP/IP
  OSI
Connections:
  Token-Ring (IEEE 802.5, ISO 8802-5)
  Ethernet (IEEE 802.3, ISO 8802-3)
  X.25

The above protocols, which are shown in Figure 2-13, will be supported across each of the above connections. All the protocols and connectivity alternatives will be supported in all SAA and AIX environments.

SNA LU 6.2, OSI, Token-Ring, Ethernet, and X.25 are already SAA components. TCP/IP is not part of SAA, and there is no indication that it will be added. However, to support interconnectivity between SAA and AIX, TCP/IP support will be provided in all SAA environments.

On the AIX side, TCP/IP was included in the AIX Family Definition from day one. IBM later added SNA LU 6.2 and OSI to the AIX Family Definition, committing to provide support for both in all AIX environments.

This means that eventually, when all this support is actually available, users will be able to pick and choose which communications protocols and interfaces to use for communicating between their AIX and SAA systems.

Network Management

Managing heterogeneous networks of different system types is one of the major problems facing most large corporations today. As IBM allows customers to network together SAA and AIX systems, managing them becomes a problem and mixed network management facilities will be a requirement. Little support is available from IBM to do this today. IBM is committed, though, to support network management of mixed SNA, TCP/IP, and OSI networks. Such support will allow MVS, VM, OS/400, OS/2 EE, and AIX systems to be managed from a single network control point.

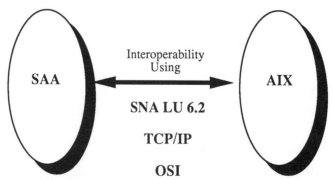

Figure 2-13. *Communications protocols to be supported between SAA and AIX environments.*

NetView will be the key product to provide such centralized network management support. IBM is intending to enhance NetView to provide network management support for TCP/IP and OSI networks in addition to SNA networks. This support will be provided under both the MVS and VM operating system environments on System/370/390-based processors and will allow mixed SNA, TCP/IP, and OSI networks to be managed from a single NetView focal point.

Distributed Database

Distributed relational database access is another area that is growing in importance. SQL is the SAA CPI database interface and is the interface that will be supported by relational database products in the AIX environments. Complete interoperability between distributed relational database systems across the SAA and AIX environments will be provided.

IBM does not yet provide relational database support under AIX, however. IBM's goal is to provide relational databases in all the AIX environments in order to support sharing of relational data between SAA and AIX systems.

The AIX Family Definition has been enhanced to include SQL distributed relational database capabilities. IBM has indicated that the relational database support will conform to the ISO and ANSI SQL standards, U.S. Government FIPS standards, and the X/OPEN SQL specifications in the X/OPEN Portability Guide Issue 3.

Shared Files

In addition to supporting relational data sharing, IBM will also support standard file sharing between SAA and AIX systems. Today, such support is accomplished using SUN Microsystem's Network File System (NFS) protocols. NFS client support is available for AIX/370 and announced for AIX/6000 and AIX PS/2. NFS Server support is available for AIX/370 and MVS and VM. It is announced for AIX/6000 and AIX PS/2.

IBM has issued a Statement of Direction indicating their intent to provide NFS Client support under OS/2 EE and NFS Server support under OS/400.

Presentation Services

Presentation services in SAA environments will be provided by SAA Presentation Managers while presentation services in AIX environments will be supported via the X Window System and AIXwindows. The X Window System and AIXwindows support will be provided in all AIX environments and as interoperability options in all SAA environments.

Mail Exchange

IBM will support electronic mail exchange between OfficeVision, an SAA application, and AIX systems. Support for TCP/IP Simple Mail Transfer Protocol (SMTP) will be provided in the AIX environments and bridge functions will be provided on MVS, VM, and OS/400 systems to support mail exchange with OfficeVision users. The MVS and VM bridge functions are actually available now from Soft-Switch, an IBM Business Partner.

In addition, the AIX systems will support the X.400 OSI mail protocols and IBM will provide another bridge function to support X.400 to OfficeVision mail. This bridge function is also available now from Soft-Switch.

Common Languages

To promote portability of source code between SAA and AIX environments, IBM will provide common language compilers for selected languages in each of the environments. The languages to be supported in both environments include C, FORTRAN, and COBOL. FORTRAN and COBOL support the existing ANSI standards for these languages and C will support the draft ANSI C standard when it is finally adopted. In addition, the compilers for these languages will also support the SAA CPI extensions for these languages.

SUMMARY

One of the major problems facing IBM's customers is the incompatibility of their different computer systems. The lack of consistency causes user-training problems, program development problems, and inhibits interoperability between systems. It also makes it difficult to distribute programs and data across a network of these dissimilar systems.

In attempting to bring greater consistency across their product lines, IBM created SAA to standardize on the interfaces to users, programs, and systems. They selected ESA/370 and ESA/390 processors, the AS/400, and the PS/2 as the strategic SAA hardware platforms. The IBM-designated SAA operating environments for these platforms are MVS/ESA and VM/ESA for ESA/370 and ESA/390 processors, OS/400 for the AS/400, and OS/2 Extended Edition for the PS/2.

SAA is subdivided into various elements, each focused on a different set of requirements. These elements are Common User Access (CUA), Common Programming Interface (CPI), Common Communications Support (CCS), and Common Applications. The CUA, CPI, and CCS elements of SAA address SAA's major goals of providing consistent user interfaces, consistent programming environments, and consistent communications support in all SAA operating environments, respectively. These SAA elements consist of components used to standardize the interfaces to users, programs, and other systems. Common Applications are built using CUA, CPI, and CCS components.

Each SAA operating environment consists of an operating system, application enablers, communications software, and applications, among other kinds of software. Each environment has its own unique products which implement these types of functions. While the various SAA products are different in each environment (i.e., they are different implementations of the same functions), consistency is achieved because the products adhere to the SAA guidelines and specifications. They provide a consistent implementation of SAA components.

SAA Common Applications span SAA environments, provide an SAA-compliant user interface, and use SAA programming services and interfaces. When communications with other systems is required, SAA CCS components are used.

IBM has chosen not to make AIX an SAA environment at this point in time. Rather, IBM is pursuing a parallel strategy. IBM's AIX Family Definition defines the support that IBM will provide across their AIX platforms. Consistent AIX and SAA environments will be provided across a range of platforms. SAA remains targeted at IBM's traditional data processing customers while AIX is targeted at the engineering workstation marketplace and other markets where UNIX is a requirement. However, IBM will provide ways to tie AIX and SAA systems together. Alternative methods of doing this will include using SNA LU 6.2, TCP/IP, and/or OSI protocols.

part 2

SAA ELEMENTS AND COMPONENTS

3

Common User Access

Common User Access (CUA) defines the interface through which users access SAA applications and system services. Prior to the introduction of SAA, IBM had no published standards for the design of user interfaces provided by its products. Since there was no cross-product standard for user interfaces, the implementors of each IBM product designed their own interfaces. This resulted in a lack of user-interface consistency across IBM's products.

Inconsistency of user interfaces across products results in user-training problems. When each application has a different interface, using one application gains the user little or no insight into the operation of other applications. It requires virtually the same level of effort for users to learn each new application, even though they might already know how to use several related applications. It is certainly desirable to leverage the investment of user training by making the knowledge of the operation of any one application largely transferable to the use of other applications.

The design of consistent user interfaces is an issue that almost everyone in the computer industry is dealing with. Virtually all vendors of computer-based products are adopting standards for user-interface design. Some examples of user-interface standardization efforts from vendors other than IBM would include Apple's Macintosh interface, NewWave from Hewlett-Packard, and Open Look from Sun Microsystems.

SAA's Common User Access is IBM's own "standard" for its SAA application platforms. While CUA and each of the other user-interface standards mentioned above is different, they all have a similar look and feel, and share many visual elements. They are all graphics-oriented, windows-based interfaces and are generically referred to as Graphical User Interfaces (GUIs). SAA also includes support for character-oriented user-interface models.

The primary objective of these user interfaces, including SAA CUA, is ease of use. This is accomplished in two ways. First, there must be consistency within applications and across applications running on any given application platform. Within SAA this would include the System/370/390 processors, AS/400s, and PS/2s. This consistency reduces the amount of training a user requires to learn new applications.

Another goal of these user interfaces is to facilitate the transfer of a user's existing knowledge to new application programs. This is typically accomplished through the use of metaphors that represent the noncomputerized system with which users might already be familiar. An example of such a metaphor might be an interface that displays information in the format of paper forms that are already in use within the organization.

Another example would be the use of icons that represent common office equipment such as file cabinets and printers. Instead of teaching the users a series of commands to print documents, the user could simply use a mouse to drag an icon that represents a document to be printed, to an icon that represents the target printer.

Another element that enhances ease of use in some applications is a high degree of user control, which allows the user to explore the applications at his or her own pace rather than requiring the user to learn the entire application on the front end. This encourages users to learn new applications incrementally.

On the other hand, there are other types of applications that require a highly structured interaction with users. These would include data-entry applications which are designed to ensure that data is entered in a very specific format.

CUA'S TARGET ENVIRONMENTS

The environments that Common User Access is targeting can be defined in terms of the types of workstations being supported as well as the requirements of the users of the systems themselves. These requirements define the two dimensions of CUA's target user environments.

Types of SAA User Workstations

One of the factors that determines the type of user interface appropriate for a given application is the level of processing power available in the user's workstation. One of the great challenges in designing user interfaces is to deal with the wide range of local processing power available in workstations today.

Processing power can range from nearly zero in nonprogrammable terminals to the mainframe-class power that is available in sophisticated workstations. The design challenge is to create a user interface that has a high degree of consistency across workstations while exploiting the tremendous processing power of modern workstations.

SAA's Nonprogrammable Terminals

While IBM does not specifically include any nonprogrammable terminals within SAA, IBM must deal with its large installed base of these devices. In the IBM product line the predominant nonprogrammable terminals are the 3270 and 5250 product lines. Both lines of terminals are designed to interface with host-based programs that provide all the application and user-interface intelligence.

The 3270 terminals are supported by System/370/390 hosts while the 5250 devices are designed to interface with IBM's midrange processors such as the AS/400, System/36, and System/38. The 3270 and 5250 terminals are important to SAA because they are the most popular workstations for users of IBM System/370 and AS/400 SAA platforms.

While there are differences between the 3270 and 5250 terminals, they are both totally reliant on the host to which they are attached. This means that any interaction that occurs with the user of that system must involve not only the terminal that is supporting the user, but also the host computer. This leads to potential performance problems, particularly when the terminal is attached to the host computer by relatively low-speed telecommunications lines. These performance considerations place severe restrictions on the types of user interfaces that can be supported by nonprogrammable terminals.

Virtually any user interface could theoretically be implemented on a nonprogrammable terminal but, as a practical matter, the user's performance expectations must be taken into consideration. Even graphics can be supported on some models of the 3270 line of display terminals, but performance suffers as large amounts of graphical data must be sent across communications lines between the terminal and its host computer. The graphical and highly interactive interfaces that many users have come to expect require a considerable amount of processing power on the workstation in order to provide an acceptable level of performance.

SAA's Programmable Workstation—The PS/2

The Personal System/2 (PS/2) is SAA's programmable workstation. It provides the processing power and graphics support that is capable of supporting any of the SAA user-interface models which are described later. The PS/2 can be used to implement either the distributed dialog or distributed function SAA cooperative processing models in situations where the PS/2 is acting as a front end to host-based applications. These cooperative processing models were described in Chapter 1.

In either case, all the user-interface processing is performed on the workstation. This means that the user interfaces implemented on these systems will generally be able to support relatively sophisticated graphics and a high degree of user interaction without serious performance problems.

SAA's distributed dialog model for cooperative processing handles most of the basic user interaction locally on the PS/2 system, but requires host-based software to actually perform application functions. This model might be appropriate when most of the application's resources reside on the host computer.

In many cases the PS/2 may have the resources required to run at least part of the application program locally. In these cases the distributed function design model can be used. This model usually results in better performance for the user because the amount of host interaction is reduced.

Interface Requirements of SAA Users

Even more varied than the capabilities of workstations is the range of users who need to interface with SAA applications. Potential users range from computer specialists who are thoroughly trained in an application to a casual user who walks up to an information terminal in a public facility such as an airport. Some users perform highly repetitive tasks like data entry while others need the flexibility to navigate through large amounts of information.

Clearly, there is no single style of interface that will meet the needs of all users. Interface designers must trade off factors like:

> Performance
> Flexibility
> Ease of use
> Ease of learning

SAA's Common User Access defines several levels of user interface that are designed to meet this range of requirements. The performance objective, for example, can be achieved in several ways.

For users of nonprogrammable terminals there is little choice other than to create a very simple interface with minimal interaction between the terminal and the host application. This results in better performance, but it will probably be lacking in flexibility and ease of learning. For users of programmable workstations, local processing power can be applied to provide acceptable performance while maintaining flexibility and ease of use.

The processing power of programmable workstations can be used to implement user interfaces that minimize the impact of these trade-offs. The combination of workstation capabilities and user requirements results in a wide range of user-interface design possibilities and trade-offs.

COMMON USER ACCESS, 1989

IBM's original 1987 definition of CUA (included as part of the initial announcement of SAA) attempted to deal with these trade-offs between workstation capabilities and user requirements, but it did not draw a clear distinction between classes of workstations and users. The 1987 CUA definition really just defined a single interface and then noted those features that were not appropriate for implementation on nonprogrammable terminals.

The burden of deciding which options should be used for each interface fell on the application designer. It quickly became evident that a single user interface could not meet the needs of all users and the variety of workstations that had to be supported. The primary goal of the CUA 1987 specifications was consistency across the SAA platforms—the lowest common denominator in effect. The capabilities of more intelligent devices was traded off for consistency.

This lowest common denominator approach, though, did not exploit the full capabilities of SAA's primary user workstation, the PS/2. In order to take better advantage of the graphics capabilities of the PS/2, in 1989 IBM enhanced and refocused the original CUA definition by more clearly defining several levels of user interface. A number of user-interface "models" were defined that were targeted at specific categories of workstations and users.

The 1989 CUA definition is subdivided into two major categories—the basic interfaces and the advanced interfaces. The basic interfaces are targeted at users of nonprogrammable terminals while the advanced interfaces are designed to support users of programmable, graphical workstations. Within both the basic and advanced categories IBM defines two interface models. Some consistency was sacrificed in order to utilize more fully the features of the PS/2. The goal was to allow the "best" user interface to be used within a given environment even though there was a trade-off in consistency.

The SAA CUA models are:

> Entry
> Text subset
> Graphical
> Workplace

These CUA user-interface models will be discussed later in the chapter. These models specify required and optional elements of interfaces that provide interface solutions for certain targeted groups of users and workstation types. Before looking more closely at each of the CUA interface models, it would be useful to discuss the different styles of user interaction that are supported.

STYLES OF USER INTERFACES

User interfaces are made up of objects and actions. Objects are the entities that users actually work with. Actions define the ways the users manipulate or modify objects. The user interface defines the way the user controls these objects and actions.

An example of an object is a spreadsheet. The spreadsheet can be manipulated via defined actions. The spreadsheet object is made up of many sub-objects such as numeric data, titles and headings, and formulas that manipulate the numeric data fields. These objects and their sub-objects create a hierarchy in which sub-objects inherit the properties of the objects that contain them. This inheritance of properties is one of the key characteristics of an object-oriented programming environment.

Actions are operations that modify the properties of objects or in some way change the objects. An example of an action involving our spreadsheet example might be the modification of the width of a column within the spreadsheet. The columns are sub-objects within the spreadsheet that have the property of width. The action is a modification of the width property. The individual cells that make up the column are sub-objects of the column and are thus modified because they inherit the property of width from the column to which they belong.

One of the major issues in user-interface design revolves around how the user interacts with these objects and uses actions to control the operation of an application program. There are two basic approaches: object-action and action-object. The selection of one approach versus the other is driven by the type of application being supported as well as by the characteristics of the user.

The Object-Action Design Approach

Users of object-action–oriented user interfaces first select an object or group of objects and then initiate some type of action on these objects. The object-action orientation is supported by all CUA user-interface models and is the preferred user interface for most new SAA applications.

The object-action orientation is suitable for applications where a high degree of user control is desired. Not only does the user get a high degree of control, but the object-action design allows users to explore new ways of using the application. This is due to the fact that a user can select an object or a group of objects and let the context of the interface show what actions can be performed on the selected objects. The user does not have to know which actions are applicable to each object type. This can be determined by the context of the user interface.

The fact that the interface can determine which actions are applicable to a given object can also eliminate the need for long sequences of hierarchical menus in applications. The user does not have to navigate through a series of action choices that might not be applicable to a target object. This contextual selection of actions can result in a greatly simplified user interface. This is particularly true in cases where there are many possible actions within an application.

Another benefit of the object-action orientation is that the user can perform multiple actions on an object without repeating the object-selection operation. This design also reduces the occurrence of action modes which are user-interface states that require the user to switch from mode to mode in order to perform multiple operations on a single object or group of objects.

The Action-Object Design Approach

The action-object–oriented interface, on the other hand, is suitable for applications that do not allow a high degree of user control. These might include applications where no user training is possible, such as a walk-up information terminal in a hotel lobby. The action-object design is often used in older applications and will continue to be used because a major rewrite of these applications is not practical.

The only CUA interface model that supports the action-object orientation is the entry model. These interfaces commonly consist of a hierarchy of menus through which the user progressively refines a request for an action and then the user chooses the object upon which the action is performed. Another common example of an action-object interface would be a command line interface like those commonly used in operating systems.

MAJOR CLASSES OF CUA USER INTERFACES

As we said earlier, two major classes of user interfaces are defined by SAA CUA 1989. The first of these are known as basic interfaces. The design goal of the basic interfaces is to support users of nonprogrammable terminals and to provide them with as much compatibility as possible with the interfaces that are defined for use on programmable workstations.

The basic interfaces must deal with the shortcomings of nonprogrammable terminals which usually include:

> Performance limitations due to host communications links
> Character-oriented rather than graphical display capability
> Lack of a pointing device such as a mouse

The basic interfaces also provide a CUA migration path for users of older application programs that are based on action-object rather than object-action interaction with users.

SAA's advanced interfaces, the second major class of CUA interface models, are designed to support users of programmable workstations. The advanced interfaces exploit the local programming power available on these workstations and their advanced graphics capabilities.

The advanced interfaces must always use the object-action style of user interaction, which frequently makes them unsuitable for use with older application programs.

Migrating Basic Interfaces to Programmable Workstations

While IBM's intent was to make the basic interfaces and advanced interfaces as consistent as is practical, the programmable workstation has capabilities that are not usually available on nonprogrammable terminals. Nonprogrammable terminals usually do not have graphics capabilities and typically cannot support visual elements such as radio buttons, icons, and resizable windows. These devices also do not support a mouse and are limited to keyboard input.

Despite the differences in capabilities between nonprogrammable terminals and intelligent workstations, migration of user interfaces is possible. If the interface is implemented using SAA's Dialog Services products, a single interface specification can be used to support both types of devices. When using nonprogrammable terminals like 3270s, Dialog Services (e.g., ISPF) implements the CUA Text Subset model, a character-oriented interface. The same interface definitions will support the graphical model of CUA, a graphical, windows-based interface, when used on a PS/2 system. The Dialog Services software (e.g., OS/2

Dialog Manager) handles the differences in the kinds of visual elements supported by each category of user device.

Each of the CUA model user interfaces will be described below.

Entry Model

The entry model interface is targeted at applications that do not give the user a great degree of control in "navigating" through the application. These applications are typically either old applications that are being upgraded to provide users with a simple SAA-like interface or new applications that are designed to rigidly control the user's actions. An example of the former would be an existing text-based, interactive host application designed for use with 3270 terminals. An example of the latter would be an application that is designed to be used by a completely untrained user such as at a walk-up information terminal in a public building. It would also be appropriate for applications that involve only repetitive data entry.

The entry model differs from all other SAA user-interface models in that it supports either object-action or action-object interaction with the user. Each of the other models supports only the object-action model of interaction. The entry model can be implemented on nonprogrammable terminals (e.g., 3270s) or programmable workstations (e.g., PS/2s with OS/2) that require an action-object style of interaction. An example of a screen layout that conforms to the entry model is shown in Figure 3-1.

Most of the visual elements used in the text subset model, which is shown in Figure 3-2, are also available for use in the entry model. The major exception is the action bar which is not available in the entry model. Another difference is

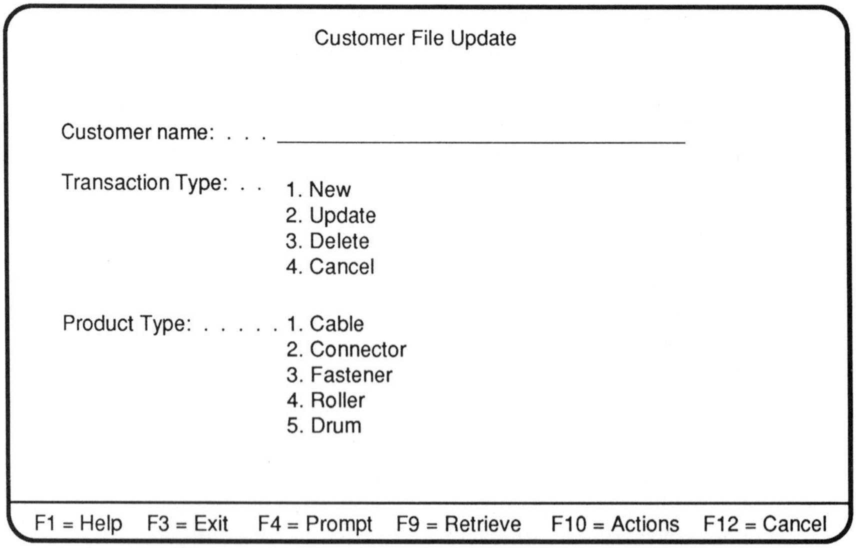

Customer File Update

Customer name: . . . _____

Transaction Type: . . 1. New
                       2. Update
                       3. Delete
                       4. Cancel

Product Type: . . . . . 1. Cable
                        2. Connector
                        3. Fastener
                        4. Roller
                        5. Drum

F1 = Help   F3 = Exit   F4 = Prompt   F9 = Retrieve   F10 = Actions   F12 = Cancel

***Figure 3-1.** Common User Access—entry model.*

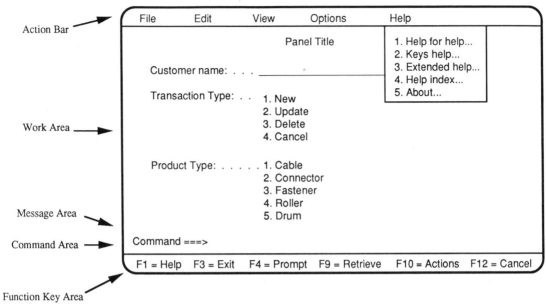

Action Bar

Work Area

Message Area

Command Area

Function Key Area

Figure 3-2. *Common User Access—text subset model.*

that the work area of the entry model can contain both objects and actions while in the text subset model only objects can appear in the work area.

Text Subset of the Graphical Model

The text subset is designed to support decision-intensive users of nonprogrammable terminals. As its name implies, the goal of this model is to provide the user with as many features of the graphical model as can practically be implemented with the nonprogrammable, text-oriented devices.

Only the object-action style of interaction is supported by the text subset model. User interfaces that are based on action-object interaction must use the entry model CUA interface design.

The text subset model includes a wide range of visual interface elements which are shown in Figure 3-2. Some of these elements are optional and may be used based on the requirements of the application. Other elements are required for all interfaces that conform to the text subset model. The visual appearance of these elements is designed to be as similar to their graphical interface counterparts as possible.

The main visual element of the text subset display is the primary window. Since the text subset model does not support windowing, the primary window covers the entire screen of the display station. All other elements of the user interface operate within the primary window. Other windows, called pop-ups, may optionally be displayed within the primary window whenever they are required by the application.

The information displays within windows and pop-ups are called panels.

Panels that are displayed in the primary window are required to contain certain elements which are shown in Figure 3-2. These elements provide the overall structure of the visual elements that the user interacts with. They also provide a degree of consistency with the advanced interfaces which are supported for users of programmable workstations.

All panels displayed in the primary window must have an action bar. The action bar is always positioned at the top of the panel and is used to select related groups of actions. The action bar contains labels that correspond to groups of subchoices which are contained in pull-down menus. There must be a pull-down menu for each choice on the action bar. The panel title should always be displayed just below the action bar.

The work area of the panel is the area set aside for the application-dependent elements of the user interface. These include the objects with which the user will be working. The choice of visual elements and their positions on the screen are based on application-design requirements rather than any rigid SAA rules.

The message area is located below the work area and is used to display three types of messages: information, warning, and action.

A command area is reserved below the message area for applications that use a command interface. The command area can be used to implement a fast-path capability which allows experienced users to bypass sequences of menus and enter entire commands directly.

The final required visual element of the text subset model is the function key area which is located at the bottom of the screen. Some of the function key definitions are common actions that are consistent across applications while others are application-specific.

Performance Issues for Nonprogrammable Terminals

While the text subset model defines many visual elements similar to those defined by advanced interface models, the designer must consider the performance impact of using some of these elements. For example, the frequent use of pull-down menus on nonprogrammable terminals involves a round-trip transmission to the host where the application program resides. The delays caused by these transmissions could become annoying to the user if they occur frequently.

Migrating to Intelligent Workstations

When an application interface is migrated from a nonprogrammable terminal to a programmable workstation, the interface designer can take advantage of several additional capabilities including: local graphics capabilities, mouse for pointing and selection, and windowing.

The local processing power of the programmable workstation can be used to eliminate most of the interactions between the terminal and the host. This is particularly true for the display of pull-down menus, pop-ups, and the scrolling of applications data.

The programmable workstation will usually provide the ability to use a mouse or other pointing device. The mouse can be used to make the use of the interface more intuitive for the user by pointing to visual objects on the screen rather than requiring combinations of keystrokes to select objects and actions.

The local processing and graphics capability of programmable workstations can also be used to implement multiple windows which are both movable and resizable. This allows the user the flexibility to arrange the information for one or more applications on the display station as described.

Graphical Model

The graphical CUA model is designed to exploit the graphics capabilities and local processing power of programmable workstations. The target SAA platform for the implementation of the graphical model is IBM's Personal System/2 running the OS/2 Extended Edition operating system.

The graphical model expands on the capabilities of the text subset model. Since the intelligent workstations that support the graphical model are assumed to have graphics capability rather than character-oriented displays, the interface designer can choose from a wider range of visual elements when designing the user interface.

The local processing power of intelligent workstations is needed to support the use of graphics and it also can reduce or even eliminate the need for interaction with a remote host computer. This local processing power allows the design of much more interactive user interfaces without imposing a performance penalty.

Major Elements of the Graphical Model

Every application that provides a user interface based on the graphical model must have a primary window. In the graphical model the primary window does not necessarily cover the entire screen because it is resizable and movable. Primary windows for multiple applications may be present on a display screen simultaneously. Figure 3-3 shows the main visual elements of a primary window which is designed according to the rules of the CUA graphical model.

The title bar is located at the top of the window. The icon on the left side of the title bar is the system menu icon which is associated with a pull-down menu that controls sizing and location of the primary window on the user's display screen. At the right side of the title bar are the window-sizing icons which can be used to minimize, maximize, or restore the previous window size.

Below the title bar is the action bar which allows users to select actions from choices listed in pull-down menus. If the primary window is resizable, it will also contain scroll bars which indicate that more information is available for display. The rest of the area within the window is called the client area. The client area contains all other application-specific information and controls required to support the user dialog.

In addition to the primary window that must be associated with each application, the designer of the graphical model user interface can also use secondary

Title Bar

Action Bar

Client Area

Scroll Bar

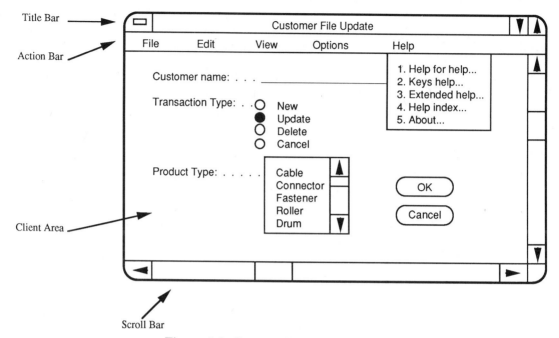

Figure 3-3. *Common User Access—graphical model.*

windows. These secondary windows must always be associated with a primary window. Like primary windows they are movable and resizable, and they contain the same basic visual elements such as the title bar, the action bar, and scroll bars. Secondary windows are used to carry on a dialog with the user that is independent of the dialog implemented in the primary window. A common example of a secondary window would be the display of help information for the dialog in the primary window.

Another window type defined by the graphical model is the dialog box. A dialog box is not resizable, but it is movable. Dialog boxes are used to carry on a serial dialog with the user that must be completed in order to continue with any other window used by the application. Dialog boxes can also be used in place of secondary windows when all the information fits into the fixed-size window without the use of scrolling.

Controls Available Within the Graphical Model

Controls are the visual elements of the interface that allow the user to enter information and make choices. These controls can range from simple text-entry fields to graphical representations of pushbuttons that can be activated by the mouse.

Figure 3-4 shows examples of three of the most common controls used in the CUA graphical model. The check boxes are used to select one or more options. Options are selected by positioning the mouse pointer over the box that corre-

Radio Buttons   Check Boxes   Combination Box

Figure 3-4. Common graphical visual control elements.

sponds to the selection being made. These boxes toggle on and off. If an option is not selected, a mouse click will select it; if an option is selected, a mouse click will deselect it. A check mark present in a box is the user's visual feedback which indicates that the option has been selected.

In cases where only a single choice must be made from a list of options, the radio buttons can be used. A mouse click on any of the buttons in a set of radio buttons will cause that option to be selected and all other options to be deselected. This always results in a single choice from the list of options.

The combination box can be used to simplify the entry of text data in a field. The user can either key the required data into the entry box or use the mouse to select one of the standard items from the list displayed below the box. The list of standard items is sequenced according to how the entry field is used and this list can be scrolled if it is too long to fit in the allocated screen space.

An example of the CUA graphical model is the OS/2 Presentation Manager. The Presentation Manager provides elements such as title bars and scroll bars, and the ability to resize windows. The Presentation Manager also provides a programming interface that allows applications to implement all the visual elements of CUA.

Workplace Extensions to the Graphical Model

CUA's workplace environment is an extension to the graphical model. This user interface model is called the workplace environment because the screen that the user interacts with is designed to look like an office workplace. The user manipulates icons that represent familiar objects found in the real office workplace.

The workplace environment is a metaphor for the typical office environment which includes objects like memos, spreadsheets, file folders, wastebaskets, and printers. These objects are represented on the user's screen by graphical icons which can be directly manipulated by the user. Icons that represent office objects are shown in Figure 3-5.

The objective of this interface model is to allow non–computer users to easily transfer their knowledge of how office environments operate to the operation of computerized systems. If the users want to print a document, for example,

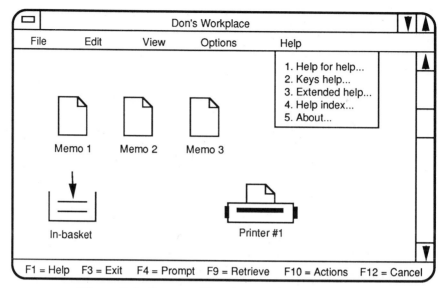

Figure 3-5. *Common User Access—workplace model.*

they simply use the mouse to drag a screen icon that represents the document to an icon that represents the printer. This direct manipulation of icons replaces the series of menus and commands that would be required if one of the other CUA interface models were being used.

The icons that the user sees on the screen represent objects within the workplace programming environment. These objects encapsulate programs and data that can be manipulated as a unit. Objects are arranged in a hierarchy where objects can be composed of sub-objects. These sub-objects inherit the characteristics of the objects to which they are hierarchically related. These relationships result in a powerful programming environment because new objects can be created simply by adding to existing objects rather than requiring a complete new implementation.

There are three major categories of objects that the users of the workplace model can manipulate. These three categories of objects are data, containers, and devices.

Data objects would include text documents, drawings, and spreadsheets. Data objects are made up of the information that is processed by an application program as well as the program itself. This is fundamentally different from a traditional programming environment where data and the application programs that process that data are separate entities.

File cabinets and in-baskets would be examples of containers. As their name implies, containers are designed to organize objects. A group of documents, for example, might be placed into an in-basket for later processing.

Devices are objects that perform some operation on another object. An example might be an input/output device like a printer. The user can drag an object such as a document to the icon that represents a printer. This results in the initiation of a print operation.

The Workplace Programming Environment

Unlike other CUA design models, the workplace environment is more than just a user-interface specification. The manipulation of icons that represent objects on the user's display screen requires the support of a specialized programming environment. The object-oriented workplace environment requires the support of an object-oriented programming environment. The result is an electronic version of an office workplace.

Object Handlers and List Handlers   Two general types of software are needed to support the object-oriented programming environment—object handlers and list handlers. Object handlers consist of software that is designed to manage objects. An object handler would be the software that implements the functions that are initiated by the direct manipulation of screen icons. For example, an object handler would initiate the printing of a document whose icon is dragged to a printer icon on a user's screen.

Container objects also require software called list handlers. A container object is an object that holds other objects. Some examples of container objects would be file folders and in-baskets, each of which is capable of holding one or more documents. List handlers display the contents of a container object and provide the ability to perform operations on the objects within the container. OfficeVision/2 implements the workplace model user interface. Figure 3-6 shows a list handler window which displays objects that are included within a container object.

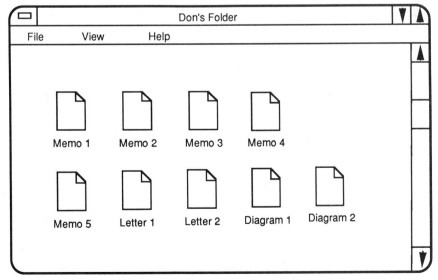

Figure 3-6. *List handler window.*

RELATIONSHIP OF CUA ELEMENTS TO SAA'S COMMON
PROGRAMMING INTERFACE

While Common User Access defines the external look and feel of SAA user interfaces, other elements of SAA are actually used to implement these interfaces. These elements are part of SAA's Common Programming Interface (CPI) and include the dialog and presentation services of CPI.

The Dialog Manager of the OS/2 operating system is generally easier for programmers to use than the CPI OS/2 Presentation Manager. Users of the Dialog Manager interact with the user through predefined panels that contain the visual element of the display screen. The Dialog Manager also has a procedural interface rather than the event-driven interface which is supported by the Presentation Manager. This makes the Dialog Manager easier for most application programmers to use.

The Dialog Manager can be used to implement the entry and text subset CUA models on nonprogrammable terminals and most elements of the graphical interface on intelligent workstations.

In order to implement the full graphical model and the workplace extensions to the graphical model on intelligent workstations, application developers must use the CPI presentation services interface. This event-driven interface gives the application programmer full control over all interactions with the user's display station. It also allows programmers to use the object-oriented application programming techniques that are required to support the workplace extensions to the graphical CUA model.

The presentation services element directly implements several of the visual elements that make up the CUA user interfaces. These include title and action bars as well as the scrolling bars and window-resizing controls.

SUMMARY

SAA is capable of supporting a wide range of user-interface styles. Common User Access defines four major levels of user interfaces. These different styles of user interfaces are described by the following models:

> Entry model
> Text subset model
> Graphical model
> Workplace model

Each of these interfaces is designed to meet a particular set of requirements. Requirements along two dimensions have influenced the design of CUA. These requirements are based on the types of users to be supported and on the power of available workstations.

Since the use of nonprogrammable terminals is still widespread, CUA defines interfaces that are simple enough to implement on these devices, but still maintain some consistency with the SAA interfaces used on more powerful programmable workstations. The interfaces that are targeted at intelligent workstation users are highly graphical and are capable of exploiting the latest object-oriented programming techniques.

CUA defines user interfaces that can provide varying degrees of user control. Some users perform highly repetitive functions or have minimal training and, therefore, require that the application control most interactions. On the other hand, many professionals who use intelligent workstations need a high degree of control over the applications. For these users SAA provides visual elements that allow flexible navigation through applications.

Within the CUA guidelines it is possible to build user interfaces that meet all these requirements. CUA gives the application designer a wide range of choices in the creation of user interfaces, but still provides a high degree of consistency across all CUA-compatible interfaces.

4

Common Programming Interface

The Common Programming Interface (CPI) element is one of the major sub-divisions of SAA, as indicated in Figure 4-1. It deals with the programming languages, system services, and programming interfaces that software developers can use in developing SAA applications. With the CPI element, IBM is attempting to standardize the software environments (i.e., the programming environments) available on SAA platforms.

Why does IBM want such standardization? There are a number of reasons for creating standard programming environments across the SAA platforms. Here are a few of the reasons:

> To allow programmers to use their skills in different environments
> To allow applications to be developed that are independent of any particular system
> To support SAA goals such as consistent user interfaces, distributed data access, and cooperative processing

Let's look at how the CPI element addresses these areas.

TRANSFERABILITY OF PROGRAMMING SKILLS

CPI defines a consistent set of programming interfaces, services, and tools which will be available on different SAA systems, making it easier to develop applications for these different systems. The availability of such common software components allows programmers to transfer their programming skills to other

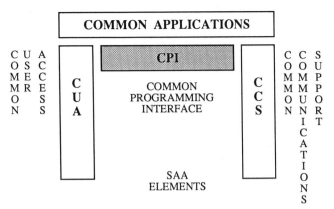

Figure 4-1. *SAA's Common Programming Interface (CPI) element.*

systems. That is, it makes it easier for programmers who have been developing programs for one system to develop programs for another system.

Rather than having to learn how to use a completely new set of program interfaces and services when developing applications that may span different systems or execute on different systems, programmers can use the same types of interfaces and services in multiple environments. This minimizes programmer training requirements and speeds up application development because familiar tools and interfaces can be utilized across systems.

The common software components that will be made available in all the SAA environments include application enablers such as programming language compilers, relational database management systems, dialog managers, and other tools. The actual application programming interfaces (i.e., the APIs) to these enablers will be the same on all systems. The programming skills learned in one SAA environment will be directly transferable to other SAA environments. For example, programs can be written in the same language and the programming to use dialog services or to access databases will be the same regardless of the SAA system for which the application is being developed.

SYSTEM-INDEPENDENT APPLICATIONS AND PORTABILITY

Another reason to create standardized programming environments is to promote portability of applications. Portability means the ability to move a program from one environment and execute it in another environment. There are varying levels of portability. In most cases, it will *not* be possible to port applications from one system to another with no changes. Usually, at least minor changes will have to be made in order to execute an application in an environment different from the one in which it was developed.

However, applications can be written in a relatively system-independent manner by using the generic SAA CPI programming interfaces to access common services that are available on all SAA systems. When moving the application code from one system to another, it is not necessary to rewrite these system-independent SAA interfaces.

SUPPORT FOR SAA GOALS

The CPI element includes components that are used to support the major SAA goals of a consistent user interface, distributed file and database access, and distributed processing across SAA environments. There are one or more CPI services and interfaces directed to each of these goals. Let's look at what is included in the CPI element and how this works.

CPI CATEGORIES

As shown in Figure 4-2, the CPI element consists of two broad categories of components: programming languages and services.

The programming languages category contains a variety of programming languages that can be used to develop SAA application programs. The services category contains a set of services that application programs can use to present information to users, access data, and communicate with other programs, among a number of other functions.

All SAA environments will support the programming languages and services included in the SAA CPI element. In developing an SAA application, one of the CPI programming languages would be used to write the program source code and the appropriate CPI services would be used for corresponding functions that may be supported by the program (e.g., accessing a database or communicating with another program). A brief description of the structure of a typical application program will clarify how this is accomplished.

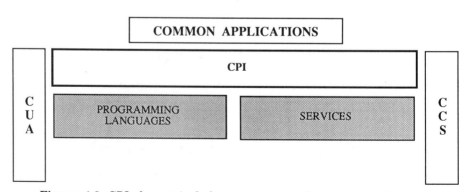

Figure 4-2. *CPI element includes programming languages and services categories.*

Typical Application Program Components

There are a number of parts of a program that are typically found in most applications, as illustrated in Figure 4-3. Usually, an application involves some type of interaction with the user of the program. This interaction involves displaying information on the user's screen and handling the user's input to the program. In other words, applications provide some type and style of user interface.

Another typical part of an application is some kind of functional processing. The program implements a function or set of functions for which it was designed. The types of functions are far ranging. The program could provide word processing functions, spreadsheet functions, specialized functional processing to support banking applications, or many other kinds of functions. It does not matter what functions the program was designed to perform. Programs of all kinds can be developed using one of the SAA programming languages.

A program's functional processing very often involves some type of data manipulation as well. This could be processing data that is input by the user or

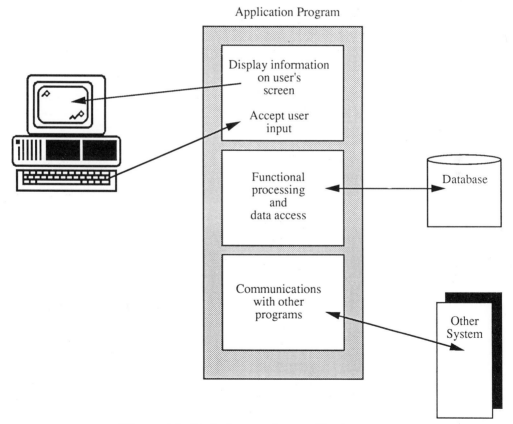

Figure 4-3. *Typical parts of an application program.*

processing data extracted from a file or database. The functional processing and data manipulation functions form the core functionality provided by the program.

An application may also involve communication with other systems. For example, if the application is attempting to access data that is physically located on some other system in the network, then a means of communicating with that other system must be provided.

SAA CPI Standards

The SAA CPI element defines standard services and interfaces for each of these parts of a program, as indicated in Figure 4-4. It standardizes the way application programs interface with their users; it standardizes the programming languages used to implement the application's functional logic; it standardizes how data is accessed by the program; and it standardizes how the program communicates

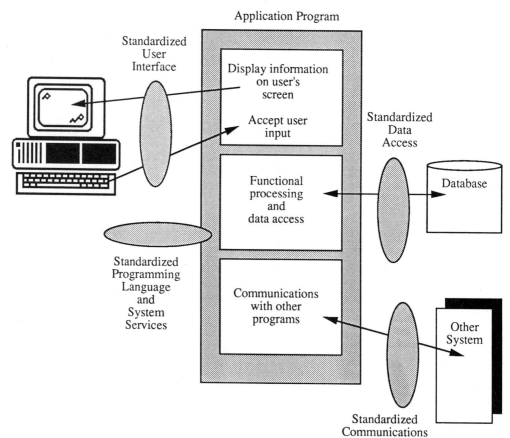

Figure 4-4. *CPI standardizes parts of a program.*

with the outside world. It also standardizes other programming aspects which will be discussed later.

An SAA application should use CPI services and interfaces in implementing the types of facilities described above. When implementing a user interface, the program should use the CPI user-interface services; when providing access to distributed data, the program should use the CPI remote-data-access services; when communicating with other programs, the program should use CPI's communications interface. The point is for all SAA applications to use the same set of programming components, services, and interfaces in order to achieve consistency across systems. The moral is: do not roll your own; do not reinvent the wheel.

Let's take a look at each of the individual components of the SAA CPI element and see how they are used to accomplish these purposes. First is a summary of all the components included in the CPI element of SAA.

CPI COMPONENTS

The components of the CPI element are summarized below by category:

> Programming Languages
>> C
>> COBOL
>> FORTRAN
>> RPG
>> PL/I
>> Application Generator
>> Procedures Language
> Services
>> Presentation Interface
>> Dialog Interface
>> Database Interface
>> Query Interface
>> Communications Interface
>> Repository Interface
>> Resource Recovery Interface
>> PrintManager Interface

Each of these programming languages and services will be discussed below.

CPI Programming Languages

As its name implies, the CPI programming languages category consists of a number of programming languages. Programming languages are included as part of SAA to ensure consistent programming language support in all SAA environments. By including a given programming language under this SAA CPI category, IBM is implicitly committing to provide support for that programming language in all SAA environments. This support may be provided by a programming language compiler, an interpreter, or an execution environment appropriate for the particular language.

As an example, COBOL is one of the languages included in SAA's CPI element, as shown in the list above. Consequently, IBM provides an SAA-compliant COBOL compiler for all their SAA environments including the mainframe's MVS and VM environments, the AS/400's OS/400 environment, and the OS/2 Extended Edition environment for PS/2 systems. Therefore, COBOL can be used to develop application programs in any of these SAA environments.

Leveraging Programming Skills

Consistent language support across systems provides a few major benefits. For one, it allows companies to leverage their programming staffs. Programmers who may have been writing programs for IBM mainframes in a language such as COBOL can also write programs for personal computers using the same programming language. They do not have to be retrained to use another programming language.

When most networks consisted of mainframes to which dumb terminals (e.g., 3270s) were attached and all applications were developed on, and executed on, mainframes, it was sufficient to have language support only on the mainframe. Now, however, most networks consist of interconnected mainframes, midrange, and personal computer systems. There is an ongoing trend to develop local applications for the midrange and personal computer systems as well as to distribute applications from the mainframe to these systems. The problem is, who is going to develop applications for these nonmainframe systems and what language will they use?

Just think of the enormous problem facing a large corporation that employs thousands of COBOL programmers who have been trained for developing host-based applications. Do all these programmers get retrained to learn how to program using C? The time, effort, and cost would be prohibitive, let alone the resistance from the programmers. Or, does the company hire new programming staff to develop applications for the different systems? The inability to find and bring onboard the needed personnel makes this a less than optimum solution.

SAA solves this problem, at least partially, by dictating that the same language support found on the mainframe will also be available on these other platforms. COBOL programmers can continue to use COBOL to develop applications that may, in fact, run on midrange or personal computer systems rather than on mainframes.

Not only will retraining not be required, but productivity should increase because of the consistent language support across systems. Many of the same programming techniques, developed over time, can be used in other environments.

Application Program Portability

A second important benefit of consistent programming language support across SAA environments is that programs developed in one environment can be more easily moved (ported) to other environments for execution. Let's see how this works.

An application program can be developed using a particular programming language such as COBOL. The sequence of COBOL statements that define the program's logic (functionality) is called the source code of the program. Each source code statement is an English language–like statement that is not directly usable or executable by a computer system. That is, the COBOL language statement is not a machine-readable statement, code, command, or instruction. It is a statement that is specific to the COBOL language, independent of any particular system on which the program may eventually execute.

In order for the COBOL source statements (the program) to be usable on a computer system, they must be translated into the machine-specific codes that are recognizable and executable by the hardware of the system. This type of translation creates what is called the program's object code and it is done by another program called a compiler.

In the case of COBOL, a COBOL compiler would translate COBOL source statements into the appropriate object code of the system on which the compiler is running. For each system on which the application is to run, a different COBOL compiler would need to be used to translate the source code.

By providing a COBOL compiler on each system, it is possible to compile the same source code on each system, provided that each compiler can handle the same language statements and parameters. This is where the CPI languages category comes into play. For a language such as COBOL, SAA defines the set of language elements (source statements) that will be supported in a consistent manner in all SAA environments.

IBM will provide consistent language compilers (or interpreters or execution environments, as appropriate) in each SAA environment for all SAA languages. There will be an SAA COBOL compiler that supports the same language elements defined in the SAA COBOL language specifications for each SAA environment.

A program written in COBOL on one SAA system can be ported to another SAA system and recompiled as shown in Figure 4-5. If there were no such standard language specifications, it might not be possible to port programs from one system to another since there would be no guarantee that the compilers (if available) on the different systems would all support the same set of language elements and parameters in the same way.

SAA Language Reference Specifications

For each programming language included as part of the SAA CPI element, IBM publishes an SAA program language reference manual. For example, for COBOL, IBM publishes an SAA COBOL Language Reference Manual and for C, IBM publishes the SAA C Language Reference Manual.

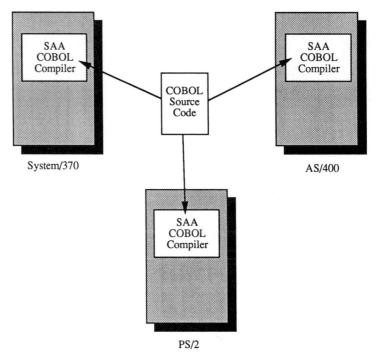

Figure 4-5. *Program source code can be ported to systems where SAA compilers exist.*

The SAA language reference manuals contain those language specifications included as part of SAA. In other words, they specify the SAA version of the language that IBM will consistently support in their SAA environments. These specifications include the language statements, elements, parameters, options, syntax, etc., that form the SAA definition. In effect, these reference manuals define the "portable versions" of the languages.

There may be other elements of a language that have not been included as part of the SAA specification for that language. These might include certain language extensions that are "nonstandard" and which IBM has elected not to support across the board on all their SAA systems.

Portability of a program's source code can be achieved by conforming to the SAA language specifications when developing the program. If a programmer uses only those elements of the language that are specified in the corresponding SAA language reference manual, then it will be possible to move that source code to another SAA environment where it can be compiled. If other language elements are used that are not included in the SAA language reference manual, there is no guarantee that support for these elements will be available in other SAA environments. Support may or may not be available.

The moral is to use only those language elements defined as part of the SAA specification for that language if portability is desired. If it is necessary to use other non-SAA language elements, isolate that portion of code so that it can more easily be modified if the program is moved to another SAA environment where such support does not exist.

One should not be misled, however, as to the ease with which programs can be ported. Consistent language support across systems does not guarantee portability. Programming language statements are just one aspect of a program. How the program performs input and output, interfaces to users, invokes system services, and accesses databases are just a few of many other aspects of a program that can affect portability. The manner in which a program does these kinds of things must also be standardized across environments in order to ensure portability or to minimize the changes required when moving a program from one system to another.

SAA CPI LANGUAGE TYPES

There are a few different types of programming languages included under the CPI element.

Most of the SAA languages are industry standard third-generation programming languages such as COBOL and C. These SAA languages are all high-level languages that are widely used in the industry today.

IBM has also included in the CPI element a fourth-generation language which it calls the Application Generator. Based on IBM's Cross System Product (CSP), the Application Generator is IBM's SAA specification for a higher-level program development tool.

A language used primarily for writing system procedures has also been included under SAA. This is the Procedures Language which is based on IBM's REXX (REstructured eXtended eXecutor) language which came out of the System/370 VM environment. REXX is a high-level, procedures-oriented language used primarily as an alternative to command list languages for developing system procedures.

The SAA programming languages are listed below according to type of language:

3rd Generation	*4th Generation*
C	Application Generator
COBOL	
FORTRAN	
RPG	
PL/I	
Procedures Language	

Before discussing why IBM has chosen these languages for inclusion under SAA, let's briefly discuss each of them individually.

C

C is a high-level, structured programming language that is widely used on a variety of minicomputer and microprocessor-based systems. It is the native language of the UNIX operating system and, hence, is the primary programming language used for developing UNIX-based software. Its flexibility allows programs to deal with low-level interfaces at the machine level which makes it suitable for developing system-level code. It also provides high-level control and data structure support which makes it appropriate for developing graphics applications, engineering and scientific applications, and commercial applications of all types.

C is well known for its portability. In addition to its basic elements, extended capabilities are added through libraries of functions. Functions in libraries are accessed via "call" statements within a program. C includes library support for input/output (I/O), math routines, string and character manipulation, dynamic memory management, and other functions.

While heavily used for PC application development, C has come to the IBM mainframe environment relatively recently just as it has recently been made available on the AS/400 system. Its inclusion in SAA and the availability of C compilers for the System/370/390 and AS/400 SAA environments will bring with it increased usage of C for developing applications in these environments as well.

The SAA C language specification is consistent with the draft proposed American National Standard for Information Systems—Programming Language—C (X3J11) standard. Since its original inclusion under SAA, the C specification has been enhanced. The C Level 2 specification adds support for record-level I/O among other features that are now part of the SAA CPI C language definition.

IBM provides SAA-compliant C language compilers in each of their SAA environments. The IBM C compiler products are summarized below.

SAA Environment		IBM C Compiler
System/370/390	MVS/ESA TSO/E	C/370
	VM/ESA CMS	C/370
AS/400	OS/400	C/400
PS/2	OS/2 EE	C/2

COBOL

The COBOL language, which has been around since the 1960s, is one of the most widely used programming languages on IBM mainframe systems. COBOL was designed for developing business applications and continues to be used for this purpose. The majority of commercial data processing applications for System/370 mainframes are written in COBOL.

COBOL's English language–like nature and its support for handling common data processing requirements and large amounts of data make it easy to use and suitable for a wide range of commercial applications. While it started out primarily as a mainframe language, it is now becoming popular for minicomputer and personal computer application development as well.

The SAA COBOL language specification is based on existing COBOL standards as well as on some IBM enhancements. Specifically, it is based on American National Standard Programming Language—COBOL, ANSI X3.23-1985 (identical with ISO standard 1989-1985), Intermediate Level and some elements of the ANSI X3.23-1985, High Level standard. In addition, IBM has included some of its own enhancements, such as COMP-3 and COMP-4 data items, to the SAA COBOL specification.

SAA COBOL compilers are available in all SAA environments. The IBM implementing products are summarized below.

SAA Environment		COBOL Compiler
System/370/390	MVS/ESA TSO/E	VS COBOL II
	VM/ESA CMS	VS COBOL II
AS/400	OS/400	COBOL/400
PS/2	OS/2 EE	COBOL/2

FORTRAN

FORTRAN is another language that has been around for a long time. It was designed by IBM to be used for developing programs involving mathematical computations. It has been primarily used, and continues to be used, for developing scientific and engineering applications and other applications requiring a lot of numerical data manipulation and computation. Not surprisingly, FORTRAN is widely used by scientists, engineers, and students.

As with COBOL, FORTRAN usage has been primarily for applications running on IBM System/370-based processors. With its inclusion in SAA, FORTRAN support will be available on the SAA midrange and workstation platforms as well.

The SAA FORTRAN language specification is based on existing FORTRAN standards with IBM enhancements. Specifically, it includes elements from the American National Standard Programming Language—FORTRAN, ANSI X3.9-1978 (FORTRAN 77) and the International Standards Organization ISO 1539-1980 Programming Languages—FORTRAN. The ANSI FORTRAN 77 and ISO FORTRAN standards specify the same level of FORTRAN. IBM has also added its own enhancements to the ANSI standard (e.g., the ability to use names up to thirty-one characters long) as part of the SAA FORTRAN language specification.

While SAA FORTRAN support was available for the mainframe and personal computer systems for some time, it was added much later to the AS/400. The table below summarizes IBM's SAA FORTRAN product support:

SAA Environment		FORTRAN Compiler
System/370/390	MVS/ESA TSO/E	VS FORTRAN
	VM/ESA CMS	VS FORTRAN
AS/400	OS/400	FORTRAN/400
PS/2	OS/2 EE	FORTRAN/2

RPG

RPG was originally designed as a report generation language noted for its ease of use. It is widely used on IBM's System/3X family of midrange computer systems including the System/34, System/36, and System/38 as well as on the AS/400 which is the successor to the System/3X family of systems. In addition to its use as a report generator, RPG is now often used for developing commercial data processing applications and is still the language of choice for many System/3X and AS/400 users.

RPG was not one of the programming languages included under SAA when SAA was first introduced. It was only added to SAA due to the outcry from IBM's System/3X customer base who were heavy RPG users. These customers felt, and rightly so, that they were being excluded from the mainstream of SAA. IBM responded by adding RPG to SAA at the time of the introduction of the AS/400, which became the midrange SAA platform (prior to the time of the AS/400 announcement and its designation as an SAA platform, IBM had always referred to the midrange SAA platform as a future offering of the System/3X family of systems).

The SAA RPG language specification is based on IBM's RPG/400 compiler which is based on RPG II and RPG III, which are primary programming languages used on the System/36 and System/38.

Since it came out of the System/3X environment, it is not surprising that IBM provides SAA RPG support on the AS/400, the successor to the System/3X family. Missing is SAA RPG support for the mainframe and workstation environments. IBM's SAA RPG product support is summarized below.

SAA Environment		RPG Compiler
System/370/390	MVS/ESA TSO/E	RPG/370
	VM/ESA CMS	RPG/370
AS/400	OS/400	RPG/400
PS/2	OS/2	—

PL/I

PL/I is another "old" mainframe-based programming language. While it never gained the industry-wide support that IBM had at one time expected, PL/I is used by a large number of IBM's mainframe customers for developing general-purpose commercial applications.

PL/I is another language that was not part of the initial SAA announcement. However, enough pressure from the installed customer base convinced IBM to add PL/I to SAA in 1989.

The SAA PL/I language specification is based on IBM's System/370 PL/I compiler.

IBM's SAA PL/I product support is summarized below for the SAA environments.

SAA Environment		PL/I Compiler
System/370/390	MVS/ESA TSO/E	OS PL/I
	VM/ESA CMS	OS PL/I
AS/400	OS/400	AS/400 PL/I
PS/2	OS/2 EE	—

Application Generator

The SAA Application Generator specification defines IBM's fourth-generation language. It defines elements that can be used for developing applications without using a traditional third-generation language such as COBOL or C.

An application generator is really a set of development tools. There are two major parts to it—an application development part and an application execution part. Using the application development facilities, users can build applications interactively using a dialog-oriented, fill-in-the-blanks approach. After completion of development, the resulting application can be executed on any systems that provide the appropriate application execution support.

The SAA Application Generator language specification is based on IBM's Cross System Product (CSP). With CSP/Application Development (CSP/AD), users can define, interactively test, and generate applications. The applications can then be executed on the mainframe using CSP/Application Execution (CSP/AE), on the AS/400 using the OS/400's application execution facility, or on personal computers using IBM's EZ-RUN product.

IBM's Application Generator product support is summarized below.

SAA Environment		Application Generator
System/370/390	MVS/ESA TSO/E	CSP
	VM/ESA CMS	CSP
AS/400	OS/400	OS/400
PS/2	OS/2 EE	EZ-RUN

Procedures Language

The SAA Procedures Language specification is based on IBM's REXX product. It is a third-generation, high-level, structured programming language similar to PL/I. It is used primarily for writing system-command procedures. The Procedures Language can be used instead of writing command lists. It allows system commands to be embedded within a program.

While the Procedures Language was originally available only in the VM environment, it is now available in other environments as well. It is characterized as being easy to learn and use. Although most usage has been in writing procedures and macros for controlling systems, it has general-purpose structured programming facilities that make it appropriate to use to develop commercial applications.

IBM's SAA Procedures Language product support is summarized below.

SAA Environment		Procedures Language
System/370/390	MVS/ESA TSO/E	MVS/ESA
	VM/ESA CMS	VM System Product Interpreter
AS/400	OS/400	Procedures Language 400/REXX
PS/2	OS/2 EE	Procedures Language 2/REXX

Why These Languages?

It is appropriate to ask why IBM has included these languages in SAA. Why not just select one language as the SAA language of choice and use it for new SAA application development? This would certainly simplify things and make it easier to provide and support an SAA language product in all SAA environments.

The answer is to allow IBM's current customers to continue using the same languages that they used in the past and are currently using for application development. Basically, it is an acceptance of the reality of the installed base. There are too many IBM customers using the various languages included in SAA for IBM to abandon them. IBM cannot leave them out in the cold. IBM's customers cannot be forced to retrain their development staffs or to hire new staff for their ongoing program development. IBM had to provide them with a migration path. IBM did this by including in SAA, sometimes reluctantly, the languages that are most widely used among IBM's existing customers.

This is demonstrated by IBM's initial inclusion of widely used languages such as COBOL and FORTRAN and the later inclusion of languages such as RPG and PL/I as responses to pressures from the AS/400 and System/370 customers, respectively.

The problem for IBM in trying to satisfy their installed customer base is knowing where to draw the line. The ideal situation, from IBM's point of view, is to support the minimal number of components. This reduces IBM's internal development and ongoing maintenance and support efforts which are duplicated for each component added to SAA. The problem is compounded because inclusion in SAA means support in all SAA environments, not just on one system.

Responding to the marketplace has led to the proliferation of SAA language components and more will probably be added to SAA in the future. This is good news for IBM customers. They will have a variety of languages to choose from in developing applications that may span SAA environments.

The reality is that many developers will continue to use the same programming languages that they have in the past. Programmers writing COBOL applications for mainframes will probably continue to use COBOL. RPG programmers writing applications for the AS/400 will probably continue to write applications using RPG. PL/I will continue to be used by PL/I programmers writing mainframe applications.

For new distributed SAA applications and local applications for OS/2 (the SAA workstation operating environment), C will become more and more widely used. This will happen for a number of reasons. A lot of personal computer applications are written in C and C is the native language of OS/2. C source code is highly portable. Most microprocessor-based development is done using C. UNIX software is heavily C-based.

Languages such as COBOL and PL/I will continue to be widely used for some time. The large numbers of programmers from IBM's traditional mainframe customer base using these languages will ensure this. And, the large number of commercial applications written in these languages will still require ongoing maintenance and enhancements.

SAA Language Product Support Summary

Following is a summary of the product support for the SAA languages.

| Language | SAA Environment | | |
	TSO/E, CICS, IMS, and CMS	OS/400	OS/2
C	C/370	C/400	C/2
COBOL	VS COBOL II	COBOL/400	COBOL/2
FORTRAN	VS FORTRAN	FORTRAN/400	FORTRAN/2
RPG	RPG/370	RPG/400	
PL/I	OS PL/I		
Application Generator	CSP	OS/400	EZ-RUN
Procedures Language	REXX	Procedures Language 400/REXX	Procedures Language 2/REXX

CPI SERVICES

The CPI services category consists of a set of system services commonly used by application programs and the programming interfaces used to access these services. Each CPI service and its corresponding programming interface will be supported in each of the SAA environments. The intent is to standardize on the interfaces that application programs will use for various services such as displaying information for users, accessing databases, communicating with remote programs, etc.

The components of the CPI element are application enablers that support application programs and provide services to them. These application enablers include compilers, dialog managers, database management systems, query and report writers, and application generators. Application enablers isolate application programs from the underlying operating system software and hardware platform on which they execute.

IBM will provide a consistent set of application enablers in all their SAA environments. The CPI element standardizes the application programming interfaces (APIs) to these enablers (services). CPI components form the building blocks for SAA applications.

Providing such consistent services and interfaces makes it easier to develop applications that provide a consistent user interface, transparent access to data, and support cooperative processing across SAA systems. The reason it makes it easier is that CPI ensures that the same types of services and interfaces will be available in every SAA environment and the interfaces/services will be supported in a consistent manner.

For example, how data is accessed from a relational database will be the same regardless of the SAA system on which the user or application resides. This implies that every SAA system will include an SAA-compliant relational database manager and the interface to the relational database manager will be the same on all systems.

This clearly benefits programmers who are developing applications on multiple platforms or who are developing distributed applications that may span systems. A programmer does not have to worry about whether a particular service can be used depending on where the application executes. The program does not have to be different because it runs in different environments. The programmer does not have to learn how to program for different services with different interfaces on different systems. The same interfaces can be used on all systems. This not only results in increased programmer productivity but also allows programmers to transfer their skills from one environment to another.

The CPI element also promotes program portability. Suppose one writes an application that displays information on a user's screen, allows the user to request access to data, retrieves the requested data from a relational database, and returns the results of the operation back to the user. The first requirement for making such a program portable to another SAA environment is to write it in one of the SAA programming languages such as C. A second requirement, though, hinges on the way that the application program requests various system services. This is what CPI addresses.

Typically, application programs request services from the operating system under which they are executing. These requests are usually some form of "call" to the appropriate operating system service routines. Unfortunately, though, every IBM operating system has its own unique set of system service interface calls. The result is that a program written using the system-unique interfaces of one operating system will not work, without change, in another operating system environment.

It will not work because the other system has it own unique set of service interfaces and does not recognize the interface calls supported by another operating system. The application becomes locked in, and dependent upon, the operating system under which it was developed. CPI comes to the rescue.

Rather than using operating system–dependent interfaces, programs can make use of SAA interfaces which are operating system–independent. Every SAA operating system will support the same set of generic CPI interface calls. Therefore, the same interfaces can be used by the application regardless of the operating system under which it is executing.

The result is that the source code for the application program does not have to be changed (at least for these interfaces) when it is moved to another SAA environment. Rather than being locked in to a particular operating system, the program is portable to multiple operating systems.

CPI Service Components

The CPI Services category includes the following programming interfaces and corresponding services:

> Presentation Interface
> Dialog Interface
> Database Interface
> Query Interface
> Communications Interface
> Repository Interface
> Resource Recovery Interface
> PrintManager Interface

Each interface is used to invoke a corresponding system service or enabler. For example, for presenting (displaying) information on a user's workstation, the Presentation Interface can be used. For accessing data in a relational database, the Database Interface can be used. For communicating with a program on another system, the Communications Interface would be used. Several of these interfaces and services are shown in Figure 4-6.

These SAA CPI interfaces form a buffer between the application program and the underlying operating system under which it is executing. The interfaces mask the internals of the underlying operating system and services from the application. While each SAA environment will have its own unique operating system, subsystems, and services implementations, the interfaces stay the same. The differences in implementation are transparent to the application.

These generic, system-independent interfaces, and the services that they invoke, are included in CPI in order to support major SAA goals such as:

> Consistent user interfaces
> Access to distributed files and databases
> Cooperative processing
> Enterprise-wide application development environment

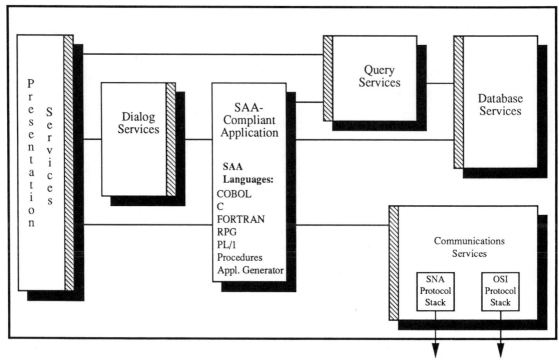

Figure 4-6. *CPI services within an SAA operating environment.*

One or more CPI interfaces are used to support the above SAA goals as shown below:

Goal	CPI Interface(s)
Consistent user interface	Presentation, Dialog
Access to distributed data	Database, Query
Cooperative processing	Communications
Application development	Repository
Standardized print services	PrintManager

As can be seen from the above table, some CPI services are related (e.g., Presentation and Dialog, Database and Query). The following descriptions will show the relationships of these interfaces as well as how they and the other interfaces are used in SAA applications.

SUPPORT FOR THE USER INTERFACE

Two of the CPI interfaces can be used by application programs to provide a user interface that conforms to SAA's Common User Access (CUA) specifications.

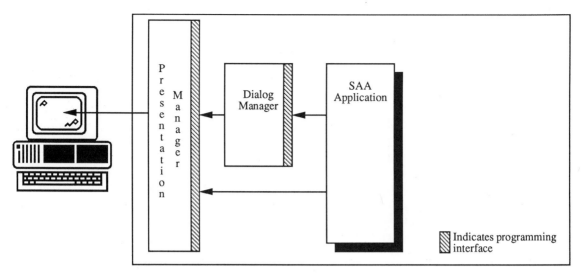

Figure 4-7. *Relationship between SAA Presentation Manager and Dialog Manager.*

These CPI interfaces, which are illustrated in Figure 4-7, are the Presentation Interface and Dialog Interface.

The Presentation Interface is a lower-level interface that gives the programmer quite a bit of direct control over the end-user interface while the Dialog Interface is a higher-level interface that is easier to use and automatically provides a degree of CUA compliance for the application.

Which interface should a programmer use? Both interfaces can be used to provide a CUA-compliant user interface. There is a trade-off between degree of control and ease of programming effort, though, and there is a difference in the types of CUA interface models supported.

The Presentation Interface allows the programmer the greatest degree of control, but is more difficult to use. The programmer is directly responsible for most levels of CUA compliance. An example of using the Presentation Interface would be writing an OS/2 application that directly uses OS/2's Presentation Manager interface.

The Presentation Interface provides device independence to the application program. The application program issues generic "calls" to the Presentation Manager which directly interfaces to the device. Device dependencies are buried in the Presentation Manager. The application program is able to determine the type of device in order to interface with it in an optimal manner.

The Dialog Interface is intended for use by menu-driven, interactive applications. An application program interfaces to a Dialog Manager, which provides dialog services such as retrieving and displaying panels and executing functions. The Dialog Manager then interfaces to the Presentation Manager for actually displaying information on a screen and receiving user keyboard input. Let's look at each of these interfaces in more depth.

SAA CPI Presentation Interface

The CPI Presentation Interface is used by application programs to display or print information on a user's device (e.g., display or printer) as indicated in Figure 4-8. There is a wide range of functions defined as part of the Presentation Interface. These include support for both nonprogrammable terminals (e.g., 3270s) using full-screen displays as well as for intelligent workstations (e.g., PS/2s running OS/2) using a windowing environment. Support is also provided for receiving keyboard and mouse input. Graphics, image (limited), and font support is also defined.

The Presentation Interface was based on IBM's mainframe-based Graphical Data Display Manager (GDDM) products and has been extended to include windowing support as provided by the OS/2 Presentation Manager. This windowing support is only provided under OS/2's Presentation Manager on PS/2 systems. It is not supported in the mainframe products.

Applications written in an SAA programming language such as COBOL or C use the Presentation Interface by issuing a set of program "calls" to invoke the functions provided. By using the Presentation Interface, applications can provide an end-user interface that conforms to SAA's Common User Access (CUA) specifications.

One of the main benefits of using a Presentation Interface is that it provides device independence. The application program displaying information on a device does not have to know about the physical characteristics of the device. All the device dependencies are buried in the Presentation Manager. The Presentation Interface masks the device characteristics from the program.

This not only makes it easier to write applications (you do not have to write device drivers) but it also provides flexibility in the devices supported. The

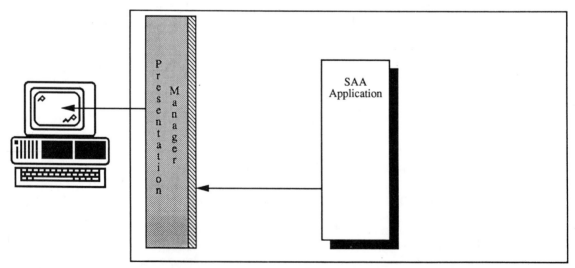

Figure 4-8. *The Presentation Interface standardizes the interface to users.*

application can be used, without change in some cases, with any device supported by the Presentation Manager.

The Presentation Interface also provides a level of SAA CUA conformance. It provides a limited degree of physical consistency (one of the goals of CUA) by ensuring consistency in selection techniques using either a mouse or a keyboard. The program issues logical requests to get input while the Presentation Manager maps these to a real physical interface with a mouse or keyboard.

For the Graphical CUA model, the Presentation Interface provides support for windows. Applications can create either main or child windows. This level of Presentation Interface, which is an event-driven interface, is most suited to highly graphical applications in which the user interacts with the graphics image, which results in processing by the program. The application program is responsible for most of the physical consistency and all of the syntactical and semantic consistency that is central to CUA conformance.

There is another level of CUA conformance supported through the Presentation Interface. By using controls and templates, applications give up more CUA responsibility to the Presentation Manager. With controls, programs describe logically the information needed from the user and the type of interaction desired to obtain the information—for example, having the user make a selection from a list of options by pushing a radio button.

A template is a collection of related controls. An application can build a panel using a template rather than specifying each individual control. With a template, the program does not have to worry about the layout of every control in the panel. The controls can be predefined and built into the template. Using templates simplifies the application but some flexibility is given up.

Here is a summary of IBM's SAA product support for the CPI Presentation Interface:

SAA Environment		IBM Product
System/370/390	MVS/ESA TSO/E	GDDM
	VM/ESA	GDDM
AS/400	OS/400	Integrated
PS/2	OS/2 EE	Presentation Manager

SAA CPI Dialog Interface

A dialog is an interaction between a program and its user. Think of it as a conversation between the user and program. Dialogs are used in interactive applications to control the interactions with the user. Typically, a dialog begins when the program displays a panel of information on the user's screen (either a full-screen display or within a single window of a multiwindow environment). The user then responds to the display with some input (e.g., a keystroke).

The user input may cause the program to perform some functional processing and then display another panel to which the user also responds by keying in some additional information or selecting some function. The program and user interact in this manner until the dialog is completed, which typically equates to the completion of a task, transaction, or unit of work.

The interaction between the program and the user, including the navigation through a sequence of multiple panels of information, is handled by a Dialog Manager. A Dialog Manager is software on a system that provides various types of dialog services that make it easier to develop online, interactive applications. Application programs use the services of a Dialog Manager by issuing program calls that are part of the application programming interface (API) provided by the Dialog Manager. An example of a Dialog Manager is IBM's Interactive System Productivity Facility (ISPF) product which provides dialog services for MVS and VM System/370/390-based mainframe application programs. Another example is the OS/2 Dialog Manager which provides similar dialog services for OS/2 application programs.

Dialog Elements

A dialog consists of a set of dialog elements. The types of elements that can be used within a dialog are listed below.

> Functions
> Panel definitions
> Message definitions
> Tables
> File tailoring skeletons
> Dialog variables

Functions are programs or command procedures that perform some type of functional processing for which the application was designed. Function programs can be written in languages such as C, COBOL, FORTRAN, PL/I, and others, and command procedures can be written using the REXX language or CLIST (command list) commands. An application could consist of multiple function programs and/or procedures, each written in a different programming or command language. Through a dialog interface, applications can request that these programs or procedures be executed, perhaps in response to some user input. The Dialog Manager will locate the named function and cause it to execute.

Panel definitions describe the content and format of panels. They describe the layout of information displayed on a user's screen. Various types of panels can be defined. These include data entry panels that allow users to enter information to be handled by the dialog program; selection panels from which the user can select from a list of options; information panels which are used to display information only; table display panels which are used to display data in tables; and tutorial panels which can be used to display "help" information.

Message definitions are used to display error messages or warning messages or just to provide information to the user. Messages could appear on the screen in response to a user input or some program process.

A table is a two-dimensional array containing data that could be for temporary use within the dialog or for permanent use, meaning it is saved across dialogs.

File-tailoring skeletons represent data organized in a sequential manner. The skeleton can be customized during the dialog, by the Dialog Manager's file-tailoring services, to create a sequential output file. This file can then be used by other processes. For example, file-tailoring skeletons are often used dynamically to configure Job Control Language (JCL) statements for submission as a batch job to the operating system.

Dialog variables contain data used by dialog functions and services. Variables are used to pass information between dialog elements.

Not all these elements are required to appear in every dialog; some are optional. Which elements are actually used depends on the type of dialog application and the manner in which it was developed. In addition to supporting these dialog elements, a Dialog Manager also provides services to the interactive application program.

Dialog Services

The Dialog Interface defines a number of services to be provided by Dialog Managers and which can be used by application programs. The defined dialog services include:

> Display services
> Select services
> Variable services
> Table services
> Message services
> Dialog control services
> Help services

Display services, quite naturally, are used to display panels of information. Included is support to retrieve named panels and perform predisplay processing if required. The retrieved panel is then displayed either as a full-screen image or within a window if the CUA windowing model is being supported. Primary, pop-up, and help windows are supported.

Variable services are provided to define, get, update, and delete variables. Variables are used to define program data which can then be communicated with the dialog interface.

Message services are used to retrieve messages from a message file and store them in variables and to display messages when the next panel is displayed.

Dialog control services are used to manage a dialog session. Services include opening and closing dialog sessions.

Help services provide contextual help facilities. Support is provided to define and display help information which conforms to CUA guidelines.

Advantages of Using a Dialog Interface

There are several advantages to using a dialog interface. These include:

> Easier to develop online, interactive applications
> CUA conformance

Device independence
Presentation Manager independence

Using a dialog interface makes it a lot easier to develop online, interactive applications for a few reasons. For one, much of the user interaction is handled automatically by the Dialog Manager. The program merely requests that panels be displayed, user input received, and functions executed by issuing calls to the Dialog Manager. Dialog services will take care of the rest. This really simplifies the core logic of a program because much of the processing does not have to be handled in the program. It is implemented outside the program in the Dialog Manager. Also, the panels of information to be displayed are defined outside the program. They are defined using the Dialog Tag Language (DTL) and then the panel definitions are stored in libraries. The program requests the display of the panel which it references by name. This not only makes the program smaller and cleaner but it makes it easier to change panel layouts. You just have to change the individual panels and replace them in the libraries. You do not have to modify program code.

Because the Dialog Manager, and not the program, controls the display of panels, CUA conformance can be enforced automatically by the Dialog Manager. The Dialog Manager controls what the panel display looks like and how the user makes selections from the panel in accordance with SAA CUA specifications. The program does not have to worry about this (the panel is defined in terms of its logical content, not its exact display format). Also, the program does not have to change when CUA changes. New Dialog Manager support will ensure conformance.

A Dialog Program Example

Figure 4-9 shows the relationship between a dialog program and the Dialog Manager. The program issues Dialog Manager calls to invoke dialog services. The names, syntax, parameters, codes, etc., of these calls are defined by the SAA CPI Dialog Interface.

The program can request that the Dialog Manager retrieve a panel from a library and display it on the user's terminal. Note that the Dialog Manager does not directly interface to the user's terminal. The Dialog Manager uses the services of the Presentation Manager to actually display the panel.

When the user enters data in response to the panel (e.g., a keystroke or series of keystrokes or a mouse pick), the Dialog Manager will present this input to the program. As a result, the program requests that a particular function be executed. The Dialog Manager will retrieve the program from a library and cause it to start executing.

CUA Conformance

Using the Dialog Interface enforces CUA compliance. As an example, the information to be displayed and its layout are defined outside the Dialog Manager.

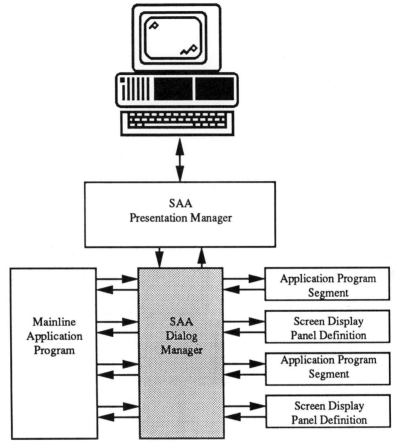

Figure 4-9. *SAA Dialog Manager provides dialog services for application programs.*

The Dialog Manager, though, controls the display of the panel, that is, how it actually appears on the user's screen.

The Dialog Interface is a procedural rather than an event-driven interface. It is most suitable for menu-driven, interactive applications. The Dialog Interface does not provide full support for the CUA graphical or workplace models. These require use of the Presentation Interface.

Following is a summary of IBM's product support for the SAA CPI Dialog Interface.

SAA Environment		IBM Product
System/370/390	MVS/ESA TSO/E	ISPF
	VM/ESA CMS	ISPF
AS/400	OS/400	—
PS/2	OS/2 EE	Dialog Manager

ACCESS TO DISTRIBUTED DATA

Another important area addressed by the SAA CPI element is distributed-data access. Distributed-data access provides the ability to access data transparently in files or databases that may be distributed across systems in a network. Transparent access means the user or application program requesting access does not need to know about either the physical location of the data or the type of system on which the data physically resides.

SAA's distributed-data access specifications fall into two major categories: distributed-file access and distributed relational database access. Both of these distributed capabilities are implemented via programming interfaces included in the CPI element and by sets of distributed services that are part of the SAA Common Communications Support (CCS) element which is described in Chapter 5.

Distributed-file access capabilities are implemented using standard local system file I/O and Distributed Data Management (DDM) which is a component of the Application Services category of SAA's CCS element. Distributed-database access is implemented via a Structured Query Language (SQL) interface, the standard CPI Database Interface, and makes use of the Distributed Relational Database Architecture (DRDA), DDM, and other related architectures specified by DRDA. All these architectures are components included in the CCS element. Below, we will expand on the relationships of the CPI and CCS elements for each of these distributed-data facilities.

Distributed-File Access

The distributed-file access services included in SAA allow users or application programs on one system to access files transparently that are located on another system in the network. The types of files supported by these distributed-file access services include byte stream files and record-oriented files such as sequential and indexed files.

The programming interface for this type of remote-file access is the standard file I/O supported in the various SAA operating environments. It is the same file I/O used by programs to access local files supported by the different file systems in the MVS, VM, OS/400, and OS/2 environments. For example, for the MVS environment, this would include Virtual Sequential Access Method (VSAM) interface calls.

The point is that to access remote files, programs would issue standard local file I/O calls such as Open, Close, Read, and Write, just as if the files being accessed were locally resident on that same system. It is transparent to the applications that the files may, in fact, be resident on some other system in the network.

This makes it easy to implement distributed-file access in programs. Programmers do not have to know or care about where files will actually be located when the program is executing. And, they do not have to be concerned with the file I/O used on another system where the files reside that may be different from the file I/O for the system on which the program is executing.

Because the same file I/O interface is used for remote-file access as well as for local-file access, IBM has not specified another new CPI interface for this type of distributed-file access. That is, there is no generic SAA file interface that is the same or consistent across all SAA environments. Rather, each system retains its standard file interfaces.

This provides a nice migration path for existing applications. Files can be distributed without having to modify the application's file I/O. On the other hand, this file I/O is unique to that system and not supported in other SAA systems, thereby limiting portability of the application.

When an application program issues file interface calls, these calls will initially be handled by the local system file software (since the call issued was a local system file I/O call) as indicated in Figure 4-10. When the local file system determines that the requested file is not local (it does not show up in the local file

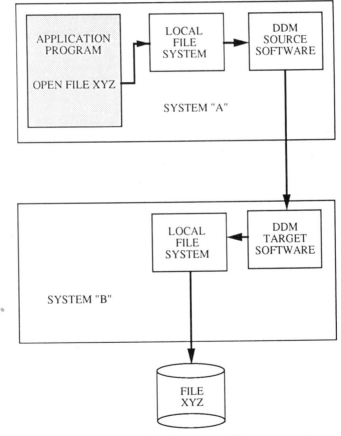

Figure 4-10. *DDM provides remote-file access services.*

directory), the call is passed to Distributed Data Management (DDM) software on that system. The DDM software will then translate the local file call to a generic DDM request which will then be sent to the remote system where the file actually resides.

DDM software on the remote system will accept the DDM request, translate it into a format that can be handled by its local file system, and will then pass it to its local file system. The remote system's file handler will then access the file. The results of the file access will then be passed back to the requesting system in a similar manner.

Note that only the local system file I/O interface calls are addressed by the SAA CPI element. The DDM services belong to the SAA CCS element. That is, the DDM commands and protocols used to distribute requests are CCS components. It is transparent to the users and applications that CCS components are actually being used. Here is a good example of the integrated usage of various SAA elements. Programming interfaces, which are the same for both local and remote functions, are part of CPI while the transaction services and protocols used to carry out distributed functions are part of CCS.

Distributed Relational Data Access

The program interfaces for remote-data access that are included under CPI are used for accessing data in relational databases as opposed to record-oriented or byte stream files. There are actually two different CPI interfaces that provide two levels of interface for remote relational data access—the Database Interface and the Query Interface. The SAA Database and Query Interfaces are related, as indicated in Figure 4-11, in much the same manner as the Presentation and Dialog Interfaces are related. The Database Interface defines a lower-level, direct interface to an SAA relational database management system while the Query Interface is a higher-level interface that uses the Database Interface for actually accessing data.

SAA Database Interface

The SAA CPI Database Interface is based on Structured Query Language (SQL). SQL, as its name implies, is a language designed specifically to allow users to define, retrieve, and manipulate information in a relational database. Users can directly type SQL statements to access relational data or SQL statements can be embedded in application programs.

Distibuted relational data access works much the same way as the distributed-file access described above. SQL calls, which are specified as part of the CPI element, are the same regardless of whether the requested data is located on the local system or on some other remote system. If the data is in a local database, then the local database management system will handle the request and provide the desired data access.

If, however, the data resides on some other system, the SQL request will be distributed (transparently to the requesting application) to the target system where the database containing the data is located. The distribution of the request

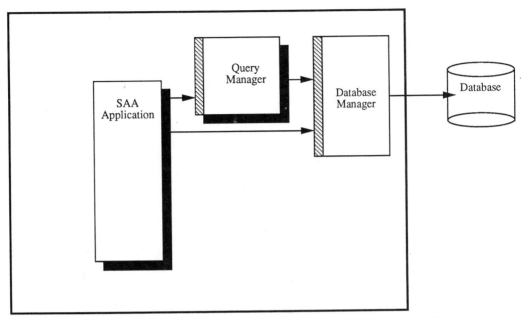

Figure 4-11. *Relationship of SAA Database Manager and Query Manager.*

is done using IBM's Distributed Relational Database Architecture (DRDA) and DDM, both of which are SAA CCS components. Once again we see that the CPI element standardizes on programming interfaces while the CCS element standardizes on the protocols used between systems.

IBM's SAA relational database products support remote unit of work level of distributed-data access. A unit of work consists of multiple, related SQL requests which are treated logically as a single unit (e.g., a transaction). With remote unit of work access, a single unit of work can be directed to a single remote database. Each SQL request within the unit of work must be handled by the same database manager. Different units of work can be handled by different database managers.

The SAA database systems will also eventually support distributed unit of work. Distributed unit of work extends remote access to multiple relational databases within a single unit of work. This allows data to be read or written to tables in different databases within a single unit of work. However, each individual SQL statement within the unit of work must refer to just one database.

IBM provides relational database management systems that support the SQL CPI interface in all SAA environments. These SAA relational database management products are:

System	Environment	Relational DB Manager
System/370/390	MVS/ESA	DB2
	VM/ESA	SQL/DS
AS/400	OS/400	integrated
PS/2	OS/2 EE	integrated

The same SQL statements are used regardless of the location of the data being accessed. The relational database in which the data resides may either be local (on the same system as the requestor) or remote (distributed on some other system in the network), as we indicated earlier.

SAA CPI Query Interface

The SAA CPI Query Interface defines a higher level of interface to relational databases (higher-level than the SQL interface). With the Query Interface, users can perform ad hoc queries into a relational database using either a query-by-example (QBE) interface or a menu-driven interface, depending on the type of interface provided by the query product being used.

IBM's query products provide both query and report writing services. They allow users to access information in a relational database and also to control how the information is presented.

IBM provides an SAA Query Manager in all SAA environments to go along with the SAA Database Managers in these environments. The following table summarizes IBM SAA Query products in the SAA environments.

System	Environment	Query Manager
System/370/390	MVS/ESA	QMF
	VM/ESA	QMF
AS/400	OS/400	Query Manager
PS/2	OS/2 EE	Query Manager

All Query Managers provide an easy-to-use interface to allow users to interact with relational databases. Users can either type in SQL commands or use the higher-level interface provided by the Query Manager.

As with the Presentation Interface/Dialog Interface relationship, there is a trade-off in using the Query Interface versus the Database Interface. The Query Interface is easier to use, requires no development effort, and can be used by nonprogrammers. However, there are some inherent limitations in the type of database access supported using queries.

The Database Interface (SQL) is more difficult to use (relatively speaking), but is also more powerful and gives users and programmers greater control over relational data access. There is also more flexibility in how access is done.

SAA's CPI Query Interface includes specifications for database queries as well as a callable query interface (a program-to-program call interface). The SAA Query Callable Interface allows programs to execute query functions. The Query Callable Interface consists of a set of macros that is the interface used by programs to request query services, the actual Query Manager that provides the query and report writing services, and a set of Callable Interface Modules that provides access to the SAA Query Manager.

SAA CPI COMMUNICATIONS INTERFACE

The SAA CPI Communications Interface (CI), also referred to as the CPI for Communications (CPIC), is a standardized LU 6.2–based programming interface that application programs can use for communicating with other application programs. CPIC is the standard SAA program-to-program communications interface.

CPIC consists of a set of calls that programs can issue in order to communicate with partner programs. The calls fall into two broad categories. There is a Starter Set which consists of the minimum number of calls needed to allow programs to set up and stop conversations and to exchange data with other programs. For very simple program-to-program communications, such as exchanging messages, the Starter Set is sufficient and is easy to use and learn.

For more sophisticated kinds of program-to-program communications, IBM has defined a CPIC Advanced Function Set. The Advanced Function Set adds calls to allow applications to synchronize and control their conversations with other programs. Calls are also available to determine the characteristics of conversations and to modify the characteristics of a conversation.

CPIC vs. APPC

A natural question is to ask about the differences between CPIC and Advanced Program-to-Program Communications (APPC). Both have to do with LU 6.2–based program-to-program communications.

APPC is the IBM marketing term for the program-to-program communications facilities defined as part of SNA Logical Unit Type 6.2 (LU 6.2). APPC and LU 6.2, then, are equivalent and the terms may be used interchangeably. APPC/LU 6.2 is discussed in detail in Chapter 7.

In order to understand the difference between APPC (LU 6.2) and CPIC, a brief discussion of LU 6.2 is needed. First of all, a distinction must be made between LU 6.2 protocols and LU 6.2 programming interfaces. From an SNA communications perspective, LU 6.2 is a particular subset of SNA session-level protocols that IBM has selected as the standard protocols to be used for program-to-program communications.

As part of the LU 6.2 definition, IBM also formally architected the interface between programs, called Transaction Programs (TPs), and the Type 6.2 LU. This interface is called the LU 6.2 protocol boundary. It is a documented set of LU 6.2 functions, called verbs, that is available to the programs using LU 6.2.

A given implementation of the documented LU 6.2 protocol boundary (set of verbs and parameters) is called an LU 6.2 application program interface (LU 6.2 API). LU 6.2 APIs are typically provided within some programming language (e.g., C) via program calls that are supported within a particular operating system environment.

Unfortunately, IBM product developers who were implementing LU 6.2 on their products did so in their own way. The result is that all LU 6.2 APIs on different systems are different from one another. They differ in the names of the functions, the syntax, parameters, options, return codes, etc.

Enter CPIC to the rescue. CPIC is the standard LU 6.2–based API that all SAA systems will support in a consistent manner. Therefore distributed applications can be developed that use the same communications interface regardless of the system on which they are executing.

When CPIC calls are issued by an application, underlying system software will generate appropriate SNA LU 6.2 protocols to support communications with a partner program as indicated in Figure 4-12. CPIC is a programming interface, not a set of SNA communications protocols like LU 6.2. In fact, CPIC calls may some day be used with OSI protocols (more on this later).

CPIC, then, is more similar to an LU 6.2 API. The difference is that it is structured somewhat differently from many LU 6.2 APIs and does not include support for all the verbs defined as part of the LU 6.2 protocol boundary.

Another important distinction to understand is that the programming interface is intended to allow two programs to communicate with one another. This is as opposed to two logical units (LUs), which represent the programs, communicating with one another. The programs that are communicating are called Transaction Programs (TPs). Each TP is supported by a Type 6.2 LU on its local system. The pair of LUs, each representing one of the TPs, communicates with one another using LU 6.2 protocols in order to carry out the program-to-program communications between the pair of TPs. This brings us to the difference between SNA LU sessions and conversations.

Conversations and Sessions

A conversation is a logical connection between two programs (i.e., two TPs). Before two programs can communicate with one another, such a logical connection (conversation) must be established between them. The conversation between

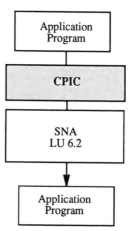

Figure 4-12. *CPI communications interface is used for communicating with other programs.*

the two partner programs is actually carried out across an underlying Logical Unit–to–Logical Unit (LU-LU) session. A session is a logical connection between a pair of LUs. Figure 4-13 illustrates the relationship between sessions and conversations.

The session between a pair of LUs can support multiple conversations between different pairs of programs. However, only one conversation at a time can be active across the session. That is, only a single pair of programs can be actively communicating across the session at a time.

In effect, the session is a serially reusable resource that is reused, in a time-sliced manner, by various pairs of programs. At any one time, the session is dedicated to a single conversation between a single pair of programs. When one conversation is completed, another conversation between a different pair of programs can become active and use the same underlying session. In this manner, multiple pairs of programs (via multiple conversations) can be supported, in a time-sliced manner, by one session between the same pair of LUs.

The CPI Communications Interface is a conversational level interface that allows two partner programs to establish connections and carry out conversations with one another. These communicating programs are not carrying out LU 6.2 protocols. The underlying LUs, representing the TPs, are carrying out LU 6.2 protocols across their LU-LU session. The CPI Communications Interface masks the LU 6.2 protocol from the application programs.

This makes it much simpler to write programs that will engage in program-to-program communications with other remote programs. These programs can use the relatively simple, high-level Communications Interface "calls" (e.g., ALLOCATE a conversation, SEND_DATA to partner program, etc.) without worrying about the details of LU 6.2 protocols (this is the job of the LUs supporting the conversation). It also makes the Communications Interface independent of the actual communications protocols being used in support of the conversation. In fact, the Communications Interface calls could be sent using OSI-based protocols instead of LU 6.2 protocols. Although IBM does not yet support this capability, it could be provided in the future, transparently to the application programs. CPIC is covered in more detail in Appendix C.

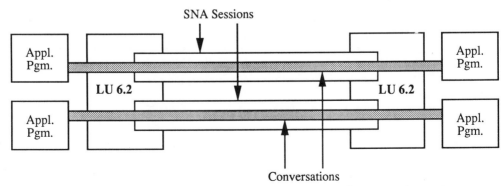

Figure 4-13. *Relationship of SNA sessions and conversations.*

Below is a summary of the CPIC support in the SAA environments.

SAA Environment		CPIC Support
System/370/390	MVS/ESA TSO/E VM/ESA	APPC/MVS IMS/ESA TM CICS/ESA
AS/400	OS/400	—
PS/2	OS/2 EE	OS/2 EE

As the summary table indicates, support for the CPIC interface is not yet available in all SAA environments. This lack of support is a drawback to developing applications that will span SAA environments since a consistent communications interface is not available. Applications can still make use of the system-dependent LU 6.2 APIs provided in the SAA environments in order to carry out program-to-program communications with programs on other systems.

SAA CPI REPOSITORY INTERFACE

The SAA CPI Repository Interface is used to interact with a Repository Manager. A Repository Manager is a set of software that provides repository services related to managing a repository. A repository is a special type of database that contains information about a business and its internal data processing.

The intent is to create a centralized location where this business and data processing information can be maintained and then accessed and shared by users and applications throughout the organization. A repository provides a single point of control for information (particularly data processing–related information) about an organization.

The type of information stored in a repository is different from the information typically stored in a company's files or databases. The information in the repository describes various types of information or objects and their relationships. The company data which is referred to and described in the repository is actually physically stored in other files and databases.

IBM's Repository Manager/MVS product, which runs under the MVS operating system on System/370-based processors, implements support for SAA's Repository Interface. SAA's Repository Interface and the Repository Manager/MVS product are key components of IBM's AD/Cycle architecture. AD/Cycle is IBM's set of offerings to be used for the development of SAA applications as described in Chapter 6.

Repository Services

One component of AD/Cycle is a set of repository services which provide centralized, shared management of all application development data. These services are implemented by Repository Manager/MVS and are built on top of DB2, the SAA relational database management system for the MVS environment.

The Repository Manager architecture includes two major sets of services (or "domains"): specification services and run-time services. Specification services allow users to define models of data and function that will be used and shared by various types of applications. Via an interactive menu-driven dialog interface, specification services allow users to specify data and function from three different points of view. These different perspectives or "views" supported by Repository Manager/MVS are the conceptual view, logical view, and storage view. Each of these views provides a different way of looking at both data and function.

The conceptual view provides a global repository perspective. This means that the descriptions defined for this view are common across all tools and functions within the repository—they are global definitions. The conceptual view is used to build a model of an organization. The model consists of definitions and data associated with those definitions. The model is built using entity-relationship (E-R) modeling techniques.

Using the menu-driven interface provided by Repository Manager/MVS, users can define types of entities (e.g., people, places, and things), attributes of these entities (i.e., facts associated with entities), and the relationships between entities. Hence, the name entity-relationship model.

A second view of information in the repository is the logical view. Unlike the conceptual view which provides a global perspective of information, the logical view is a tool-specific view. A "tool" is a program or set of programs that performs a particular type of repository-related task. A tool is actually composed of various repository functions. Tools are used to store, retrieve, and/or manipulate information that has been modeled and mapped to DB2 databases.

The logical view is a subset of the conceptual view to which a particular tool has access. The logical view includes specifications as to how a tool processes data and interfaces with a user.

The third view supported by Repository Manager/MVS is the storage view. This view indicates how information in the repository is actually physically stored in a separate file. The storage view specifies the mapping of the conceptual view information to physical storage. Repository Manager/MVS uses DB2 for this function.

Run-time services are invoked by different development tools and repository functions. The services provide the support to allow tools to access the information stored in the repository.

Some examples of run-time services include adding, deleting, or updating entity-relationship instances; requesting repository functions; and calling other repository functions.

The various views described above are supported by the SAA CPI Repository Interface. This CPI interface is supported by the Repository Manager/MVS product. Following is a summary of IBM's support for the CPI Repository Interface.

SAA Environment	Repository Interface Support
MVS/ESA TSO/E	Repository Manager/MVS
VM/ESA CMS	—
OS/400	—
OS/2 EE	—

CPI RESOURCE RECOVERY INTERFACE

The Resource Recovery Interface (RRI) provides two-phase commitment control required when multiple resources are being updated simultaneously. RRI provides a consistent way to develop SAA applications that need to ensure data integrity. Such applications can use RRI to implement two-phase commit in order to ensure that changes made to multiple resources will be made simultaneously to all resources or not at all.

An example would be when multiple distributed databases are being updated by a single transaction. It must be ensured that all databases involved are successfully updated. If not, any updates must be backed out.

Support for RRI is provided in IMS/ESA Transaction Manager Version 3 Release 2 and VM/ESA Version 1. In VM/ESA, the RRI implementation is called Coordinated Resource Recovery (CRR). RRI support is not yet provided in the other SAA environments.

Following is a summary of RRI support in the SAA environments.

SAA Environment	RRI Support
MVS/ESA	IMS/ESA Transaction Manager
VM/ESA	CRR
OS/400	—
OS/2 EE	—

CPI PRINTMANAGER INTERFACE

The PrintManager Interface provides a consistent method of requesting print services in SAA environments. It allows applications to dynamically control and specify print options, to validate selected options prior to sending the data to be printed, and the ability to retrieve and place resources in-line with a print job.

By allowing common print options to be set and controlled from within an application, it simplifies and provides a consistent method for sending printer output to a system spool. Printing requests then become independent of the operating environment. Applications using the PrintManager Interface can be moved between environments without having to change the print services interface.

Listed below is a summary of support for the PrintManager Interface.

SAA Environment	PrintManager Interface Support
MVS/ESA	SAA PrintManager
VM/ESA	SAA PrintManager
OS/400	SAA PrintManager/400
OS/2 EE	—

AN SAA MODEL

A "model" SAA environment would include support for the types of programming services we have been discussing, including:

> Presentation Services
> Dialog Services
> Database Services
> Query Services
> Communications Services
> Repository Services
> Resource Recovery Services
> PrintManager Services

These types of services are implemented by "managers" in an SAA environment. A "manager" is a set of software that implements a particular set of services. Therefore, a model SAA environment would include the following types of service managers:

Service Provided	Type of Manager
Presentation Services	Presentation Manager
Dialog Services	Dialog Manager
Database Services	Database Manager
Query Services	Query Manager
Communications Services	Communications Manager
Repository Services	Repository Manager
Resource Recovery	Recovery Manager
PrintManager Services	Print Manager

Each manager would provide support for the corresponding set of SAA services. For example, the Presentation Manager would provide presentation services and the Database Manager would provide database services.

As you can see from the list above, there is a manager for each of the services included in SAA's CPI element. The CPI element standardizes the application programming interfaces (APIs) that application programs use to access the services provided by the various managers. Thus, there is a corresponding CPI interface for each manager providing the various CPI services.

The following list shows the CPI interfaces that would be supported by managers in each SAA environment.

CPI Service	CPI Interface	Supported By
Presentation	Presentation Interface	Presentation Manager
Dialog	Dialog Interface	Dialog Manager
Database	Database Interface	Database Manager
Query	Query Interface	Query Manager
Communication	Communications Interface	Communications Manager
Repository	Repository Interface	Repository Manager
Recovery	Resource Recovery	Recovery Manager
Print	PrintManager Interface	PrintManager

This model can be mapped on top of each of IBM's SAA operating environments. Since IBM has designated environments which existed prior to SAA (e.g., MVS and VM), the products that implement the CPI services and interfaces in these environments are not named "managers." As an example, the MVS-based product that implements CPI relational database services and supports the CPI Database Interface is DB2—it is not named the MVS Database Manager.

With the newer IBM operating systems that have been designated SAA environments, however, there is greater consistency in the names given to the software that implements CPI services and interfaces and the names of those interfaces. For example, in the OS/2 Extended Edition environment, the OS/2 Presentation Manager supports the Presentation Interface and the OS/2 Database Manager supports the Database Interface.

The point is not to look for the name "Manager" in trying to identify which software in certain SAA environments provides CPI support. Those operating environments in which most of the SAA support is integrated as part of the operating system (e.g., OS/2 EE and OS/400) have a closer correspondence than do the operating systems where separate program products implement the different CPI components (i.e., the CPI support is not integrated). These latter environments are the MVS and VM SAA operating environments.

Several of the CPI services are illustrated in Figure 4-14, which represents a model SAA environment. Let's take a look at how the SAA model maps onto various SAA operating environments.

OS/2 Extended Edition

OS/2 Extended Edition (OS/2 EE) provides the "best" match to the SAA model discussed above. Following is a comparison of OS/2 EE to the SAA model.

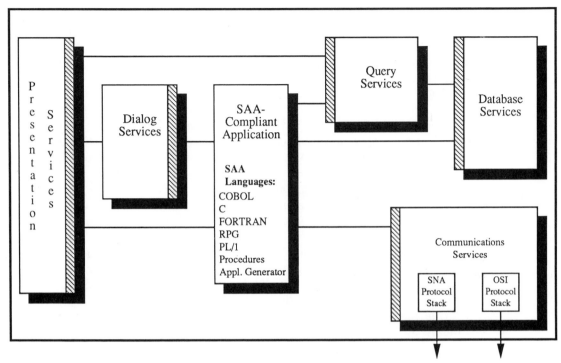

Figure 4-14. *CPI services available in SAA environments.*

SAA Model	OS/2 EE
Presentation Manager	Presentation Manager
Dialog Manager	Dialog Manager
Database Manager	Database Manager
Query Manager	Query Manager
Communications Manager	Communications Manager
Repository Manager	—
Resource Recovery Manager	—
PrintManager	—

Notice that a Repository Manager is missing from OS/2 EE. This is because IBM has positioned its repository as being host-based. Repository Managers will only be provided in SAA host environments such as MVS and VM for mainframe systems and OS/400 for AS/400 hosts. OS/2 EE workstations can access the host-based repositories but actual repositories are not directly supported on these workstations.

As of this writing, OS/2 EE also lacks support for an SAA Resource Recovery Manager and a PrintManager which were added to SAA in 1990. This support will be provided in the future releases of OS/2 EE.

All other SAA services are implemented via integrated SAA "managers" in

OS/2 EE. The OS/2 Presentation Manager provides support for the SAA CPI Presentation Interface. OS/2 applications can directly use the Presentation Manager by issuing Presentation Manager calls. The OS/2 Presentation Manager supports the CUA Graphical Model. This is a windows-based, graphical user interface.

The OS/2 Dialog Manager provides support for text-based interactive applications. OS/2 applications of this type can directly interact with the OS/2 Dialog Manager via Dialog Interface calls. The Dialog Interface is a simpler interface than the Presentation Interface and the Dialog Manager automatically provides a substantial degree of CUA compliance for applications.

The trade-off is that applications have less control over the user interface when using the Dialog Manager than when using the Presentation Manager. Also, the Dialog Manager only supports text-based applications and is procedural rather than event-driven.

Both the OS/2 Presentation Manager and OS/2 Dialog Manager are included as part of OS/2 Standard Edition even though OS/2 Standard Edition is not a designated SAA environment (OS/2 Extended Edition is the SAA operating environment for PS/2 workstations).

This means that SAA-compliant applications can be developed for OS/2 Standard Edition as well as for OS/2 Extended Edition. Missing from OS/2 Standard Edition, however, is any support for other SAA components such as database and communications services.

OS/2 EE's Database Manager provides relational database services and supports SAA's Database Interface (SQL). OS/2 EE also includes a Query Manager which allows users to query OS/2 databases. OS/2 EE Query Manager users can either enter SQL commands directly or they can use the Query Manager's menu-driven interface.

On the languages side, IBM also provides compilers for OS/2 EE for many of the SAA programming languages. These include C/2, COBOL/2, FORTRAN/2, and Procedures Language 2/REXX.

OS/2 EE also includes a Communications Manager which provides a wide range of both SAA and non-SAA communications support. SAA communications support includes LU 6.2, Node Type 2.1, Token-Ring, SDLC, and X.25.

As you can see, OS/2 EE provides a rich SAA operating environment. It provides the "fullest" range of SAA CUA support, supports several of the SAA languages, and includes support for most of the SAA services. Also, the structure of OS/2 EE matches closely the structure of the model SAA environment.

OS/400

OS/400 is another of the SAA operating environments that closely matches the generic SAA model. The summary on the next page shows the level of SAA CPI services support available in OS/400.

SAA Model	OS/400
Presentation Manager	GDDM
Dialog Manager	—
Database Manager	SQL/400
Query Manager	Query Management
Communications Manager	APPC/APPN Subsystem
Repository Manager	(Statement of Direction)
Resource Recovery	—
PrintManager	SAA PrintManager/400

Although support is provided for most of the CPI services in OS/400, the level of support is not the same as provided in OS/2 EE. One area where OS/400 lacks the level of SAA support provided in OS/2 EE is in the user-interface area.

OS/400 provides a much more limited level of SAA CUA support than does OS/2 EE. For example, the OS/400 Presentation Manager supports only the CUA Entry Model. This model assumes that nonprogrammable terminals are being used, which would be 5250 terminals in this case (or PCs that use 5250 emulation). The OS/400 Presentation Manager does not provide CUA Graphical Model support. This windows-based support is provided only in OS/2 EE.

The significance of this is that OS/2-based workstations are required to be connected to AS/400s if full CUA Graphical Model support is desired. PS/2 workstations running OS/2 can attach to AS/400s using the AS/400 PC Support program.

An SAA-compliant Dialog Manager is not yet available for OS/400. Although dialog type services are provided by OS/400, they are not totally CUA compliant and are not at the level of OS/2's Dialog Manager or the Query Management Facility (QMF) products for the mainframe SAA environments.

OS/400, like OS/2 EE, does include an integrated relational database manager. Support for the SAA Database Interface is provided via a separate product called SQL/400. SQL/400 interprets SQL calls and then interacts with OS/400's relational database manager which provides the database services.

Query services are also provided by OS/400 but, again, these are not full SAA query services. The OS/400 query services will be upgraded to comply with the SAA Query Interface and to be consistent with the query services provided in OS/2 EE and the mainframe SAA environments.

OS/400 includes a rich set of SAA communications support. This includes support for LU 6.2, Node Type 2.1 (LEN), DIA, SNA/DS, DDM, SNA/MS, all SAA data link interfaces, and object and data stream components included in SAA's CCS element.

OS/400 will eventually support host repository services and resource recovery services but this support is not yet available as of this writing.

MVS/ESA

MVS/ESA contains widespread SAA component support. The MVS/ESA CPI support is summarized below.

SAA Model	MVS/ESA
Presentation Manager	GDDM
Dialog Manager	ISPF
Database Manager	DB2
Query Manager	QMF
Communications Manager	ACF/VTAM
Repository Manager	Repository Manager/MVS
Resource Recovery	DB2
PrintManager	PrintManager/MVS

The Graphical Data Display Manager (GDDM) product is the "manager" that provides presentation services and supports the SAA Presentation Interface in the MVS/ESA environment. In fact, the initial Presentation Interface was based on GDDM.

GDDM, however, does not support the CUA graphical model as does the OS/2 Presentation Manager. GDDM supports other CUA models used with 3270 terminals or systems providing 3270 emulation. For full CUA Graphical Model support, OS/2-based workstations are required.

The initial SAA Dialog Interface was based on the Interactive System Productivity Facility (ISPF) product. ISPF is the MVS/ESA Dialog Manager. It provides dialog services and supports the SAA Dialog Interface which can be used for developing text-based, menu-driven, interactive host-based programs.

IBM's Database 2 (DB2) product implements SAA relational database services and supports the SAA Database Interface for MVS/ESA. The SAA Database Interface was based on the SQL support provided by DB2.

The Query Management Facility (QMF) product provides query services and support for the SAA Query Interface for MVS/ESA. Again, the initial SAA Query Interface was based on QMF. QMF provides a query-by-example user interface that allows users to perform ad hoc queries into relational databases managed by DB2. QMF interacts with DB2 in order to carry out the requested access.

Repository services and support for the SAA Repository Interface are provided in the MVS/ESA environment by the Repository Manager/MVS product. In fact, this is the only repository manager support available from IBM today.

SAA communications support for the MVS/ESA environment is provided primarily by VTAM. For interacting with remote systems, VTAM interacts with the Network Control Program (NCP) software running in a front-end 37XX

Communications Controller. Support is provided for LU 6.2, Node Type 2.1, and Token-Ring LAN connections, among other SAA CCS components.

VM/ESA

VM contains CPI support similar to that provided in MVS/ESA. The VM CPI support is summarized below.

SAA Model	VM
Presentation Manager	GDDM
Dialog Manager	ISPF
Database Manager	SQL/DS
Query Manager	QMF
Communications Manager	ACF/VTAM
Repository Manager	(Statement of Direction)
Resource Recovery Manager	CRR
PrintManager	PrintManager

The GDDM and ISPF products provide SAA Presentation and Dialog support in VM as well as in MVS, as discussed above.

VM's SAA database manager is Structured Query Language/Data System (SQL/DS). Like DB2 in the MVS environment, SQL/DS provides SAA relational database services and supports SQL, the SAA Database Interface.

A VM version of the QMF product described above provides SAA query services and support for the SAA Query Interface for VM as it does for MVS.

VTAM also runs in the VM environment, providing SAA communications support as it does in the MVS environment. VTAM is the "communications manager" for both the MVS and VM environments.

IBM does not yet provide a Repository Manager product for VM.

SUMMARY

The goal of the SAA CPI element is to standardize the programming environments provided on each SAA platform. This includes providing support for a standard set of programming languages which can be used to develop SAA applications and a standard set of programming interfaces that applications will use to access services in each environment.

By using the SAA CPI interfaces and services, applications are able to provide CUA-compliant user interfaces, access SAA relational databases, support SAA cooperative processing, and support other SAA-related functions.

The result of this consistent support across SAA environments is that applications are less dependent on a particular operating environment, programmers are able to transfer their programming skills from one environment to another, portability of programs is enhanced, and cooperative processing is possible, among other benefits.

5

Common Communications Support

Common Communications Support (CCS) defines the communications protocols, data streams, and related components that will be used to interconnect SAA application platforms in networks. The object of CCS is to provide a standard level of interoperability among all SAA platforms. These CCS protocols are also important for any equipment that will coexist with SAA platforms in networks because compatibility with CCS results in the ability to interoperate with SAA platforms.

SAA includes support for two different sets of communications protocols. These protocol "stacks" are IBM's own proprietary networking architecture, Systems Network Architecture (SNA), and the vendor-independent international networking standards for Open Systems Interconnection (OSI). SAA users can choose to implement either or both of these sets of communications protocols in their SAA networks.

THE SCOPE OF SAA COMMUNICATIONS

SAA communications deals not only with basic connectivity among systems, but also with the definition of standard application level services and the data streams that are exchanged among SAA systems. The CCS protocols support a cooperative processing environment where some parts of applications or some application resources might reside on one SAA platform while other application processing software and resources reside on other platforms within the network.

The scope of communications issues that SAA addresses is similar to that described by networking models like the ISO Reference Model for Open Systems Interconnection and IBM's Systems Network Architecture (SNA). These models define seven sets of networking functions that are usually represented by the functional layers which are shown in Figure 5-1. These seven layers address issues ranging from basic physical interfaces to the definition of application data streams that will be exchanged by users. The basic connectivity issues are addressed by the lower functional layers of these models while the upper layers deal with issues that are related to the applications and users that are communicating.

THE SAA NETWORKING MODEL

SAA defines its own functionally layered model which creates a structure for the elements of Common Communications Support. The major differences between the SAA model and the others is in the structure of the layers or functional categories within the model.

The lowest layer of SAA's CCS is the Data Link Control category which deals with connectivity between adjacent nodes in an SAA network. The data link layer provides error checking and correction for all data flowing between SAA

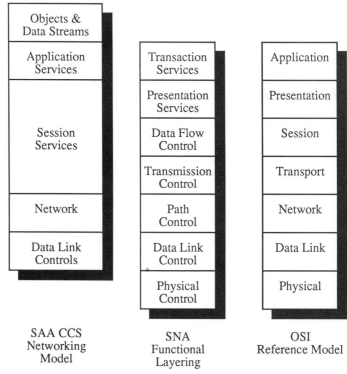

Figure 5-1. *Common Communications Support networking model.*

systems. It also provides protocols for initiating and terminating the operation of data links. The data link level connections can be across either wide area networks (WANs) or local area networks (LANs).

The CCS Network category consists of components that describe the level of network connectivity required of SAA platforms. In an SAA network, support must be provided for peer-to-peer connectivity among all systems in the network.

The logical connections between end users of SAA systems is provided by the CCS Session Services category. The CCS Session Services component defines and enforces the end-to-end protocols that provide a logical connection between users. These components also provide protocols that can be used by the communicating users to carry on a structured conversation.

The Application Services category consists of components that can be used to provide generic services such as electronic mail and remote file access which standardize these services across SAA systems. This ensures interoperability between SAA systems that need to share data and other services.

The CCS Data Streams category defines the formats of data that is interchanged between SAA systems in the network. CCS defines several data stream types, each designed for a specific purpose. For example, one data stream is used to send print data streams to intelligent printers while another data stream is designed to support the interchange of documents that can be revised by text-processing systems.

The CCS Objects category defines the formats of several standard types of data that can be carried in the CCS Data Streams. Each object contains not only data but also information that can be used by the recipient of the data stream to interpret that data properly.

SAA SUPPORT FOR SNA AND OSI COMMUNICATIONS

The generic CCS networking model that we have just described acts as a framework for structuring the use of real communications protocols. Within SAA there is currently support for two alternative sets of communications protocols. The first protocol stack that is supported is IBM's own Systems Network Architecture (SNA). Support for this proprietary IBM networking architecture was included in the original SAA architecture that was announced in 1987 and it remains the primary method of networking SAA systems.

In 1989 IBM added support for OSI standard communications protocols to SAA. Users of SAA-compatible systems can now choose to use either the SNA or OSI protocols for communications.

THE RELATIONSHIP BETWEEN SAA AND SNA

SNA is strictly a networking architecture which deals only with communications issues while SAA also defines user interfaces and an application programming environment. Therefore, the scope of SAA and SNA are quite different from one another. SNA is the basis for just one of the major elements of the SAA architecture—CCS element.

SNA was originally introduced by IBM in 1974 and is designed to support a wide range of communications requirements. These requirements include both hierarchical networking required to support the attachment of nonprogrammable terminals to host application processors and peer-to-peer networks which support connections between intelligent applications processors.

Since SAA is primarily targeted at users of intelligent workstations and host computers, IBM selected SNA's peer-to-peer networking capability for use within SAA. Therefore, the SAA definition includes only SNA's peer-to-peer communications capability and omits support for SNA's earlier hierarchical communications between hosts and nonprogrammable terminals.

The apparent lack of support for IBM's older hierarchical SNA networking protocols does not mean that those hierarchical connections between terminals and SNA hosts are obsolete. In fact, communications between terminals, particularly 3270-type terminals, and SNA hosts are still the predominant type of communications in most SNA networks. SAA systems will continue to support the hierarchical SNA protocols in order to achieve backward compatibility with the huge installed base of 3270 applications that currently exists.

DATA INTERCHANGE BETWEEN SAA SYSTEMS

The implementation of cooperative processing applications depends heavily on the interchange of data among the application platforms in a network. SAA addresses this requirement by defining two sets of architectures, object content architectures and data stream architectures. The object content architectures define the formats of several different types of data (objects) that can be interchanged among SAA systems. These object content architectures define standard formats for the representation of text, type font, image, and graphics information. Each object is really a package of information that includes not only the data itself, but also information that will ensure that the data is interpreted correctly by the recipient.

The interchange of data between SAA systems frequently involves multiple objects and multiple types of objects. These collections of objects are packaged as data streams. Each data stream defines a logical collection of objects such as a document or a transaction that updates a database.

SAA defines several types of data streams. Each data stream will contain one or more data objects and each data stream carries information that is specific to the type of operations to be performed on the data by its recipient. For example, one type of data stream carries data to be printed on an intelligent printer, while another is designed to describe data that will be stored in a library.

SAA OBJECT CONTENT ARCHITECTURES

SAA currently includes five Object Content Architectures (OCAs). Each OCA defines the format for a specific type of data along with the information needed to interpret the data properly. The Object Content Architectures are:

Presentation Text Object Content Architecture (PTOCA)—Describes text objects that are in a format suitable for presentation (not revisable)

Image Object Content Architecture (IOCA)—Describes the content of image data

Graphics Object Content Architecture (GOCA)—Describes the content of graphics data and operations to manipulate that data

Font Object Content Architecture (FOCA)—Describes digital fonts used to print and display text objects

Formatted Data Object Content Architecture (FDOCA)—Describes format of tables used to represent data in relational databases

Presentation Text Object Content Architecture

Text data is represented by the Presentation Text Object Content Architecture (PTOCA). These objects are device-independent representations of text data that are intended for output on devices like display stations and printers. These text objects are not in a format that is suitable for revision; they are only intended for final output.

Presentation Text Objects, which are shown in Figure 5-2, are made up of a Presentation Text Descriptor which describes the size and shape of the text object. The area within which the text will be displayed is called the Object Space. The Presentation Text Data contains the graphic characters to be displayed within the Object Space. Also contained within the Presentation Text Data are control sequences that position the text within the Object Space. Control sequences also determine display characteristics like color.

PTOCA defines subsets of capabilities which can be selectively implemented in products. Implementation of the base set of functions is always required. Base functions include the ability to interpret PTOCA control sequences and to detect exception conditions during processing of text objects. A subset called PT1 contains a minimal set of basic control sequences for text positioning and orientation.

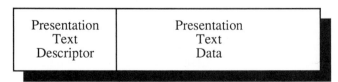

Presentation Text Descriptor	Presentation Text Data

Figure 5-2. *Presentation Text Object Content Architecture data stream format.*

The implementation of the PT1 subset is a requirement for SAA compliance. Additional control sequences are contained within the PT2 subset which includes all of the control sequences defined by the PT1 subset. The PT2 subset adds additional functions like overstrikes and underscores.

Image Object Content Architecture

Raster image data is described by IBM's Image Object Content Architecture (IOCA). This type of image data is made up of image points. Each image point describes a single point within the image area. These images can be bilevel (black and white), grey scale, and color. For a bilevel image, each image point will indicate whether the image is either black or white at that point. For grey scale and color images, each image point will be assigned a specific shade of grey or a color, respectively.

The IOCA architecture is subdivided into subsets that are called function sets. SAA will require support for Function Set 10 when IOCA is used within either IPDS or MO:DCA-P data streams which are discussed below. Function Set 10 supports only black-and-white images which can be compressed using IBM's MMR compression algorithm or the CCITT T.6 G4 facsimile compression algorithm.

If the IOCA data is to be exchanged within the MO:DCA-L data stream (for library support), Function Set 20 is required which can represent up to 24 bits-per-pixel color images.

These image points are, in turn, represented by one or more bits of information which are called Image Data Elements (IDE). The IDEs describe the image at each image point.

The data structure defined by IOCA is shown in Figure 5-3. In order to interpret image data properly, certain information must be conveyed, including the size of the image area, its resolution, the number of bits used to represent each IDE, and any compression algorithms being used. This information is included within an IOCA data structure called the image data parameters.

Graphics Object Content Architecture

Vector graphic images are represented within CCS by the Graphics Object Content Architecture (GOCA). Rather than representing the final image as is done by the previously discussed IOCA, GOCA uses a series of drawing commands (primitives) and attributes to describe how the image should be drawn. These primitives describe lines, characters, and arcs which make up the image. The attributes describe characteristics like the orientation of the primitives and the width of lines.

The GOCA architecture is defined by subsets of primitives and attributes called function sets. The relationship between these function sets is shown in Figure 5-4. The level of GOCA support required by SAA depends on the type of data stream being supported. When GOCA data is carried in a Mixed Object: Document Content Architecture data stream which is targeted for final output,

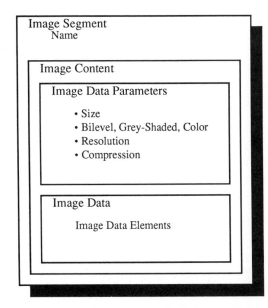

Figure 5-3. *Image Object Content Architecture data structure.*

support for GOCA's DR/2V0 function set is required. When the library version of the MO:DCA data stream is being used, the DR/3V1 function set must be used.

Font Object Content Architecture

The Font Object Content Architecture (FOCA) is used to carry information about type fonts which are used to represent text data in SAA data streams. FOCA data structures contain various parameters that define font resources. These parameters generally fall into three categories. The first category identifies the font. The second contains information on how the characters will be positioned for final

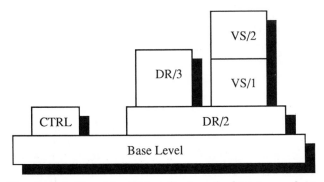

Figure 5-4. *Graphics Object Content Architecture subsets.*

output. The third category consists of parameters that define the shape of the characters.

Text formatting software that must determine where text characters will appear on a presentation medium will access the character positioning information. Presentation software which creates the final display of the document will access the character-shape information to create the graphic characters.

Other SAA object architectures such as Presentation Text Object Content architecture (PTOCA) and Graphics Object Content Architecture (GOCA) can include references to font information. Products can store font information in any internal format that is appropriate, but the FOCA format is used to interchange font information among products.

Formatted Data Object Content Architecture

The Formatted Data Object Content Architecture (FDOCA) defines a data stream that carries tabular data between SAA platforms. This data can be of various types including text and numeric data and is arranged in a two-dimensional matrix. FDOCA supports heterogeneous matrices whose elements can be of various sizes.

FDOCA is particularly important for supporting distributed relational databases. This is due to the fact that the information in these databases is always viewed as two-dimensional tables. When these table are exchanged between distributed database managers, the information is contained in FDOCA data streams.

Product Support for SAA Objects

The SAA object content architectures are currently used by several of IBM's office product lines. In some cases the objects are used internally, within the product, and in other cases they are used to interchange information from system to system. IBM's DisplayWrite/370 text-processing package runs on the System/370 processor and supports the PTOCA, IOCA, and GOCA architectures. The IOCA and GOCA architectures are also used by IBM's Graphical Data Display Manager (GDDM) which runs on System/370/390 hosts and drives both local and remote graphical devices such as printers. The FOCA architecture is used by the IBM host-based Print Services Facility.

The operating systems of the PS/2 and AS/400 platforms also make use of the object content architectures. OS/400 uses the IOCA and GOCA while the OS/2 Extended Edition operating system uses both of these architectures plus FOCA.

DATA STREAM ARCHITECTURES

All of the SAA object content architectures are self-contained descriptions of individual pieces of data, but they are used in conjunction with SAA's Data Stream Architectures. The Data Stream Architectures create packages of information that include one or more data objects along with additional data used to perform specific functions. Each of the Data Stream Architectures is designed to support a particular type of information interchange.

When groups of objects that are related to one another, such as within a compound document, are moved from application to application (usually across a communications network) they are carried in one of the SAA data streams. The type of data stream is determined by the operations to be performed on the data. For example, if the data is being sent to an intelligent printer, the Intelligent Printer Data Stream would be appropriate.

The data stream provides an envelope to carry the objects and it contains the information that describes how the objects are related to one another. In the case of Intelligent Printer Data Stream (IPDS), the data stream would contain information that describes the positioning of each object on the printed page and how that information should be displayed. The data stream and the objects are separate entities. The data stream, for example, could be changed to reposition an object on the output page without requiring any changes to the object itself.

The data streams defined by SAA standardize the formats of data that can be used by applications on a single SAA platform or interchanged among SAA application platforms. SAA's Common Communications Support includes the following data streams:

> Intelligent Printer Data Stream (IPDS)
> 3270 Data Stream
> Mixed Object: Document Content Architecture (MO:DCA)
> Revisable Form Text: Document Content Architecture (RFT:DCA)
> Character Data Representation Architecture (CDRA)

Each of these data streams has a specific purpose within SAA. IPDS is used to send compound documents created by application programs and text processors to intelligent laser and dot matrix printers. The 3270 Data Stream is used to communicate with users of nonprogrammable terminals which are either 3270s or products that emulate 3270s. The MO:DCA data stream defines a generalized data stream that can be used to define a document that is suitable for final output or to be stored in a library where it can be accessed by other data streams. The RFT:DCA data stream is used to exchange documents between text processors on the various SAA application platforms. CDRA is used to implement distributed databases and provides a standard way of representing character sets across dissimilar systems.

Intelligent Printer Data Stream

The Intelligent Printer Data Stream (IPDS) is used to send the data created by an application program to what IBM refers to as an all-points-addressable (APA) printer. An APA printer is capable of handling text as well as graphics and image data. These are typically dot matrix or laser printers.

The IPDS is made up of commands and the data to be printed. The data can include not only text, but also graphics, images, and bar codes. The

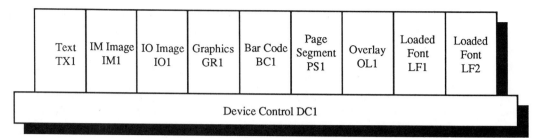

Figure 5-5. *Intelligent Printer Data Stream command subsets.*

IPDS commands and data are organized into subsets called command sets. Each command set handles a specific type of data. The command sets which are supported under SAA are shown in Figure 5-5.

The Device Control command set is always required. It provides the basic commands needed to set up and manage the printer operations. The Text command set contains the commands and data required to display text data on a page. The Image command set is used to write bit-mapped graphics images on a page. The image data is in a format defined by Image Object Content Architecture (IOCA).

The Graphics command set handles the drawing orders needed to display vector graphics on the page. The graphics data is in a format defined by Graphics Object Content Architecture (GOCA). The Bar Code command set handles the presentation of machine-readable bar codes on a page.

In order to be SAA-compliant, an SAA platform implementing IPDS must support the required Device Control command set which is called the DC1 command set. In addition, at least one of the optional IPDS command sets shown in Figure 5-5 must also be included.

The optional IPDS command sets each focus on support for a particular type of data to be output on the printer. Each of these subsets includes not only the command subsets required to print each type of data but also support for the SAA object content architecture which describes the format of the data itself. These data stream formats are referred to as the IPDS data towers as shown in Figure 5-6.

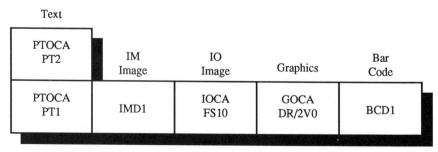

Figure 5-6. *Intelligent Printer Data Stream data towers.*

Support for text data is provided by the TX1 command set. The supported text data towers are defined by the Presentation Text Object Content Architecture (PTOCA). Both the PT1 and PT2 subsets of PTOCA are supported.

The printing of raster image data is controlled by the IO1 command set of IPDS. The format of the image data is defined by the Image Object Content Architecture (IOCA). The FS10 subset of IOCA is supported by IPDS.

Vector graphics support is defined by the IPDS GR1 command set. The format of graphics data within IPDS is defined by the DR/2V0 subset of Graphics Object Content Architecture (GOCA).

IPDS also includes support for the printing of bar-code data. The IPDS BC1 command set supports the printing of bar codes. Since IBM has no separate object content architecture that defines bar-code data, IPDS includes its own BCD1 definition of bar-code data formats.

IPDS is currently used by the OS/400 operating system and by the mainframe-based Graphical Data Display Manager (GDDM) and the Print Services Facility.

3270 Data Stream

The set of 3270 data stream functions that is required by SAA is referred to as the Extended Function Base Support (EBASE). In addition to standard 3270 commands and orders, it supports various structured fields including the structured fields needed to send these 3270 data streams over an LU 6.2 session as required by SAA.

The following EBASE elements are required for 3270 data stream support under SAA:

> Query Replies:
>> Character Sets
>> Implicit Partition
>> Null
>> Summary
>> Usable Area
> Structured Fields:
>> Read Partition
>> Erase/Reset
>> Outbound 3270 Data Stream
> Basic 3270 Commands:
>> Erase All Unprotected
>> Erase/Write
>> Erase/Write Alternate
>> Read Buffer
>> Read Modified
>> Read Modified All
>> Write
>> Write Structured Field

Basic 3270 Orders:
Start Field
Set Buffer Address
Program Tab
Insert Cursor
Repeat To Address
Erase Unprotected To Address
3270 Controls/Special Characters:
NUL, SUB, DUP, FM, FF
CR, NL, EM, EO

3270 Data Stream Support in IBM Products

The 3270 data stream is widely supported across the IBM product line. Some of the most significant SAA-related products that use the 3270 data stream include the 3270 emulation software on the AS/400 and the OS/2 Extended Edition operating system. On System/370/390 processors 3270 data streams are used by all the SAA environments, including CICS, IMS, TSO/E, and GDDM.

Mixed Object: Document Content Architecture

The Mixed Object: Document Content Architecture (MO:DCA) is defined as part of SAA's Common Communications Support (CCS), but only part of its role within SAA really has to do with communications. MO:DCA is used as a generalized vehicle for interchanging objects among SAA applications regardless of whether those applications reside on the same system or are distributed across a network.

Two subsets of MO:DCA have been defined so far. Within this architecture IBM refers to these subsets as interchange sets. One interchange set has been defined for libraries and another for presentation. The library interchange set (MO:DCA-L) is a format that is designed to be used to save data for later use by an application program.

An example of the use of this library interchange set is in the OS/2 Presentation Manager. The Presentation Manager creates files called metafiles which are created by application programs via calls to the Presentation Manager interface. These metafiles are in MO:DCA-L format.

The other interchange set that is currently defined within MO:DCA is the presentation interchange set (MO:DCA-P). This interchange set is used to create data streams that are intended for output on intelligent workstation displays and printers. There is also a revisable version of MO:DCA, but support for this format is not currently included in SAA.

In order to be SAA-compliant, an implementation of MO:DCA must support all the base functions in either MO:DCA-L or MO:DCA-P plus at least one type of object as defined by SAA's object content architectures.

The SAA object content architectures that can be included within the MO: DCA-P data stream are:

The PT1 subset of Presentation Text Object Content Architecture (PTOCA)
The DR/2V0 subset of Graphics Object Content Architecture (GOCA)
The FS10 subset of Image Object Content Architecture (IOCA)

The object architectures that are supported within the MO:DCA-L data stream are:

The DR/3V1 subset of Graphics Object Content Architecture (GOCA)
The FS20 subset of Image Object Content Architecture (IOCA)

These objects represent the actual data to be either displayed, printed, or stored in libraries while the MO:DCA architecture provides the vehicle for describing how these objects relate to one another and how they will be displayed. It is important to remember that the objects and the MO:DCA data streams which carry the objects are very distinct from one another. One can be changed without affecting the other.

Figure 5-7 shows the structure of a typical MO:DCA data stream. Structured fields identify and delimit the entire MO:DCA data stream which is made up of one or more pages of data. Each page, in turn, is delimited by the Begin Page and End Page Structured fields. The Active Environment Group field describes the environment in which the data is to be presented and the data is made up of one or more objects, each of which describes an individual data object. Different types of objects, such as text and graphics, can be included on a single page of information.

The MO:DCA data stream is supported by the OS/400 and OS/2 Extended Edition operating systems and IBM's ImagePlus program product on the System/370/390 platform.

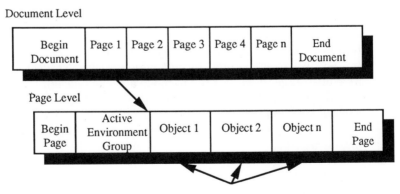

Figure 5-7. Mixed Object: Document Content Architecture data stream.

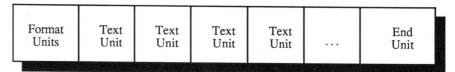

Figure 5-8. *Revisable Form Text: Document Content Architecture data stream.*

Revisable Form Text: Document Content Architecture

When documents whose format can be revised are interchanged among SAA platforms, the Revisable Form Text: Document Content Architecture (RFT: DCA) is used. These documents consist of only text data. This is the SAA standard data stream format that is used by many of IBM's text-processing software packages. RFT:DCA is also supported by text-processing products from many other vendors and has thus become an industry standard in itself.

Within SAA networks, RFT:DCA support includes all the major elements of RFT:DCA documents. The data structure defined by RFT:DCA is shown in Figure 5-8. The Format Units, which appear at the beginning of documents, control the overall format of the document including page size, margins, and global default value for text formatting. The Text Units are the pages of text within the document. Text Units contain the text information along with embedded formatting commands that control the display of the text within the page. Any number of Text Units can be included within an RFT:DCA document. The End Unit delimits the end of an RFT:DCA document.

The RFT:DCA data stream is used by all of IBM's key text-processing packages including DisplayWrite/370 and the PS/2-based DisplayWrite 4/2 and 5/2 products.

Character Data Representation Architecture

The different hardware platforms that are supported by SAA each have their own internal data representations which may be different from those used by the other SAA platforms. Differences might include ways the numeric information is represented. For example, numeric data on System/370 processors can be represented in packed decimal format which packs two decimal digits into a single byte of storage. If we wanted to move a packed decimal field to a PS/2 system we would have to perform a data conversion operation because the PS/2 is not capable of handling packed decimal fields. The CDRA data stream provides a standard method for performing this and other data conversions between SAA platforms.

SAA APPLICATION SERVICES

The role of the Application Services category of CCS is to provide generic distributed application services to users of an SAA cooperative processing network.

SAA specifies a standard set of services and protocols for electronic mail, remote file access, remote database access, and network management. These cross-system services are based on the following SAA Application Services Architectures:

> Document Interchange Architecture (DIA) for electronic mail and document archiving
> SNA/Distribution Services (SNA/DS) for store-and-forward networking
> Distributed Data Management (DDM) for remote file access
> SNA/Management Services (SNA/MS) for network management

Both the electronic mail and remote file access protocols use SNA's Logical Unit Type 6.2 session level protocols to support peer-to-peer connectivity among SAA platforms.

While DIA and SNA/DS support was part of the original SAA announcement in 1987, the addition of DDM support for remote file access was added in 1988.

Each of these architectures will be described briefly below. More detailed information on these Application Services is provided in Chapter 9.

Document Interchange Architecture

IBM's Document Interchange Architecture (DIA) provides the application-level protocols required to support the interaction between a user, or requester, system and a server that provides electronic mail and document library services.

DIA is used within IBM's SAA OfficeVision product line to link users of the Personal System/2 with servers that reside on all three SAA hardware platforms—the System/370/390 processors, the Application System/400, and the Personal System/2.

Like most of IBM's communications architectures, DIA is designed to be implemented on a wide range of products. In order to tailor the architecture to the requirements of these products, the DIA architecture is made up of subsets called function sets. These function sets are defined within the DIA architecture and each addresses a specific set of DIA services and the protocols needed to support those services.

SAA's Definition of DIA Compatibility

All SAA platforms must implement DIA Function Set 10 which provides the basic session services needed to connect DIA requesters and servers and to update session information such as passwords. The other SAA function sets that are supported by SAA are optionally implemented based on the requirements of specific products.

It is important to remember that the list of function sets supported is only a partial measure of a product's DIA compatibility. The other key element is whether the product provides either server or requester support for each function set. Requester support defines the protocols needed to issue requests for DIA services from a user's system to a server that will actually provide the requested services. The server capability provides the DIA protocol handling required for a system that is providing services like electronic mail and document library services.

In addition to the basic requirement to support DIA Session Services, an SAA-compliant platform must support at least one of the DIA function sets that provide electronic mail, document library, and application-processing services to network users. The following DIA function sets are implemented based on the product's need to provide the associated services.

> Function Set 10—Session Services
> Function Set 8—Document Library Services
> Function Set 2—Electronic Mail Server Capability
> Function Set 5—Electronic Mail Requester Capability
> Function Set 9—Application Services

All DIA implementations must include Function Set 10 which supports Session Services. This Session Services support allows users to update the session parameters such as passwords which control access to DIA Document Distribution and Library services. In addition to the required Function Set 10 support, each SAA product that implements DIA must include at least one of the following additional DIA function sets.

Document library support, Function Set 8, defines protocols used to file documents in server-based libraries, and to search those libraries and retrieve the documents when needed.

SAA's electronic mail services are implemented by two DIA function sets. Function Set 2 defines the DIA protocols needed to deliver documents from a DIA server node, also known as an Office System Node (OSN), to a user's system which is also referred to as a Recipient Node. This function set also includes protocols that allow the user to perform mail-management functions like checking the contents of the user's mailbox and the delivery status of documents that have been sent.

Function Set 5 contains the protocols that allow a user to initiate the distribution of documents from his workstation, also known as a Source Node, to an electronic mail server which will actually perform the document distribution on behalf of the user.

Finally, Function Set 9 supports DIA's application-processing services. This allows users to initiate the execution of application programs which convert the format of documents, update the descriptions of documents which are filed in libraries, and other user-defined functions.

DIA is currently supported by IBM's OfficeVision software running on all three of the SAA platforms. IBM's Distributed Office Support System (DISOSS) package on the System/370 processor is also a key DIA implementation. IBM's Personal Services line of office products for the System/370, System/36, System/38, and PC, also support DIA services.

SNA/Distribution Services

SNA/Distribution Services (SNA/DS) is IBM's store-and-forward networking technology. It uses the underlying services of SNA's LU 6.2 to provide basic connectivity between SNA/DS network nodes.

SNA/DS is most often used in conjunction with DIA to provide electronic mail services to network users. Document distributions that only involve users connected to a single electronic mail server are handled completely by DIA alone. When document distributions involve multiple servers, however, those servers use SNA/DS protocols to transfer the documents between servers.

While electronic mail is currently the primary user of SNA/DS's store-and-forward networking capability, SNA/DS is a generalized technology that can be used for a wide range of purposes. The latest use to which IBM is putting SNA/DS is to support the distribution of software in large-scale SNA networks. For example, SNA/DS is now being used to deliver microcode updates and configuration information to remote 3174 Control Units. The distributions are initiated and managed by the NetView Distribution Manager. We expect this capability, which is particularly important in cooperative processing networks, to be extended to support all SAA platforms in the near future.

SAA does not specify any particular restrictions on the implementation of SAA-compliant SNA/DS platforms. Any appropriate combination of SNA/DS functionality can be implemented in SAA networks.

SNA/DS is implemented within the OS/400 operating system and on the System/370/390 processors within DISOSS and the NetView/DM packages.

Distributed Data Management

Another major application-level service which is defined within SAA networks is remote file access. This means real-time, file-level or record-level access to files that can reside anywhere in the network. The IBM communications architecture that supports this service is Distributed Data Management (DDM).

Systems that implement DDM can provide either source or target capability, or both. A DDM source system is one that is capable of accessing remote files on behalf of local application programs. The DDM target systems are essentially file servers that respond to requests for file services from DDM source systems.

An SAA-compliant platform must support the source or target, or both DDM roles, and comply with a list of specific SAA requirements. These SAA requirements specify support for sequential, direct, and keyed files. More specifically, the following list of required DDM access-method managers shows the types of access that are required for each file type.

Relative access by record number for sequential and direct files
Random access by record number for direct files
Combined access by record number for direct files
Relative, random, and combined access by key for keyed files

SAA also requires DDM support for SNA LU 6.2 communications as well as the DDM lock and security manager. Support for fixed-length records is an SAA requirement.

Over and above these basic requirements, SAA allows optional support for DDM features like variable-length records and byte stream files.

DDM has recently been enhanced to include support for distributed relational databases. This DDM Level 3 support is combined with other application-level architectures within IBM's Distributed Relational Database Architecture (DRDA), which is a component of SAA.

DDM is currently available on System/370/390 processors in the DDM/CICS program product and it is built into the OS/400 operating system.

SNA/Management Services

The final application-level service that is included in SAA's Common Communications Support (CCS) is network management. IBM's SNA/Management Services (SNA/MS) defines a number of categories of network management services including configuration management, problem management, and performance management. SAA currently only requires support for the problem management category of SNA/MS.

The problem management category deals with the reporting of exception conditions as they occur in SNA networks. These exception conditions are reported to network management focal point products via alerts which carry the problem management data in a format prescribed by the SNA/MS architecture. SNA/MS is discussed in more detail in Chapter 10.

SNA SESSION AND NETWORK SERVICES

The basic system-to-system connectivity required to support all the SAA Application Services as well as all user-written SAA applications which require communications is provided by the Session and Network Services of CCS. The CCS Session layer provides a logical connection between application programs that are distributed across an SAA network.

The Network layer provides connectivity between the individual systems within the SAA network. Both the Session and Network layers provide peer-to-peer connectivity among any SAA systems in a network. This permits SAA networks to be configured in any way that is appropriate to support the users and applications within the network.

Logical Unit Type 6.2

The session services layer of the SAA communications protocol stack uses SNA's Logical Unit Type 6.2 protocols to provide end-to-end connectivity between users of an SAA network. Logical Unit 6.2 is described in detail in Chapter 7.

A basic requirement of any LU 6.2 implementation is to support the base set of LU 6.2 protocols. Support for this base set of protocols is, therefore, a basic SAA requirement.

Most SAA platforms will need to support SAA's standard application programming interface for communications, known as the Common Programming Interface for Communications (CPIC), which is described in Chapters 4 and 7. In order to support this interface, SAA defines some additional LU 6.2 services and protocols which are required. In addition to the base set, the following option sets are required in order to support the Communications Interface defined within SAA's CPI element.

101 Flush the LU's send buffer
102 Get attributes
105 Prepare to receive
106 Receive immediate
110 Get conversation type
203 Immediate session allocation
245 Test for request-to-send received
290 Logging of data in a system log

The exact definition of each of these LU 6.2 option sets and the base set can be found in IBM's SNA Transaction Programmer's Reference Manual for LU Type 6.2, GC30-3084.

Network Connectivity

The network layer of CCS defines the level of network connectivity required on SAA platforms. The IBM technologies included in CCS are Low-Entry Networking (LEN) and Advanced Peer-to-Peer Networking (APPN) End Nodes, which are provided in IBM's Node Type 2.1 SNA systems. The characteristic of Low-Entry Networking that is most significant within SAA is its ability to support direct peer-to-peer connections between any pair of systems in a network. LEN, APPN, and Node Type 2.1 are described in detail in Chapter 8.

The specific features of Node Type 2.1 which are required for SAA CCS compatibility include:

SDLC, X.25, and Token-Ring LAN support
Switched and non–switched link connections
Data link activation and deactivation by either peer system
SNA session activation and deactivation by either peer system
Support for independent logical units
Link station role negotiation

These features of Node Type 2.1 collectively support a communications environment that supports peer-to-peer connectivity directly between any of the SAA application platforms which include System/370 processors, AS/400s, and PS/2s. They also support decentralization of basic network configuration operations.

SAA DATA LINK CONTROL

The data link category of SAA's CCS defines connectivity between adjacent SAA application platforms in a network. There are three technologies included in this CCS category that are used to support both local and wide area networking at this level:

> Token-Ring LAN
> Synchronous Data Link Control (SDLC)
> X.25 Packet-Switching Interface

IBM's Token-Ring architecture is based on the IEEE 802.2 and 802.5 standards which correspond to the ISO 8802-2 and 8802-5 standards. In order for Token-Ring support to be SAA-compliant, IBM has specified that the following functions must be implemented:

> Dynamic window flow control in LLC
> Source routing for Token-Ring bridging
> The MAC layer enhancement for Token-Ring architecture
> Early token release for the 16-mbps Token-Ring

For X.25 and SDLC wide area networking within SAA, IBM has not really supplied any new requirements. They simply refer to existing specifications for supporting X.25 with SNA.

The relationship between X.25 and SNA is a little more complex than that of the other SNA data link layer standards. This is due to the fact that X.25 is more than just a data link protocol. As shown in Figure 5-9, X.25 provides an interface to another entire network, specifically, a packet-switched network. IBM has defined a logical data link protocol which extends across the packet-switched network and ties the two SNA devices together at the data link level. Below this logical link control layer is an implementation of X.25 which, in itself, is a three-layer protocol. Despite the fact that X.25 is much more than just a data link protocol, SNA treats it as if it were simply a point-to-point data link.

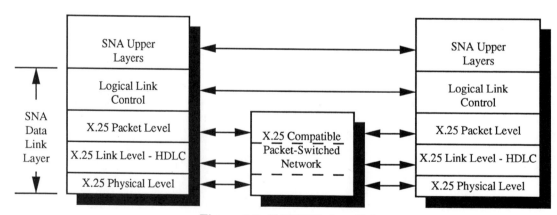

Figure 5-9. X.25/SNA data link support.

For SDLC, the only specific SAA requirements are those for link station role negotiation capability. In general, SDLC must be implemented in its entirety in SAA products.

OSI COMMUNICATIONS SUPPORT

IBM has also included the OSI communications protocol stack as an alternative to SAA's support for SNA. IBM has not yet defined its SAA support for OSI communications protocols in as much detail as it has for the SNA protocol stack. In particular, there are no specific definitions of data streams or objects at the Application Layer. IBM has included support for the international standards that are included within most of the international OSI profiles that are designed to promote interoperability among OSI systems. These profiles include:

> U.S. Government OSI Profile (GOSIP) Version 1
> UK GOSIP Version 3.0
> European Norms ENV 41-104 Part 2
> Interoperability Technology Association for Information Processing (INTAP)

Figure 5-10 shows how all the OSI standards that are supported by CCS relate to one another and layers for which more than one optional set of standards exists.

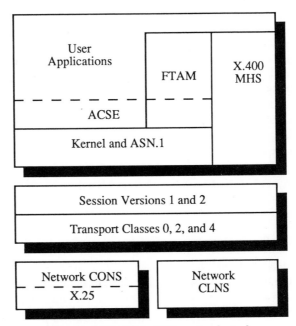

Figure 5-10. *SAA OSI protocol stack.*

Application Layer Support for OSI

The OSI application services that are defined by SAA include File Transfer, Access, and Management (FTAM) and the X.400 Message Handling System. FTAM supports access to remote files and is, therefore, the OSI counterpart to SNA's Distributed Data Management (DDM). X.400 provides electronic mail and messaging to users of the OSI protocol stack. The SNA counterparts to the X.400 Message Handling Systems would be Document Interchange Architecture (DIA) and SNA/Distribution Services (SNA/DS). There is currently no OSI counterpart to the document archiving and retrieval capabilities of DIA.

The OSI Application Layer also supports the Association Control Service Element (ACSE) which defines a standard way for applications to start, stop, and abort application-level connections across an OSI-compatible network.

SAA Session Layer Support for OSI

Both SAA's Common Communications Support (CCS) and the OSI Reference Model define a Session Layer, but these layers have a different role within each protocol stack and this can lead to considerable confusion. The Session Layer defined by the SAA protocol stack includes several SNA and OSI functional layers which are used to support logical end user–to–end user connections.

In the SNA protocol stack these would include the Transmission Control, Data Flow Control, and Presentation Services layers. In SNA, these three layers collectively define Logical Units through which end users of the SNA network communicate with one another. In the OSI protocol stack, the Transport, Session, and Presentation layers would be included within SAA's Session Services category.

The OSI Transport layer supports the logical connections between end users of open systems. This layer establishes and manages the logical connections and controls the sequence and flow of data on these connections. SAA supports Transport Layer Classes 0, 2, and 4 as defined by the ISO 8073 standard.

The OSI Session layer is responsible for managing connections between communicating applications. Protocols are provided to synchronize and manage dialogs between network users. SAA includes support for the ISO 8327 standard versions 1 and 2.

The representation of data is addressed by the OSI Presentation layer. SAA supports the Kernel and Abstract Syntax Notation (ASN.1) which is defined by the ISO 8823 and 8825 standards.

Network Layer Support for OSI

The OSI Network layer is responsible for network routing. This routing involves source, intermediate, and destination nodes. Facilities for blocking and segmenting data are also provided. There are two major classes of Network layer services that are supported. The Connectionless Network Services (CLNS) using Internet provides connections that do not have to be preestablished. CLNS is defined by the ISO 8473 standard. The Connection-Oriented Network Service (CONS) is also supported. CONS works with X.25 to support connections across packet-switched networks and conforms to the ISO 8878 standard.

Data Link Layer Support for OSI

SAA includes support for both wide area and local area networking using the OSI protocol stack. For wide area networking the X.25 packet-switching interface is supported. SAA supports the X.25 Packet-Level Protocol (PLP) which is defined by the ISO 8208 standard. The LAPB Procedures defined by the ISO 7776 standard are also included in SAA's support for X.25.

There is also support for local area networks which conform to the ISO 8802-3 CSMA/CD and 8802-5 Token Ring standards. SAA's LAN support also includes the ISO 8802-2 Logical Link Control standard.

Mainframe OSI Communications Support

IBM's first complete OSI protocol implementation on an SAA platform is the OSI/Communications Subsystem (OSI/CS) product which runs on the System/370 processors. OSI/CS is a VTAM-based communications subsystem that implements OSI functional layers 3 through 6. OSI/CS is the foundation for OSI communications support on System/370 processors. Application services like FTAM and X.400, as well as user-written applications, are supported by OSI/CS.

As shown in Figure 5-11, the OSI/CS software uses both VTAM and X.25 facilities that have been used to implement SNA protocols on IBM mainframes

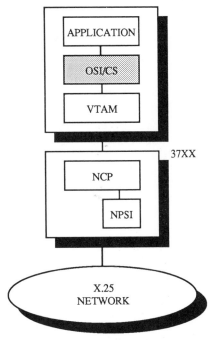

Figure 5-11. *OSI/Communications Subsystem software structure.*

for many years. The X.25 support is provided by the NCP Packet-Switching Interface (NPSI) software which runs in IBM 37XX Communication Controllers along with the Network Control Program (NCP).

The basic NPSI X.25 support has been used to provide the ability to connect SNA devices to mainframes over X.25 virtual circuits. The combination of VTAM, NCP, and NPSI has always had the ability to support higher-level protocols other than SNA over X.25 virtual circuits, but this required user-written programs to provide the upper-layer support. The OSI/CS package is an off-the-shelf implementation of the upper-level OSI protocols.

VTAM and NCP support the lower three layers of the OSI reference model as defined by the X.25 packet-switching standard. The OSI/CS package completes the layer 3 protocols and adds support for layers 4 through 6. OSI application services reside at layer 7 along with ACSE support and, therefore, use the underlying services of OSI/CS. An example of an OSI service provided by IBM is the FTAM support contained in the OSI/File Services program product. OSI/FS is an application that uses the OSI/CS communications services.

SUMMARY

SAA products can implement either the SNA or OSI protocol stacks for communications. Each provides functions ranging from physical connectivity through application-level services. IBM has provided a more detailed definition of its SNA protocol stack which includes definitions of data streams and objects that are standardized across IBM SAA and non-SAA products.

Both protocol stacks include support for networking function which ranges from the application level down to basic physical connectivity issues. The higher-level applications services provided by both protocol stacks include electronic mail and remote file access services. Within the SNA protocol stack electronic mail support is provided by DIA and SNA/DS while X.400 supports OSI electronic mail services. DDM provides remote file and database access for SNA users. Within the OSI protocol stack only remote file access is provided by FTAM.

Communications between SAA platforms is addressed by the middle layers of both protocol stacks. SNA uses LU Type 6.2 and Node Type 2.1 for peer-to-peer support. The OSI protocol stack also provides peer-to-peer communications among platforms. Both protocol stacks also provide connectivity to both wide area and local area networks.

6

Common Applications

What is an SAA Common Application? Actually, there is no single answer. An SAA Common Application can have various characteristics and various levels of SAA component support. SAA Common Applications will vary in their degree of "SAA-compliance" or "SAA-conformance." In general, SAA Common Applications have one or more of the following characteristics in common:

> Will provide a user interface that conforms to one of the SAA user-interface models
>
> Will use standard SAA components and interfaces for programming services addressed by SAA
>
> Will use standard SAA communications components when communicating with other systems
>
> Will run in one or more SAA operating environments
>
> Will be structured for cooperative processing (where appropriate)

The first three items in the list above indicate that an SAA Common Application can be looked at primarily in three general areas: the user interface provided, the programming interfaces and services used, and interoperability with other applications. These areas just happen to match the three major elements of SAA as indicated below:

SAA Common Application	SAA Element
User Interface	CUA
Programming Interfaces	CPI
Communications/Interoperability	CCS

By conforming to the SAA standards in these areas, an SAA Common Application will have a user interface that is SAA CUA-compliant (i.e., it will have the same look and feel as other SAA applications); it will run in multiple SAA environments where appropriate; and it will support cooperative processing where appropriate.

Not all SAA Common Applications will have all these characteristics. For some applications, one or more of these areas may not be addressed by the application at all. For example, a word processing application may provide an SAA CUA-compliant user interface and execute in all the SAA environments, but it might not support communications with other programs because this is not a function addressed by the application—it is a standalone application.

Another characteristic of an SAA Common Application (its ability to run in multiple SAA environments) derives from either the ability to split the application across environments or to port the application across environments.

The point is that SAA applications are built using components or following guidelines included in the SAA CUA, CPI, and/or CCS elements. CUA, CPI, and CCS standards, therefore, form the basis or framework for developing SAA applications as indicated in Figure 6-1.

How much the application uses components or follows guidelines from the CUA, CPI, and CCS elements will determine its level of SAA conformance. The range of conformance will vary by application. Some applications will conform in all areas while others may conform only in certain areas. Within a particular area there may be varying levels of conformance as well. Each of these areas will be discussed in more detail below.

The reality is that SAA Common Applications will also include non-SAA elements and will use non-SAA interfaces and components. These non-SAA elements may be used because the particular area for which the non-SAA element is used may not be addressed by SAA; or system-dependent value-added facilities may be used in order to exploit capabilities of a particular system or environment in which the application will execute. Of course, the more usage of non-SAA or system-dependent facilities used, the less portable the application becomes and the less consistent with other SAA applications.

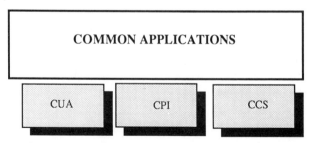

Figure 6-1. *Common Applications are built using CUA, CPI, and CCS components.*

THE ENVIRONMENT

An SAA application will run in one or more of the SAA operating environments. A fully conforming SAA Common Application will actually run in all the SAA operating environments.

One of the first choices an application designer makes is selecting the environment(s) in which the application will execute. The application may execute in any of the designated SAA environments listed below:

Operating System	Subsystem
MVS/ESA	TSO/E
	CICS/MVS
	IMS/VS DC
VM/ESA	CMS
OS/400	
OS/2 EE	

These are the operating environments in which IBM has committed to provide SAA support. An SAA Common Application, therefore, can be written to run in one or more of these environments, as shown in Figure 6-2. The choice of environment will be influenced by the type of application, the installed base of systems, and the structure of the application, among a wide range of other considerations.

Actually, the choice of environments is rarely this objective. The reality is

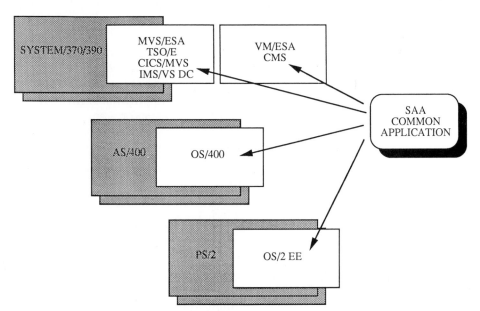

Figure 6-2. *Common Applications span SAA operating environments.*

that the installed base of systems and environments will usually determine the environment in which the applications being developed must execute. For example, a company that has one or more System/370 mainframes running MVS will probably develop new applications for the MVS environment and certainly there will be a requirement to continue using the existing MVS applications.

It is unlikely that such a company would make a wholesale switch from MVS to VM or that AS/400s or PS/2s would totally replace the mainframe, although there would be an ongoing downsizing trend in which applications that were typically mainframe-based would be migrated to midrange systems and workstations. Often this will involve splitting the application across systems rather than totally eliminating the mainframe. We will discuss this in more detail below.

In any case, an SAA Common Application should be as independent of any of the above operating environments as possible. That is, the application should minimize any operating-system dependencies that make it difficult or impossible for the application to be ported to or execute in other environments.

This can be done by ensuring that the application is developed using an SAA language, makes use of SAA CPI interfaces available, and isolates any system dependencies to sections of code or separate modules that are easily identifiable and can be replaced or modified as necessary in order to move the application to another environment.

STRUCTURE OF THE APPLICATION

As we said above, the structure of the application will also determine to some extent the environments in which it executes. Two very general ways to structure an application are standalone and cooperative. These structures are illustrated in Figure 6-3.

A standalone application is one that runs self-contained within a single SAA operating environment. A standalone application could execute in every SAA environment, but the application is not split across environments nor does it directly interact with other distributed applications. An example of a standalone application is a word processing application or a spreadsheet application that is used on a particular system and does not involve any distributed processing.

There are actually two classes of standalone applications:

> An application that runs on a host system and is accessed via nonprogrammable terminals
> An application that runs on a programmable workstation

The mainframe-based MVS and VM environments and the OS/400 environment for AS/400 systems are positioned as SAA host environments. In the first case, the standalone application could run on a System/370 mainframe under either MVS or VM and can be accessed by 3270 terminal users. Or, it could be an application running on an AS/400 accessed by 5250 terminals.

These are the kinds of applications typically found in most companies today and are reflective of traditional mainframe-based SNA hierarchical networks. In

STANDALONE APPLICATION:

COOPERATIVE PROCESSING APPLICATION:

Figure 6-3. *Common Applications can be either standalone or structured for cooperative processing.*

the second case, the standalone application would run on a PC or PS/2 workstation under OS/2 Extended Edition. The application user would be the local PC or PS/2 user. No other host system is involved.

An application structured for cooperative processing, on the other hand, will span SAA environments. The processing is distributed across multiple environments, such as between a programmable workstation and a host. A good example of this type of cooperative application is one that is used on an intelligent workstation and presents a graphical, windows-based user interface that provides an easy-to-use means of accessing the "back-end" of the application that is being executed on a host system to which the workstation is attached.

Unlike standalone applications, which could be used via nonprogrammable terminals, cooperative processing applications require programmable workstations (PS/2s running OS/2 EE) because the application processing is split between the workstation and one or more host systems. This type of cooperative processing application will almost always involve PS/2 workstations since OS/2 EE is the only SAA environment that provides CUA Graphical Model support.

This is the real target for SAA. The programmable workstation serves as the window into the network. Workstation users are provided highly graphical interfaces that allow them to easily and transparently access applications and other resources distributed throughout the network.

A typical SAA cooperative processing application will involve an OS/2 EE-based PS/2 workstation connected to a host System/370/390 or AS/400 system. SAA CCS components such as LU 6.2 will be used to provide the communication between the workstation and the host. The decision to go cooperative probably means using the OS/2 EE environment, at least in an SAA framework.

THE USER INTERFACE

The style of user interface is another test of an application's SAA compliance. The design of the user interface is typically one of the first considerations when designing an application. The user interface is how the application will actually appear to its users, that is, its look and feel. Because the user interface is the most visible part of an application, its conformance to SAA often will be judged quite heavily on how closely its user interface is consistent with SAA guidelines.

An SAA Common Application must provide a user interface that conforms to the guidelines and specifications described by SAA's CUA element. The intent is for SAA applications to have consistent user interfaces in order to make them easier to learn and use.

As we saw in Chapter 3, the SAA CUA element defines various user-interface models that can be used as the basis for developing the user interface for the application. The designer of an SAA application must decide which of these models to use in defining the application's user interface. Each model has its own characteristics and each is targeted at different types of users and applications. The choice of which model to use will depend on the type of application, the type of users, and the type of terminal or system on which the application will be used.

SAA CUA defines two main types of interfaces: basic interface and advanced interface. These interfaces support various CUA user-interface models. The user-interface models addressed by these interfaces are:

> Entry Model
> Text Subset (of the Graphical Model)
> Graphical Model
> Workplace (extension to the Graphical Model)

The user-interface models, shown in Figure 6-4, are designed to support either or both of the following:

> Nonprogrammable Terminals (NPTs)—3270s, 5250s
> Programmable Workstations (PWSs)—PS/2s with OS/2

The user-interface models are designed for use not only with the above devices but also for the following broad categories of applications:

> Data-Entry-Intensive Applications
> Decision-Support-Intensive Applications

The Basic Interface guidelines support both nonprogrammable terminals and programmable workstations. Either the Entry or Text Subset model can be used with nonprogrammable terminals but programmable workstations are only supported via the Entry Model.

In effect, the programmable workstation is being treated like a non-

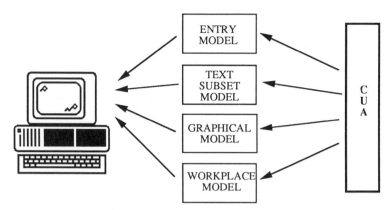

Figure 6-4. *Common Applications provide a user interface that conforms to one of the CUA models.*

programmable terminal, assuming it has no windows-based graphics support or application-processing capability. This would be the case when the programmable workstation is emulating a terminal such as a 3270 terminal. The different CUA models are described in detail in Chapter 3.

What this all boils down to is this: If a windows-based, graphical user interface is desired, then OS/2-based workstations are required and either the CUA Graphical Model (for Presentation Manager applications) or Workplace Model (for OfficeVision/2 applications) can be used. These user interfaces are not supported on nonprogrammable terminals.

If it is a requirement to support nonprogrammable terminals (or to use intelligent workstations in terminal emulation mode), then either the Entry or Text Subset model can be used.

Designers need to know which types of terminals and workstations need to be supported by the application and the level of user-interface consistency required for the different types of devices.

PROGRAMMING COMPONENTS

An SAA Common Application will be developed using one of the SAA programming languages and the services included in the CPI element which are shown in Figure 6-5. The choice of language will be dictated by

1. The availability of language support on the system on which the application is being developed (not all SAA systems support all SAA languages)
2. The developer's familiarity with a particular language (COBOL programmers may choose to develop using COBOL rather than C)
3. The type of application being developed (a business application may be easier to develop using COBOL while an application using lower-level system services may be better written using C)

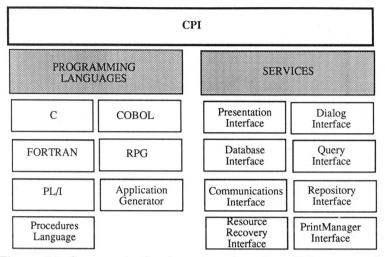

Figure 6-5. *Common Applications are written in a CPI programming language and use CPI interfaces and services.*

4. The degree of CPI interface support provided by the SAA language compilers
5. The degree of portability desired (C and COBOL would be more portable than RPG today because of the lack of RPG compilers on other than the AS/400)

Other issues affecting the decision are whether to use a third-generation language such as COBOL or C or a fourth-generation development tool such as Cross System Product (CSP), IBM's product implementation of the SAA Application Generator language.

Developers have the choice of using the following SAA languages:

C
COBOL
FORTRAN
RPG
PL/I
Application Generator (Cross System Product)
Procedures Language (REXX)

The choice of an SAA programming language is not as objective and open-ended as it appears. The reality is that applications written for VM- or MVS-based mainframe shops that are heavily COBOL-oriented will probably also be written in COBOL.

CPI SERVICES

An SAA Common Application will use CPI programming interfaces to access CPI services as much as possible. For example, for displaying information on a user's screen and interacting with the user, the application should use the SAA Presentation and Dialog interfaces.

For interacting with relational databases, the SAA Database or Query interfaces should be used. For communicating with other applications, the SAA Communications Interface should be used. For interacting with a repository, the Repository Interface should be used.

The CPI services are application "enablers" that provide underlying services to the application. An application program interacts with the enablers by using the system-independent CPI programming interfaces. Using these interfaces promotes the portability of applications and provides for the development of integrated applications that span SAA environments.

Decisions must be made as to which CPI interfaces and services will be used by the application. The list below summarizes the choices the developer has:

Functional Area	CPI Interface
User Interface	Presentation
	Dialog
Database Access	Database
	Query
Communications	Communications
Repository Access	Repository
Printing	PrintManager

The availability of support for these CPI interfaces and services in a particular SAA operating environment in which the application will execute, will determine whether or not the application can actually make use of the interface. As an example, the Repository Interface is not yet supported in OS/400.

SAA COMMUNICATIONS SERVICES

Another characteristic of SAA Common Applications is that they may involve cooperative processing with other applications. If so, SAA Common Communications Support (CCS) components should be used for communications and interoperability between environments.

The CCS components that provide these kinds of services include Application Services such as DDM, DIA, and SNA/DS; LU 6.2 program-to-program communications protocols, Node Type 2.1 peer-to-peer support; and data link protocols such as SDLC, Token-Ring, and/or X.25.

Standardized data streams and standardized object formats are used to exchange information between SAA environments. All SAA environments include support for these CCS components. The total set of SAA CCS components is shown in Figure 6-6.

SAA Common Applications do not always directly make use of these CCS components in order to carry out cooperative processing with other environ-

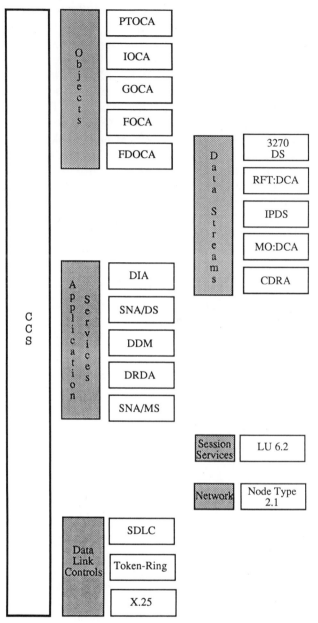

Figure 6-6. *Common Applications use CCS components for communicating with other systems.*

ments. Most of the communications support is carried out "under the covers," transparently to the application.

A good way to illustrate this is to show what happens when an application requests access to data in a database that is physically resident on some other remote system in the network. The SAA Common Application does not have to implement support for CCS components directly in order to carry out the distributed request.

Instead, the application is written as if the data being accessed were locally resident on the same system. The application, therefore, would issue SAA CPI Database Interface (SQL) calls to access the data. These SQL calls would be handled by the local system's Database Manager. When the local system's Database Manager determines that the requested data is not local, it will distribute the request to the appropriate remote system, using the standard CCS components for this type of distribution (e.g., LU 6.2, DRDA, DDM).

The distribution of the request is unknown to the application. The results of the distributed request are eventually returned from the remote system back to the local system. The local Database Manager will then complete the application's SQL request just as if it had been serviced locally. The distribution and use of CCS protocols is totally transparent to the application. Note that the application program did not have to use the Communications Interface for this distributed processing.

For applications that need to perform specialized distributed processing with other applications, the SAA CPI Communications Interface (CPIC) can be used. The application will issue CPIC calls to communicate with remote programs. The CPIC interface provides LU 6.2–based program-to-program communications facilities.

SAA COMMON APPLICATION MODEL

Figure 6-7 shows an SAA Common Application using CPI interfaces for various types of services. For interacting with the user, the application will issue Presentation Manager and/or Dialog Manager calls. These are the CPI interfaces used for the application's user interface because of their support for SAA's CUA.

For accessing data in relational databases, the application would issue calls to the local Database Manager or to the Query Manager. These programming calls would conform to the CPI Database Interface and Query Interface, respectively.

The actual data being accessed may or may not be locally resident. That is, the data may not be on the same system (local) on which the application is executing. The data may, in fact, physically reside on some other remote system in the network. The actual location of the data is transparent to the application, as discussed above. The application does not have to issue any communications calls in order to get at data that may be distributed on a remote system.

The application issues the same Database Interface (SQL) calls or Query calls regardless of where the data resides. If the data is local, the local Database Manager will handle the request. If the data is on a remote system, the local Database Manager will distribute the request to the remote system's Database Manager who will then handle the request. The results will be passed back to the local system's Database Manager who will complete the request to the application just as if it had been serviced locally.

The application may also gain access to data in a relational database using the higher-level Query Interface. In this manner, the application would issue Query calls rather than SQL calls. A local Query Manager would handle the

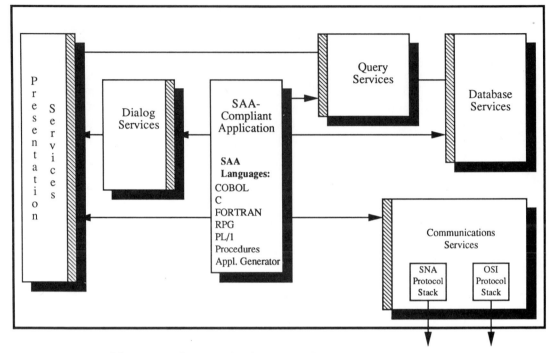

Figure 6-7. *Common Application within a model SAA operating environment.*

Query calls and convert them to appropriate SQL calls for interacting with the local Database Manager. Transparent access to the data would be provided in the same manner as discussed above for the Database Interface.

For communicating with remote programs, the application can issue CPI Communications Interface calls. These LU 6.2–based calls support program-to-program communications between the local program and a remote program. The Communications Interface can be used to support special distributed processing functions implemented by the application.

For interacting with a Repository, the application can issue Repository Interface calls. This interface allows applications to define entities and their relationships, and to store and retrieve information in the repository.

The level and type of SAA communications compliance supported by cooperative processing applications is determined by which CCS components are used to carry out the cooperative processing services (even though the application itself might not directly implement these services).

CCS components are broken down into the following components, which are shown in Figure 6-6:

> Objects
> Data Streams
> Application Services

Session Services
Network
Data Link Controls

Cooperative processing should involve the use of components from each of these categories.

The Objects category consists of Object Content Architectures (OCAs) that define the format and structure of objects that can be transferred between systems. Formatted Data Streams are used to carry objects between systems. Application Services consist of architectures used to provide distributed services such as electronic mail, document distribution, remote file and database access, and others. Session Services provide program-to-program communications support. The Network category defines the level of connectivity and networking support. The Data Link Controls category includes the different types of data link interfaces that can be used to connect systems.

Back to the Model

The SAA Common Application uses these kinds of CPI programming interfaces to get access to the various kinds of CPI services we have been discussing. It is implied that the SAA operating environment in which the application will execute includes support for the CPI interface calls.

What is more important is that it is implied that the SAA operating environment includes support for the CPI services being accessed via the CPI interface calls. Interpreting the calls is one thing; actually carrying out the services requested is another.

The CPI services are implemented in an SAA operating environment by CPI "managers" as we discussed in Chapter 4. There is a manager to support each of the CPI interfaces used by the application.

The application itself does not have to implement all these CPI services. The managers do this; they are system enablers. The applications merely request access to these services via the SAA CPI interfaces.

The SAA Common Application source code can therefore be moved to another SAA operating environment, assuming this other environment also includes support for the CPI interfaces and the underlying services managers being accessed by the application. Let's take a look at one of IBM's SAA Common Applications.

OFFICEVISION

When IBM first introduced SAA on March 17, 1987, they indicated that it was their intent to develop common applications that would span the SAA operating environments. One of the first common applications IBM indicated they would develop was to focus on office functions. This future application offering would include support for common office functions such as:

Document creation and processing
Document library services
Personal services
Mail
Decision support

True to their word, IBM fulfilled this promise on May 16, 1989, when they announced their "SAA Office" offering, the OfficeVision Family of products.

OfficeVision was IBM's first SAA Common Application. It is actually a family of products consisting of a series of products for each of IBM's major SAA operating environments. The OfficeVision Family includes the following series of products:

Platform	OfficeVision Product	Operating System
System/370/390	OfficeVision/MVS Series	MVS/ESA
	OfficeVision/VM Series	VM/ESA
AS/400	OfficeVision/400 Series	OS/400
PS/2	OfficeVision/2 LAN Series	OS/2 EE

Each series consists of a base product plus a number of optional products. The base product in each series includes connectivity support for both OS/2 EE and DOS workstations. Enhanced terminal support is also provided.

Not surprisingly, the OfficeVision products provide support for common office functions, just as IBM had promised. These include functions for:

Document processing
Library services
Calendar management
Address book
Mail
Decision support

Following is a brief description of each of the OfficeVision Series of products for the major SAA environments.

OfficeVision/MVS Series

As its name implies, the OfficeVision/MVS Series is the set of OfficeVision products for the System/370 MVS environment. The base product for this series is OfficeVision/MVS. Along with the base OfficeVision/MVS product, a number of other optional host features are available. These include the Document Writing and Document Composition features and the software for OS/2 and DOS workstations. The workstation software is packaged as "features" of the host package. These workstation features include the OS/2 Office Feature, the OS/2 Office DOS Requester Feature, and the DOS Office Direct Connect Feature.

OfficeVision/MVS Series also includes a number of optional host products.

These include the Distributed Office Support System (DISOSS), DisplayWrite/ 370, and Application System (AS).

In addition to these optional host products, a number of additional optional workstation products are also available as part of the OfficeVision/MVS Series. The optional products for OS/2 are:

> DisplayWrite 5/2
> DisplayWrite 5/2 Composer
> DisplayWrite Dictionaries
> SearchVision/2
> OS/2 Image Support
> Personal AS

Optional DOS-based products are DisplayWrite 4, DisplayWrite Dictionaries, and Office Facsimile Application.

OfficeVision/VM Series

This series is the set of OfficeVision products for the System/370/390-based VM environment. It is structured similar to the OfficeVision/MVS Series. There is a base product called OfficeVision/VM with optional features of this offering. There are also other optional VM-based host products and there is a set of optional products for OS/2 and DOS workstations.

The OfficeVision/VM optional features are the OS/2 Office Feature, the OS/2 Office DOS Requester Feature, and the DOS Office Direct Connect Feature. Other optional VM host products are DisplayWrite/370, Application System (AS), and Executive Decisions.

The same OS/2 and DOS products listed above for the OfficeVision/MVS Series are workstation options for the OfficeVision/VM Series as well.

OfficeVision/400 Series

The AS/400's OfficeVision package is the OfficeVision/400 Series. This series provides OfficeVision support for the SAA OS/400 operating environment. It is structured similar to the OfficeVision/MVS and OfficeVision/VM Series discussed above. It consists of a base offering called OfficeVision/400. Optional features associated with the base offering are the OS/2 Office Feature, the OS/2 Office DOS Requester Feature, and AS/400 Language Dictionaries.

There are no other optional AS/400 host products offered as part of this series. The optional OS/2 and DOS products are the same as those for the OfficeVision/MVS and OfficeVision/VM Series.

OfficeVision/2 LAN Series

This series provides OfficeVision facilities for the OS/2 Extended Edition environment and includes DOS support as well. The base offering of this series is OfficeVision/2. Its optional features include the OS/2 Office Feature and the OS/2 Office DOS Requester Feature.

As with all the OfficeVision series, this series includes the same optional OS/2 and DOS products as listed above. Let's take a closer look at the OS/2 Office Feature.

OS/2 Office Feature

This software provides office functions for OS/2 EE and DOS workstations connected via a LAN. Its user interface is an implementation of SAA's CUA Workplace extension to the Graphical Model.

OS/2 Office can function either as a requester or server. OS/2 Office requesters can request services from an OS/2 Office server connected to the LAN. DOS-based systems can also act as requesters, using the OS/2 Office DOS Requester software. Therefore, an OS/2 Office server provides office services both to OS/2 and DOS requesters.

OS/2 Office provides support for the following office functions:

> Mail
> Calendar
> Address Book
> Correspondence Processor
> Composite Correspondence Processor
> File System
> File Cabinet
> Library
> Telephone
> Print Support
> Decision Support
> Online Help and Tutorials

OS/2 Office actually provides an application platform for office applications. It provides services for applications such as object services, display services, application services, communication services, and system services. These OS/2 Office services are accessed via programming interfaces supported by OS/2 Office. These are not SAA programming interfaces but are, rather, interfaces unique to OS/2 Office. Applications are developed specifically to run under this environment.

Using the OS/2 Office services makes it easier to write applications for the OfficeVision environment. For example, display services make it easier to provide a graphical user interface that conforms to OS/2 Office's Workplace extension interface. Applications using these services can also achieve different levels of integration with OS/2 Office, including applications that are integrated via direct icon manipulation.

An Evolutionary Offering

OfficeVision was the successor to IBM's existing Distributed Office Support System (DISOSS) and Professional Office System (PROFS) products for the MVS and VM environments, respectively. It was IBM's intent to provide a migration path for their DISOSS and PROFS office customers to OfficeVision.

OfficeVision was truly an evolutionary offering. In most cases it was based on existing IBM products. OfficeVision/MVS was built on the existing Application Support Facility (ASF), Personal Services/CICS (PS/CICS), and the Personal Manager products. In addition, the first release of OfficeVision/MVS required DISOSS in order to communicate with OfficeVision/2 users that were LAN connected to the OfficeVision/MVS host.

OfficeVision/VM was basically a new release of PROFS and the PROFS Application Support Feature. Not only was OfficeVision/400 based on an existing AS/400 product, the AS/400 Office, but it actually *was* the AS/400 Office product. All IBM did was rename AS/400 Office to OfficeVision/400.

While very little new was offered with the OfficeVision host series of products, there were some interesting new facilities provided with the OfficeVision/2 LAN Series. All the exciting things were happening at the workstation end. Probably the most notable new feature provided in OfficeVision/2 was its iconic, windows-based, graphical user interface. OS/2 Office's user interface conforms to the SAA CUA Workplace extension to the Graphical Model described in Chapter 3.

The most significant aspect of this user interface is that it provides for integration of applications via direct icon manipulation. For example, a document can be printed directly and automatically by dragging the icon representing the document to the icon representing the printer. It is not necessary to invoke a word processing program, open the document, and then select the printer function. This is a step beyond the basic Graphical User interfaces supported by OS/2's Presentation Manager and provided on systems such as the Apple Macintosh.

OfficeVision's SAA Characteristics

What qualifies OfficeVision as an SAA Common Application? Let's look at its SAA characteristics. For one thing, OfficeVision products span the major SAA operating environments on IBM's SAA mainframe, midrange, and workstation platforms, as indicated above.

OfficeVision's user interface complies with SAA CUA specifications. OfficeVision/2, which runs as a Presentation Manager application under OS/2 EE, supports the CUA Workplace Model user interface as indicated above. This is the most advanced of the CUA models. It builds on the standard CUA Graphical Model support provided by the OS/2 Presentation Manager (action bars, pulldowns, pop-up windows, mouse interaction, etc.) and adds support for application integration via direct icon manipulation.

In addition to providing an SAA CUA-compliant user interface, OfficeVision products also make use of other SAA components and programming interfaces. For example, portions of OfficeVision/2 are written in the SAA C and REXX languages. Document interchange is supported using DIA protocols (DIA is a component of the CCS element).

OfficeVision is structured for cooperative processing. Distributed services such as electronic mail, document distribution, remote file access, remote calendar management, distributed database access, and others are supported across the OfficeVision offerings on the different SAA platforms. OfficeVision products cooperate with one another in carrying out these distributed services transparently to OfficeVision users and applications.

OfficeVision is just one example of SAA Common Applications. Other applications such as ImagePlus, which provides image-processing facilities that span the SAA environments, are also available and more applications will be provided by IBM in the future. Third-party vendors will also develop SAA Common Applications that will be available for each of the SAA environments.

A major push by IBM has been in trying to make it easier and quicker for itself as well as other developers to create SAA Common Applications. IBM has created an umbrella strategy just for this purpose.

AD/CYCLE

IBM has defined a broad strategy that can be followed in developing SAA applications. This strategy is called Application Development/Cycle (AD/Cycle). It represents IBM's approach and entry into the Computer-Aided Software Engineering (CASE) arena. AD/Cycle is much more than just a set of CASE tools, though. It is a broad framework for developing SAA applications and addresses support to be provided throughout the life cycle of an application's development. The development life cycle covers everything from the initial requirements planning, to designing the application, to actually producing the application, through supporting and maintaining the application.

AD/Cycle was formally introduced by IBM in September 1989. It was targeted at solving the problem of the large and growing backlog of applications that many of IBM's largest customers were facing. These customers have not only a backlog of applications to develop but have huge ongoing maintenance costs for existing and new applications. This, coupled with the inability to find enough qualified programmers or, in some cases, faced with budget constraints that limit hiring, has led to another push towards improving programmer productivity. Hence, the growing trend towards CASE as a possible solution.

These problems have been exacerbated over the years as applications have grown in complexity. This is especially true with new applications that involve cooperative processing and access to distributed resources. No longer are applications isolated from and independent of other applications and systems.

Another set of problems arises when the initial requirements specifications and design information prove to be inadequate or incorrect. This ultimately results in loss of time and budget overruns as applications need to be redesigned and redeveloped in some cases.

Even when applications are initially specified, designed, and developed correctly, it is inevitable that changes and enhancements will be required over time. Managing these changes is a real challenge, especially when large numbers of applications are being used.

Although there have been a number of various CASE tools provided by different vendors in the past, one problem is that there has been a lack of integration of these tools. Better integration would allow tools from different vendors to be mixed and matched and tools could be acquired to address all the issues discussed above. This is one of the targets of AD/Cycle.

In fact, all the issues we have been discussing are addressed by AD/Cycle. It is an approach to aid in improving programmer productivity, improving the quality of applications, and making it easier to manage the development life cycle.

A major goal of AD/Cycle is to provide an integrated application development environment that will allow the development of applications that can be ported across or span SAA environments.

An important requirement is to provide customers with a migration path into using CASE technologies and tools. This means that existing third-generation development languages and tools can continue to be used in some cases. While protecting their customers' investments in IBM products, the AD/Cycle strategy must also allow new application development technologies to be employed.

The approach IBM has taken with AD/Cycle is to support a cooperative processing development environment. PS/2 workstations can be used for front-end development tasks. Centralized control and management of application data will be provided via host-based repositories and Repository Managers.

IBM is openly soliciting the support of third-party vendors. These vendors will provide many of the CASE tools needed for AD/Cycle to be viable. IBM realizes they cannot go it alone in this area.

The Development Life Cycle

AD/Cycle provides the framework, shown in Figure 6-8, for developing SAA applications. Included under the AD/Cycle umbrella is a set of development tools and support facilities that can be used across the life cycle of an application program's development. AD/Cycle encompasses the following application development life-cycle phases:

> Requirements
> Analysis and Design
> Producing the application
> Building and Testing
> Production and Maintenance

The first activity addressed by AD/Cycle is building a model of a company's business and the data processing activities in support of the business. This is referred to as enterprise modeling. Such modeling will allow users to define an accurate, up-to-date set of application program requirements that is consistent with the enterprise's strategies and data processing requirements.

Using various modeling techniques, analysts and other nontechnical personnel (i.e., other business professionals) can define, establish relationships, and validate data and processes that are or will be used. These data and process requirements are stored in a centralized repository. They form the enterprise

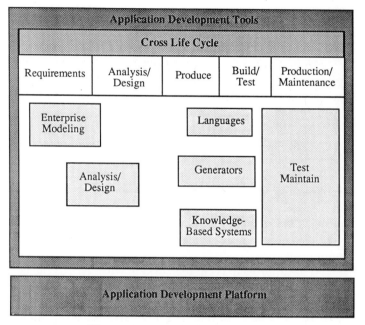

Figure 6-8. AD/Cycle framework.

model data which can then be used by other development tools and processes throughout the remainder of the development life cycle.

A major benefit of this type of enterprise modeling is that prototyping can be done at this very early stage in the development of applications. Problems can be uncovered before actual program development begins. This, of course, can lead to substantial cost savings in the long run.

Another advantage is that the modeling can be done by individuals who are knowledgeable about the enterprise's business activities. That is, nontechnical business professionals rather than programmers can model the business. This can result in models that more accurately reflect the enterprise's business activities.

Once the requirements have been determined from the enterprise modeling, AD/Cycle analysis and design tools can be used to develop the design specifications for the application. Tools will be available to support various types of design methods such as using decomposition diagrams, data-flow diagrams, entity-relationship diagrams, and data structure diagrams. The particular set of tools selected will be determined by the design methodology chosen.

For actually developing applications, users can select from among a number of third-generation programming languages (e.g., COBOL) or fourth-generation application generators (e.g., Cross System Product). Knowledge-based development tools will also be supported.

The programming languages that developers can select within the AD/Cycle framework are those languages included in SAA's CPI element. These include C, COBOL, FORTRAN, PL/I, RPG, and Procedures Language (REXX). SAA's Application Generator language, Cross System Product, can also be used.

Tools will also be provided that can be used for testing and maintaining the applications. Examples of such tools are the Software Analysis Test Tool product that provides test-coverage analysis for PL/I and COBOL programs, and the Workstation Interactive Test Tool that provides regression-testing support for interactive applications.

In addition to tools used within each of the various phases of the development life cycle, there are also requirements to support activities that span the entire life cycle. Therefore, tools will be available to support cross-life-cycle activities.

Examples of such cross-life-cycle tools would be those to assist in project management, documentation, and changes made throughout the development process. As we have said, both IBM and third-party vendors (e.g., IBM Business Partners) will be providing AD/Cycle tools.

AD/Cycle Concepts

As we saw earlier, AD/Cycle covers all phases of a program's development. For each phase, tools will be provided to support the activities performed at that stage. In addition, tools used to support general activities that span these phases will also be provided. These are the cross-life-cycle tools. In order for this to work effectively, the tools must be integrated to some extent. Users must be able to access all the tools in a similar manner. Tools must be able to share related information. Output from one tool must be usable as input to other tools.

This is accomplished through AD/Cycle. There are really two major portions of the AD/Cycle framework shown in Figure 6-8: a set of integrated tools and an application development platform that provides services for the integration of these tools.

Application Development Platform

The application development platform provides the services needed for the integration of the individual tools used throughout the phases of the development life cycle. The following services are included as part of the application development platform:

> Services and specifications for the user interface
> Workstation services
> Repository services
> Information-model specifications
> Common tool services

Workstation-based AD Cycle tools will provide a user interface that conforms to SAA's Graphical Model CUA specifications. These workstation-based tools will operate under OS/2 Extended Edition (the workstation SAA operating environment) and use the OS/2 Presentation Manager for the CUA Graphical Model support. This will be true of both IBM tools and tools provided by other vendors. AD/Cycle workstation tools, therefore, will operate in a graphical, windows-based environment and will provide transparent access to host AD/Cycle services.

As indicated above, AD/Cycle assumes cooperative processing. PS/2 workstations, running OS/2 Extended Edition with various AD/Cycle tools, will interact with host-based systems. Workstation services provide the workstation cooperative processing support. The workstation becomes the window into the network.

Some AD/Cycle tools will run only in the workstation while others will run only in host systems. Workstation users will have access to the host-based tools. In addition, some tools will run in a cooperative manner between workstations and hosts.

Typically, front-end tools will run on workstations. This includes modeling, design, and program-development tools. Such tools can take advantage of OS/2's graphics capabilities, for example, to provide modeling and diagramming facilities. Activities later on in the development cycle very often will be done at host systems. This includes activities such as system testing and building and distributing applications.

AD/Cycle Repository

A major component of the AD/Cycle platform is a repository. The repository is the AD/Cycle information database. The repository will contain information about an enterprise's application development, business, and data processing–related activities and procedures. Information in the repository will be shared by all the AD/Cycle tools. The repository, then, is the central point of control for the administration, definition, storage, and retrieval of all application development information.

A set of repository services will be provided for defining and storing information in the repository and for providing access to this information. The information stored in the repository will be in entity-relationship (ER) format. This information is defined and stored using ER modeling techniques and, as discussed above, tools will be provided for this purpose.

An information model will also be supplied as part of AD/Cycle. The AD information model is the architected interface between AD/Cycle tools and the application development information managed by the repository.

The last area covered by AD/Cycle is a set of tool services. Services include library and administration functions and common functions such as copying, deleting, and moving objects to and from workstations; retrieving information from the repository; adding information to the repository; creating relationships among objects; and many others. The use of these tool services will make it easier to design and implement different tools and will make these tools more consistent. This will also make it easier to integrate tools.

AD/Cycle and SAA

As we said earlier, AD/Cycle is the strategy and framework for developing SAA applications. AD/Cycle tools and services will provide an SAA CUA-compliant user interface. Support will be provided for SAA programming languages including C, COBOL, FORTRAN, PL/I, RPG, and the Procedures Language (REXX).

AD/Cycle products use SAA CPI programming interfaces for services such as accessing databases.

The SAA CPI Repository Interface is supported by the Repository Manager/MVS, a major AD/Cycle component which implements AD/Cycle repository services. The SAA applications developed using AD/Cycle tools can span the SAA operating environments.

AD/Cycle will evolve over time as IBM and other vendors fill in the holes in the various areas covered by AD/Cycle. Third-party tool developers, especially, will play an important part in this evolution. This evolution will take a long time and is just in its infancy. AD/Cycle sets the framework for developing SAA applications throughout the 1990s.

SUMMARY

An SAA Common Application is an application that exhibits a number of SAA characteristics. Support for the Common Application will be available in all SAA operating environments. The application will provide an SAA CUA-compliant user interface. It will be developed using SAA CPI components and will use standard SAA CCS components for communicating and interoperating with other applications and environments. An SAA Common Application might also support cooperative processing.

Not all SAA Common Applications will necessarily have all these characteristics. The level of SAA conformance will be determined by the level and type of support for SAA components included in the application. SAA Common Applications will very often also include non-SAA elements.

AD/Cycle is IBM's SAA application development strategy. AD/Cycle covers the entire life cycle of application development from defining requirements via enterprise modeling to producing and maintaining the applications. IBM and third-party vendors will provide AD/Cycle tools needed throughout the life cycle.

part 3

SAA DISTRIBUTED SERVICES

7

Logical Unit 6.2 and Cooperative Processing

Logical Unit 6.2 is the key SNA LU type used to support SAA cooperative processing. In fact, as shown in Figure 7-1, LU 6.2 is the *only* SNA LU type included in SAA as of this writing. This means that LU 6.2 will be used for all SAA-based cooperative processing, as we will see throughout this chapter. First, let's explain some terms.

First of all, what is meant by cooperative processing? In the context of SAA, cooperative processing means that multiple programs, typically on different systems, cooperate with one another in order to carry out some type of distributed processing. Sending mail between users on different systems, distributing documents or programs between systems, or accessing files or databases distributed across systems are all examples of this type of distributed, cooperative processing.

Chapter 1 discussed cooperative processing as the primary goal of SAA. This follows the desire of many large corporations to distribute resources and processing (e.g., files, databases, programs) across systems in their networks and to allow transparent access to these resources from any system in the network. This, in a nutshell, is what cooperative processing is all about—providing transparent access to distributed resources. Cooperation among systems at a number of levels is needed for this type of processing to be carried out successfully. We will explore below in detail how this is actually accomplished using LU 6.2 and related technologies.

Another term related to LU 6.2 that needs to be defined is Advanced Program-to-Program Communications (APPC). There has been a lot of confusion as to the meaning of APPC and its relationship to LU 6.2. Some of the confusion has come about because of inconsistent usage of these terms by IBM. Also, IBM has

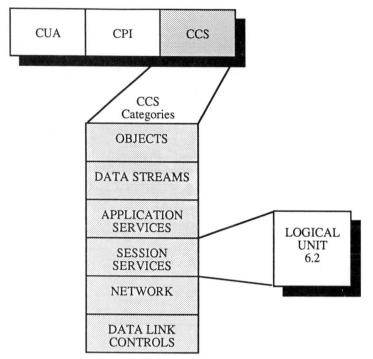

Figure 7-1. *LU 6.2 is the single SNA-based Session Services component.*

slightly altered its definition of these terms over time to conform more closely to the market perception it was trying to promote. In addition, widespread mis-understanding of these terms and related technologies is pervasive throughout the industry.

APPC and LU 6.2 really have the same meaning in terms of the functionality they imply. As its name indicates, Advanced Program-to-Program Communications has to do with programs communicating with other programs. Whether this is "advanced" or not is debatable. It is advanced relative to terminal-oriented communications, as we will discuss below.

APPC is the IBM marketing term for the program-to-program com-munications facilities provided by LU 6.2, the SNA architectural/technical term for this capability. APPC and LU 6.2, therefore, may be used interchangeably. In most cases we will use LU 6.2 to refer to the program-to-program com-munications technology being described in this book since the SNA LU 6.2 protocols are used to implement this capability. Where the term APPC is used, it implies SNA LU 6.2 protocols.

LU 6.2'S STRATEGIC IMPORTANCE

IBM has elevated LU 6.2 to a position of major strategic importance. As we said above, it is the *only* SNA LU type included under SAA as of this writing. LU 6.2 is the single component under the Session Services category of the Common

Communications Support (CCS) element of SAA, as Figure 7-1 indicates. Excluded from SAA are all of IBM's other SNA LU types, including the most widely used LU type, LU 2, which is used for 3270 communications.

It is clear that IBM's future SAA applications involving cooperative processing across a network of systems will be based on LU 6.2. IBM's Application Services components of SAA (e.g., DIA, SNA/DS, and DDM) use LU 6.2 for their program-to-program communications.

LU 6.2 has taken on this strategic role due to a number of factors. One factor is the evolution of IBM communications from simple terminal-to-host connections to distributed transaction processing. This evolution has been driven by the proliferation of personal computers and the growth of LAN usage throughout organizations. Earlier SNA LU types lack some of the LU 6.2 facilities needed for this more intelligent type of communications between programs. Its importance has also grown because of the problems caused by incompatibilities built into the earlier LU types. LU 6.2 provides a common set of SNA protocols that will bring compatibility at a program communications level.

With SAA and the move towards cooperative processing among dissimilar systems, the need for a consistent set of communications protocols and a consistent communications programming interface grows. Again, this is provided with LU 6.2. These factors will be discussed in more detail later in this chapter.

STANDARD SNA

One of the most important things to realize about LU 6.2 is that it is standard SNA. IBM has not invented a new communications architecture or new communications protocols with LU 6.2. LU 6.2 is one particular type of SNA LU. It makes use of standard SNA protocols such as chaining and bracketing to carry out its functionality. This means that LU 6.2 sessions can be used across any of the standard types of connections supported by SNA. These include remote SDLC connections, Token-Ring LAN connections, local channel connections, 3270 coaxial connections, and even X.25 connections, among others, as shown in Figure 7-2.

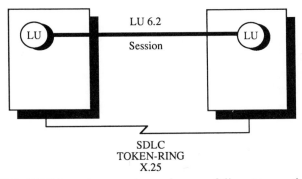

Figure 7-2. *LU 6.2 sessions can be used across different types of wide area and local area network connections.*

Because LU 6.2 deals only with SNA session-level protocols, as do all other LU types, it is independent of the underlying connections used. There is nothing in LU 6.2 that ties it to any particular physical connectivity or restricts it from being used with any types of physical connections. LU 6.2 sessions could easily be used over other LANs such as Ethernet LANs or other types of connections such as async connections.

Because LU 6.2 is a standard SNA LU, it is supported by standard SNA node types such as Node Type 2 and Node Type 2.1, which IBM used to call Physical Unit (PU) types (e.g., PU 2 and PU 2.1). When used in a hierarchical host connection, the remote system on which LU 6.2 is running looks like a standard Type 2 node (cluster controller) to the mainframe—just as if it were using LU 2 3270 sessions. In fact, both 3270 LUs and LU 6.2 sessions can be concurrently active on these nodes.

When used in a peer-to-peer connection, Node Type 2.1 support is required. This allows two such nodes to communicate directly with each other on a peer-to-peer basis, without host involvement. LU 6.2 is the only type of LU supported across these peer-to-peer connections.

LU 6.2 fits very nicely into the SNA networking environment and can coexist with other standard SNA LU types. As with all other LU types, LU 6.2 shares the underlying SNA path control network which provides connectivity between the various systems in the network. LU 6.2 goes beyond just hierarchical connections by supporting peer-to-peer communications as well. The relationship of LU 6.2 and Node Type 2.1 is discussed in detail in Chapter 8.

There are three areas that differentiate LU 6.2 from other LU types and that have led IBM to select LU 6.2 as the LU type of choice:

> LU 6.2 defines a common subset of SNA session-level protocols
> LU 6.2 was designed for program-to-program communications
> LU 6.2 defines an architected program interface

A Common Subset of SNA Protocols

LU 6.2 defines a common subset of SNA protocols that all systems are to implement in order to achieve SNA communications compatibility with other systems. At first glance this may seem to be what SNA provides in general. It is true that SNA was designed to bring communications compatibility to IBM's diverse set of products but, prior to LU 6.2, this had not been totally achieved. What SNA had accomplished was providing widespread connectivity among products.

However, real intelligent communications compatibility between systems or programs was still lacking. Incompatibilities resulted because different IBM developers elected to implement different subsets of SNA in their systems and products. Therefore, even though each of the systems uses SNA, they are not necessarily able to conduct meaningful communications with other SNA products.

A brief description of SNA and LU types in general will make this clearer. The SNA architecture defines a wide range of SNA commands and protocols used for a variety of different kinds of communications and networking facilities. No IBM product implements the entire architecture. Each product implements that subset of the SNA architecture needed for it to carry out its particular set of functions or role in the network. A product's role is determined by the type of product it is and how IBM has positioned the product.

IBM mainframes (e.g., System/370-compatible processors) and front-end communications controllers (e.g., 3745 controllers), which are represented as Type 5 and Type 4 nodes respectively, provide a much broader range of SNA support than do peripheral node products (e.g., 3174), which are represented as Type 2 nodes or midrange systems (e.g., AS/400), which may be represented as Type 2.1 nodes. This is because the role of mainframes and communications controllers, from a networking point of view, is to provide full network connectivity and routing and to support the attachment of a wide range of devices and systems. These nodes are referred to as SNA subarea nodes. The peripheral nodes, on the other hand, have a much more limited set of SNA support. These types of peripheral nodes do not have full network routing capability; they support a limited set of connectivity options and have limited network management support.

All nodes contain a Physical Unit (PU) and host (Type 5) and peripheral nodes (Type 2 and 2.1) typically also contain one or more LUs. The LUs represent the applications or end users of the node. The node type defines the subset of SNA capability supported at the lower levels of the architecture. This includes the physical connectivity, data link control, and path control support as shown in Figure 7-3.

For example, a Type 2 node, by definition, supports only a single physical

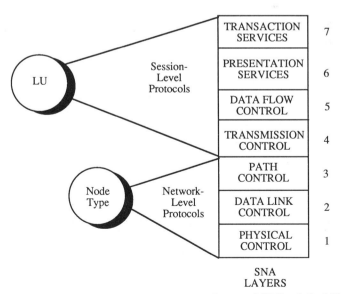

Figure 7-3. *Node types deal with the lower layers of SNA while LUs deal with the upper layers.*

data link connection and supports secondary SDLC protocols only. On the other hand, a Type 2.1 node, which is an extension to the Type 2 node, supports multiple physical data links and both primary and secondary SDLC capabilities. The differences between Type 2.0 and Type 2.1 nodes are discussed in more detail in Chapter 8.

The LU type, on the other hand, defines the subset of SNA commands and protocols supported at the higher layers of SNA—Transmission Control (TC), Data Flow Control (DFC), and Presentation Services (PS), as Figure 7-3 indicates. These upper SNA layers make up the session-level commands and protocols used to support programs and devices, the end users of the network. For each active SNA session, there would exist an instance of TC, DFC, and PS working in conjunction with each other.

Whereas the PU component of SNA has to do with managing a node's resources and providing support for the lower-level connectivity and networking capabilities, the LU component has to do with supporting users of the network. These users may be persons, devices, or programs. Older LU types such as LU 2 are used to support devices such as 3270 terminals; LU 6.2 is intended to support programs which IBM calls Transaction Programs (TPs).

The SNA architecture defines separate commands and protocols at each of these upper layers supported by the LU. As with the architecture in general, there is a wide range of commands and protocols defined at each layer. No product implements the entire set of commands and protocols. Again, products support various subsets of the commands and protocols at each layer depending on the functionality to be provided and the product's role in the network.

The particular subset of SNA commands and protocols supported at a given layer is specified in profiles, as indicated in Figure 7-4. There are several different profiles (subsets) defined by IBM for each of these upper LU layers. Each profile is assigned a unique number to identify and refer to it easily. The profiles that describe the subsets of SNA commands and protocols used at the Transmission Control layer are called Transmission Subsystem (TS) profiles. The profiles that describe the subsets used at the Data Flow Control layer are called Function Management (FM) profiles, and the profiles that describe the subsets used at the Presentation Services (PS) layer are called Presentation Services (PS) profiles.

A particular LU type is the combination of the TS, FM, and PS profiles used at the TC, DFC, and PS layers, respectively. For example, LU 2 (used for 3270 display station sessions) might consist of TS 3, FM 3, and PS 2. TS Profile 3 would describe the subset of TC commands and protocols used on the LU 2 session. FM Profile 3 would describe the subset of DFC commands and protocols used on the session. PS Profile 2 would describe the subset of PS commands and protocols used on the session.

Unfortunately, early IBM product implementors elected to use different subsets of the SNA commands and protocols at these higher layers and hence the proliferation of different LU types. Some programmable products implemented a subset of SNA protocols now referred to as LU 0; the subset now called LU 1 was developed to support 3770 RJE terminals and a limited variation of LU 1 was

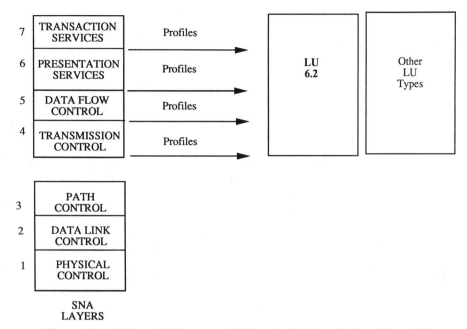

Figure 7-4. *Different LUs support different subsets, called profiles, of the session layers.*

used to support 3270 SNA Character String (SCS) printers; LU 2 was used for 3270 display station support; LU 3 was used for standard 3270 printers; and LU 7 became the subset of protocols for 5250 workstations.

Applications developed for these systems and devices had to support the particular LU protocols used. The result was that even though all the products implemented SNA protocols, none of them was really compatible because they each implemented a different subset of the commands and protocols.

LU 6.2 is an attempt to correct this. IBM has focused on and defined the particular subset of SNA commands and protocols at the upper SNA layers that all products should support. The particular subset defined by LU 6.2 consists of the SNA commands and protocols at the TC, DFC, and PS layers described by TS Profile 7, FM Profile 19, and PS Profile 6.2. For example, TS Profile 7 specifies that the TC commands SDT, CLEAR, RQR, and STSN are not supported. FM Profile 19 specifies that the only DFC commands supported are SIGNAL, LUSTAT, BIS, and RTR. In addition to the SNA commands supported, the profiles also specify which SNA protocols and options are supported.

The SNA subset used by LU 6.2 is actually a smaller and less complex set of SNA commands and protocols than are used for 3270 (LU 1, 2, and 3) communications. Even though LU 6.2 provides more sophisticated capabilities, it is not necessarily more complex. Much of the lower-level processing, in fact, is similar to the processing required for LU 2 sessions. This is good news for manufacturers trying to support LU 6.2, especially if 3270 LU type support is already provided.

DESIGNED FOR PROGRAM-TO-PROGRAM COMMUNICATIONS

A second important aspect of LU 6.2 is that it was designed specifically for a distributed transaction processing or cooperative processing environment utilizing program-to-program communications. Most earlier LU types (e.g., 1, 2, 3, 7) were designed to support dumb terminals used to access host-based application programs (i.e., terminal-to-program communications).

LU 6.2 is intended to be used by intelligent, distributed transactions for their interprogram communications rather than for terminal emulation, as shown in Figure 7-5. Because of this, LU 6.2 includes more sophisticated capabilities needed when two programs are communicating with each other.

For example, a different style of error recovery is required when two programs are in communication with one another versus a terminal operator that is in communication with a host-based application program. In the case of the terminal-to-host application connection, error recovery may be as simple as the host application releasing the operator's keyboard so that information can be reentered and the screen image rewritten. Because a human operator is involved, the operator can visually see that error recovery is occurring and can manually retry the operation.

With two programs such error recovery is not possible. Facilities must exist that will allow both programs to perform some level of error recovery. As an example, if a distributed database transaction is in process and an error occurs, it is necessary to be able to back-out any partial updates that may have been made

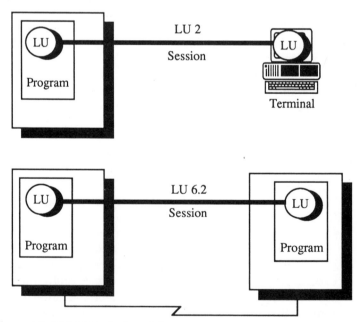

Figure 7-5. *LU 6.2 is designed for program-to-program communications as opposed to terminal-to-program communications.*

to the database. This must be done automatically without human knowledge or intervention. LU 6.2 provides for this type of capability.

LU 6.2 also provides for the dynamic interaction that may occur between two distributed programs. This includes starting and stopping conversations (logical connections) between programs, sending and receiving information between programs, and synchronizing event processing. One important added capability provided by LU 6.2 that you do not get with the terminal-oriented LU types is support for both primary and secondary LU processing. The terminal-oriented LU types are limited to acting as secondary LUs. The host applications always act as the primary LUs in these terminal-to-host connections.

The limitation is that only primary LUs can activate and deactivate sessions. Secondary LUs can request activation/deactivation (e.g., via LOGON and LOGOFF) but the actual session activation/deactivation (via SNA BIND/ UNBIND commands) must be sent by the primary. While this is less a restriction in a terminal-to-host hierarchical connection, it becomes more of a problem in distributed transaction processing. With distributed programs, either system should be able to dynamically activate or deactivate sessions when needed. While older LU types are restricted to hierarchical connections in most cases, LU 6.2 can be used across either hierarchical or peer-to-peer connections.

In a peer-coupled connection where no host mainframe is involved, either system needs to be able to support primary or secondary capabilities. Typically, the system initiating the connection would assume the role of primary while the other system defaults to secondary.

LU 6.2 provides generalized program-to-program communications support that is usable by a wide range of different types of distributed processing applications. This includes applications such as file transfer, document distribution, remote database access, network management, electronic mail, and others. IBM currently supplies LU 6.2–based products providing many of these capabilities.

The relationship of LU 6.2 and other SAA components is also revealed here. For each of the types of distributed services listed above, IBM has defined a separate architecture that is the framework on which the corresponding service will be implemented in the SAA operating environments. These architectures are components of the Application Services category of SAA's CCS element. They include Document Interchange Architecture (DIA), SNA/Distribution Services (SNA/DS), Distributed Data Management (DDM), Distributed Relational Database Architecture (DRDA), and SNA/Management Services (SNA/MS).

All these architected services are implemented in basically the same manner—via pairs of Transaction Programs (TPs) in different SAA environments that communicate and cooperate with one another in order to carry out the particular service for which they were designed. As an example, a DIA TP on one system would communicate with a partner DIA TP on another system in order to exchange documents between the systems. Similarly, a DDM TP on one system would communicate with a DDM TP on another system in order to support remote file access services between the systems.

Each of these pairs of TPs communicate using LU 6.2 protocols. LU 6.2 is the common set of SNA session-level protocols that all SAA Application Ser-

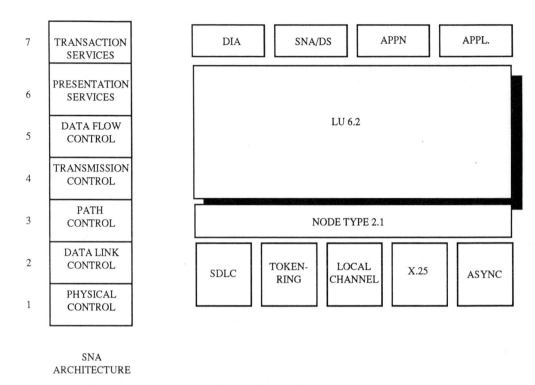

Figure 7-6. *LU 6.2 can be used by a wide variety of transaction programs.*

vice architectures will use for their interprogram communications, as shown in Figure 7-6.

A STANDARD API

A third major aspect of LU 6.2 is that IBM has formally architected the interface between the programs using LU 6.2 and the LU itself. This architected interface is called the LU 6.2 protocol boundary. It consists of a set of "verbs" which specifies the functions and parameters that are used by a transaction (application) program to interface to LU 6.2. Each verb consists of a generic name (e.g., ALLOCATE) and a set of associated parameters that may be required for the verb function to be carried out.

When these LU 6.2 verbs are actually implemented in a particular programming language on a particular system, the interface is called an Application Programming Interface (API). An LU 6.2 API, then, is typically a set of function calls (e.g., C language "calls") or macros that a transaction program can issue in order to interface to the LU supporting it, as shown in Figure 7-7. The LU provides the SNA LU 6.2 protocol processing for the transaction program. By its nature, an LU 6.2 API is language and system dependent. That is, the API is

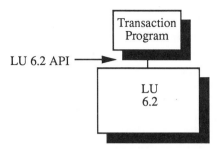

Figure 7-7. *An LU 6.2 API is the interface between a TP and the LU supporting it.*

provided in some programming language (e.g., "C" or assembler) on some system (e.g., PC-DOS on a PC).

This brings us to a major problem with LU 6.2 in the IBM world today. Unfortunately, IBM has not provided consistent or compatible LU 6.2 APIs on their various systems that provide LU 6.2 support. As an example, LU 6.2 APIs are provided in IBM mainframe systems (CICS/VS for MVS and TSAF for VM), System/36, System/38, Series/1, PC (APPC/PC), and others. None of these APIs is compatible with any other. They each have different function call names, parameters, calling sequences, syntax, etc.

The actual interface "calls" provided in a particular LU 6.2 API may or may not have the same or similar names as corresponding LU 6.2 protocol boundary verbs. Also, there may not be a one-to-one relationship between an API function call and an LU 6.2 verb. In some cases, a single API call may perform the function of multiple LU 6.2 verbs.

Although the LU 6.2 APIs on these systems are not consistent, the systems can still communicate with each other since the LU 6.2 protocols generated and sent between systems are compatible in most cases. Theoretically, an API may take any form and as long as correct LU 6.2 protocols are supported externally between systems, then LU 6.2 compatibility is achieved. However, when developing distributed transactions across systems, it would be much easier if the APIs on each system were consistent.

The lack of a consistent LU 6.2 API across systems makes it impossible to design a program using an LU 6.2 API that can be ported without change to another system. None of the existing IBM LU 6.2 APIs uses the same function call names, the same syntax, the same parameter lists, etc. Since SAA holds out the promise of porting applications across systems, this is a major limitation today.

IBM's solution to the problem is the SAA Common Programming Interface for Communications (CPIC). This interface is based on LU 6.2 and is an attempt to standardize on the names, syntax, and calling sequences of LU 6.2 functions provided in the interfaces supported on different systems. Doing this makes it much easier to develop cooperative processing applications that span systems.

LU 6.2 Verbs

The LU 6.2 protocol boundary that has been formally architected by IBM consists of three different types of verbs—basic conversation verbs, mapped conversation verbs, and control operator verbs. The basic and mapped conversation verbs provide the same type of functionality but are intended for use by different types of LU 6.2 programs.

The basic conversation verbs are intended for use by IBM service transaction programs. These are IBM-supplied transaction programs that make use of LU 6.2 for their program-to-program communications with a distributed partner transaction program. Examples of such service transaction programs are DIA, SNA/DS, and DDM. Architecturally, IBM describes these service transaction programs as actually being part of the LU itself.

Mapped conversation verbs, on the other hand, are intended for use by user application programs. A major difference between the basic and mapped conversation verbs is that transaction programs using basic conversation verbs must present data in a Generalized Data Stream (GDS) format (consisting of structured fields), while transactions using mapped conversations may present data in any format they desire. Then, by pointing to a particular named map, the data may be mapped (reformatted) into GDS format. This relieves the application from having to deal directly with GDS formats. The application can deal with its own proprietary formats and have the LU automatically perform mapping when mapped conversation verbs are issued. This is especially appropriate for applications coded in high-level languages such as COBOL.

Following is a summary of the basic and mapped conversation verbs included under the LU 6.2 protocol boundary.

Basic Conversation Verbs	Mapped Conversation Verbs
ALLOCATE	MC_ALLOCATE
CONFIRM	MC_CONFIRM
CONFIRMED	MC_CONFIRMED
DEALLOCATE	MC_DEALLOCATE
FLUSH	MC_FLUSH
GET_ATTRIBUTES	MC_GET_ATTRIBUTES
POST_ON_RECEIPT	MC_POST_ON_RECEIPT
PREPARE_TO_RECEIVE	MC_PREPARE_TO_RECEIVE
RECEIVE_AND_WAIT	MC_RECEIVE_AND_WAIT
RECEIVE_IMMEDIATE	MC_RECEIVE_IMMEDIATE
REQUEST_TO_SEND	MC_REQUEST_TO_SEND
SEND_DATA	MC_SEND_DATA
SEND_ERROR	MC_SEND_ERROR
TEST	MC_TEST

Type Independent Verbs
BACKOUT
GET_TYPE
SYNCPT
WAIT

As you can see, the basic and mapped conversation verbs provide basically the same set of functions. Some of the mapped verbs include a map name parameter to identify the map that should be used to map data from the application format to the GDS format. The mapped verbs include some other minor differences as well. The type-independent verbs are common to both basic and mapped conversations.

Let's briefly describe each of these verbs and then look at a simple example of how they can be used for communication between two transaction programs.

ALLOCATE is used to establish a logical connection between the Transaction Program (TP) originating the request and the partner TP to which the connection is desired. This logical connection between the pair of TPs is called a conversation. When the conversation is established, a unique conversation ID is assigned to it. This ID is then used to identify the particular conversation when subsequent verbs are issued.

Just as ALLOCATE sets up the conversation between a pair of TPs, DE-ALLOCATE is used to terminate the conversation. This is typically the last verb issued when the conversation is ready to be ended.

Two verbs can be used to provide a level of synchronization of processing between the TPs. CONFIRM results in a confirmation request being sent from the requesting TP to the partner TP. It is a solicitation for the partner TP to send an indication (i.e., a reply) when it has reached a certain point in its processing (this point is product dependent). CONFIRMED is used by the partner to send back this confirmation indication. The use of these two verbs in this manner allows the two programs to synchronize their processing.

FLUSH is used to ensure that any information that has been buffered by the LU, but not yet sent to the partner TP, will actually be sent. In other words, it results in send buffers being flushed out. The data that may be buffered up, waiting to be sent, could be data associated with previous SEND_DATA verbs issued by the requesting TP.

GET_ATTRIBUTES is a verb that returns information about the conversation. This information could include the mode name, the name of the remote LU supporting the partner TP, and the synchronization level set for this conversation.

The POST_ON_RECEIPT verb is used to request that the requesting TP be posted when information is available for it. Information that might cause such posting could be end-user data, conversation status, or a confirmation or sync point request.

PREPARE_TO_RECEIVE is used to change the state of the conversation from send to receive. This would prepare the requesting TP for receiving information from the partner TP. As a result of this verb, a SEND indication is sent to the partner which then causes the partner TP to change itself to send state.

RECEIVE_AND_WAIT allows the TP to wait for information from the partner TP. If information is already available when the RECEIVE_AND_WAIT is issued, no waiting will occur. The local TP will get control back immediately. If no information is available, the TP will be suspended until information does arrive. Again, this information could be user data, conversation status, or requests for confirmation or sync point.

Another receive-type verb is RECEIVE_IMMEDIATE. As its name implies, the requesting TP will get control back immediately regardless of whether any information is available or not. When control is given back, an indication is provided as to whether there is, in fact, any information.

REQUEST_TO_SEND, as it name implies, is a request to the remote TP to allow the local TP to go into send mode. This assumes that the local TP was in receive mode and the remote TP is in send mode. Since LU 6.2 is half-duplex, only one TP can be sending at a time. REQUEST_TO_SEND is issued when a TP in receive mode wants to enter send mode in order to send information to the partner TP that has control over the direction of data flow.

SEND_DATA is used to send user data from the local to the remote TP. The data consists of logical records which consist of a length field and a data field.

SEND_ERROR is used to send information as opposed to sending end-user data.

The TEST verb is used to test the conversation to determine if it has been posted or if a request-to-send indication has been received.

The type-independent verbs can be used with both basic and mapped conversations. These verbs include SYNCPT, BACKOUT, GET_TYPE, and WAIT.

SYNCPT results in all protected resources being advanced to the next synchronization point. These protected resources and sync points are unique to a given application.

BACKOUT is used to back-out any partial updates made to a protected resource. It restores all protected resources to their status as of the last synchronization point.

GET_TYPE is used to determine the type of conversation, either basic or mapped, that is being used.

WAIT is used to put the requesting TP into a wait state, waiting to be posted when any information becomes available.

CONVERSATIONS BETWEEN TPS

As discussed above, the ALLOCATE and DEALLOCATE verbs are used for establishing conversations between distributed transaction programs (TPs). A conversation is a logical connection between a pair of TPs. This is an important distinction between the conversation between the TPs and the underlying SNA session between the pair of LUs supporting the conversation.

The SNA session is the logical connection between LUs which are both Type 6.2 LUs in this case. The LU 6.2 session between the pair of LUs is a standard SNA LU session established by a BIND command and terminated by an UNBIND command and controlled by standard SNA session-level protocols (e.g., bracketing, chaining, pacing, change direction, etc.). The LUs can negotiate the use of LU 6.2 session-level commands and protocols to be used during the session at BIND time. Once the session is established, conversations between TPs can be supported across the session.

The SNA session is a serially reusable resource. A single conversation at a time may be active across the session. A conversation is a time-slice of a session. Multiple conversations can be interleaved over the session in a time-sliced manner with the session dedicated to a single conversation at a time. The LU manages these conversations and allocates the session resource as necessary to various conversations. The distinction is important because the LU 6.2 verbs used by TPs to interact with the LU are applicable to a conversation rather than for the session.

For example, the ALLOCATE verb is used to establish a conversation between the TP issuing the ALLOCATE and the distributed TP named in the ALLOCATE request. If an SNA session is not currently active, it would have to get established before the ALLOCATE function can be carried out. Verbs such as SEND_DATA are intended to send information from one TP to another via the conversation between themselves. The information actually flows across the underlying SNA session between the LUs supporting the TPs on each system.

The advantage of this approach is that individual TPs are relieved from having to deal directly with SNA LU protocols. Each TP is written as if it is in direct contact with a partner TP. Simple, high-level function calls such as ALLOCATE, SEND_DATA, and RECEIVE_DATA are issued by the TP to communicate with its partner. It is the LU that must translate these function calls into appropriate SNA protocols. The LU must manage multiple conversations that may be active.

A pair of Type 6.2 LUs may engage in either a single session with each other over which one or more conversations can be supported, or they may engage in multiple, concurrent parallel sessions with each other. Each individual parallel session operates as an independent session, with its own session-level protocols and state management, and over which one or more conversations may be supported. This LU 6.2 parallel-session capability is supported only in Type 2.1 nodes. Parallel sessions are not supported in Type 2 nodes.

AN LU 6.2 EXAMPLE

Figure 7-8 illustrates a simple example of an LU 6.2 exchange between two distributed transaction programs. In this example, TP "A" gets invoked on its system by some action, possibly the user explicitly starting it up. Once started, TP "A" issues an ALLOCATE verb to establish a conversation with TP "B" which has been identified in one of the parameters of the verb. (The actual function call issued: its name, syntax, parameters, etc., is dependent on the LU 6.2 API provided by the system on which TP "A" is executing.) Another parameter that may also have been included is the synchronization level desired for this conversation.

Upon receiving a return code indicating that the ALLOCATE verb has completed and has been successfully processed by its local LU (the ALLOCATE is not sent to TP "B"), TP "A" can send information to TP "B" by issuing a SEND_DATA verb and pointing to the information to be sent. A return code will indicate whether the LU supporting TP "A" has accepted this information. If TP

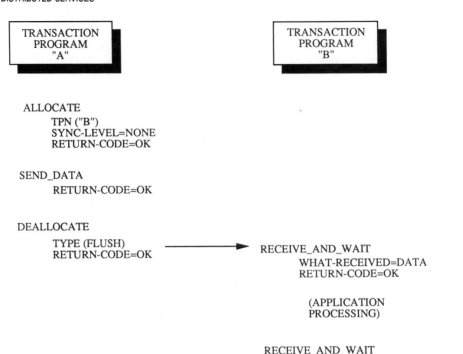

Figure 7-8. *An example of LU 6.2 usage between distributed TPs.*

"A" has no further information to send and no further processing to do, it can terminate its end of the conversation via a DEALLOCATE command. Again, a return code will indicate whether this was accepted without error from the local LU.

Note that no information flowed across the communications link between the two systems on which TP "A" and TP "B" are executing until TP "A" issued the DEALLOCATE. The prior LU 6.2 verb calls did not directly result in transmission of any data across the connection. The LU supporting TP "A" interpreted the verb calls, translated them into appropriate SNA protocols, and buffered the information in its send buffer(s). Only when an indication was given that transmission was required (via the DEALLOCATE with a FLUSH option) did physical transmission take place. This buffering is an implementation option and will vary from system to system, but LU 6.2 allows for this type of processing.

It is important to understand that the LU 6.2 verbs issued by the transaction programs are not actually flowing across the conversation between these programs. The verbs are not SNA commands. The LU translates these verb calls, which are the interfaces between the application and the LU, into standard SNA commands and protocols. If one were to look only at what flowed across the communications link between the programs it would not necessarily be apparent what calls were actually issued by the transaction programs.

For example, TP "A" 's ALLOCATE request results in an SNA Function Management Header (FMH) being built by its local LU and stored in the send buffer. TP "A" 's local LU interprets the ALLOCATE call and uses the associated parameters to build this special Type 5 FMH (called an ATTACH FMH) which will eventually be transmitted to the LU supporting TP "B." TP "A" 's local LU will also set begin bracket (BB) bits and chaining bits in the Request Header (RH) portion of the SNA message unit to be transmitted. The BB bit will eventually be used to establish the conversation between TP "A" and TP "B" since bracketing is the standard SNA means of delimiting conversations on an SNA LU-LU session.

Note that as TP "A" is issuing requests, TP "B" is not even active yet. TP "B" will get dynamically activated by the local LU supporting it upon receipt of the ATTACH FMH. TP "B" 's local LU will then allocate various resources (e.g., control blocks, storage, etc.) for TP "B." These services of invoking programs and allocating resources are typical services provided by operating systems, which is one reason why IBM refers to LU 6.2 as a "distributed operating system." In this case, the LU becomes more than just a port for end users into the SNA network.

When TP "B" begins executing, it issues a RECEIVE_AND_WAIT verb in order to receive information from TP "A." TPs that participate in distributed transaction processing will be developed in a coordinated manner. In this example, TP "B" knows that its role is to receive and process requests from another TP. The RECEIVE_AND_WAIT verb call will be completed when the LU supporting TP "B" moves the data it received into the appropriate receive buffer and sets a return code indicating that data has been successfully received.

TP "B" will perform whatever processing it was designed to do and then issue another RECEIVE_AND_WAIT. It does this because it does not know whether or not any other data will be forthcoming from the remote TP. Since no additional data was sent from TP "A," the RECEIVE_AND_WAIT is completed by TP "B" 's LU with a return code indicating that the conversation should be terminated. TP "B" then issues the DEALLOCATE verb to terminate its end of the conversation.

Although this is an extremely simple example, it does highlight some important points about LU 6.2 processing. For one, TPs are logically connected via a conversation which is managed by the LUs supporting them, using SNA LU 6.2 session-level protocols. The TPs never engage directly in any SNA session-level protocol processing themselves. In fact, the TPs may be sharing the underlying SNA session between their supporting LUs with other pairs of TPs that may also be engaged in conversations. The LUs will manage one conversation at a time between a single pair of TPs over the LU session and interleave the conversations between other TP pairs.

The TPs issue LU 6.2 verbs (i.e., function calls made available by their system's LU 6.2 API) as if they were communicating directly with their partner TP. The verb calls are the interfaces between the TP and its local LU. The local LU is responsible for accepting the calls, interpreting them, translating them into appropriate SNA protocols, and transmitting the appropriate information to the remote LU. The verb calls do not flow between LUs or TPs. SNA message units flow that may contain FMHs, bracket, chaining, change direction, and pacing bits, to name just a few that are used to control the LU-LU session supporting the TPs.

The verb interface makes it much easier to write distributed transaction programs because the programs do not have to deal directly with SNA protocols such as bracketing, chaining, change direction, etc. They deal only with the high-level verb calls for requesting simple functions from the LU such as allocate a conversation with a partner program, send data to the distributed program, receive data, etc.

Because the LU 6.2 verb calls are not directly related to the SNA session-level protocols they do not necessarily require that SNA protocols be used. That is, the LU 6.2 API becomes a generalized program-to-program interface independent of the underlying protocols and physical connections being used between systems. This makes it possible, therefore, to transparently use protocols other than SNA protocols.

This is actually what might happen with the SAA CPIC interface in the future. Application programs could be written to the CPIC interface. If the application were to run in an SNA environment, the interface calls would be translated to SNA LU 6.2 session-level protocols as was done in our example. If, however, the application were used in conjunction with some other OSI system, the interface calls could be translated into OSI protocols, as shown in Figure 7-9. This would be transparent to the application that uses the same interface regardless of the underlying protocols being used.

BASE AND OPTION SETS

As with most of IBM's architectures and technologies, the LU 6.2 functionality is subdivided into different levels of support. A base level of LU 6.2 is required of any LU 6.2 system. This base level is the minimum level of LU 6.2 capability that all systems must support in order to engage in LU 6.2 sessions with other systems. The base set should not be confused with the basic conversation verbs. The base set is actually a subset of basic conversation verbs and options.

In addition, there are a number of LU 6.2 option sets (or towers) that provide enhanced functionality that a system may choose to support. Examples of option sets include support for mapping, sync-point processing, program-initialization parameters, security, and performance options, among others.

The actual set of options to be used during a session is determined when the LU 6.2 session is established by the SNA BIND command. Only those LU 6.2 functions included in the base set and the selected options may be used during the session. If the session is terminated and then reestablished between the same pair of LUs, a new set of options may be used. The ability to negotiate some BIND parameters is another added capability of LU 6.2 that is not supported by most of the earlier LU types.

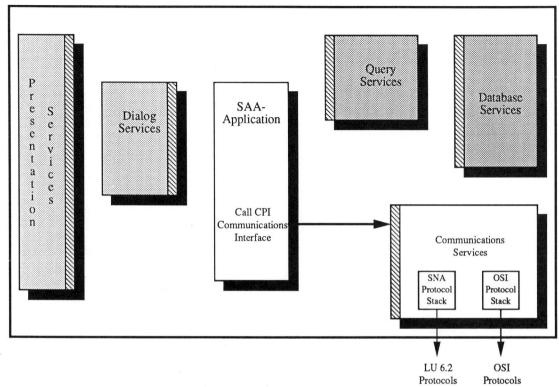

Figure 7-9. *CPIC could be mapped to either SNA or OSI protocols.*

If one LU supports options while another LU supports only the base set, the LUs can agree to communicate using just the base set of LU 6.2 functions. The base set provides the minimum level at which communications can take place. This still allows more intelligent products to communicate with less intelligent products. Value-added capabilities can be built into products without necessarily restricting them to connections with other products that also implement the same value-added capabilities.

HIERARCHICAL AND PEER-TO-PEER CONNECTIONS

LU 6.2 protocols can be used over both hierarchical and peer-to-peer connections, as indicated in Figure 7-10. Contrary to what many believe, LU 6.2 does not require Node Type 2.1 connections although more recent IBM documentation mentions only Node Type 5 and 2.1 as supporting LU 6.2 sessions. This is probably to keep more in line with future requirements for peer-to-peer capability (Node Type 2.1 supports both peer-to-peer and hierarchical connections), as indicated by SAA's requirement for Type 2.1 node support.

The significance of Node Type 2.1 support is that this is the level of networking capability included under SAA today. This means that SAA systems must

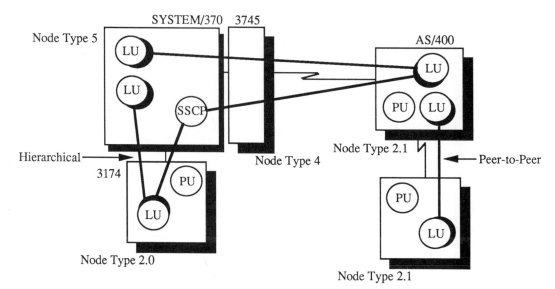

Figure 7-10. *LU 6.2 can be used over either hierarchical or peer-to-peer connections.*

support both hierarchical and peer-to-peer connections as well as parallel sessions.

The requirement for peer-to-peer support becomes more important in the local area network environment where communications directly between workstations on the LAN is peer-to-peer by nature. It is also a recognition by IBM for the need to make SNA less hierarchical in general.

LU 6.2 IN IBM PRODUCTS

There is widespread support for LU 6.2 protocols in IBM systems. This is not surprising since LU 6.2 has been around for some time—it was introduced in 1983. Current IBM systems that support LU 6.2 include System/370/390 processors, System/36, System/38, AS/400, Series/1, 8100, 5520, S/88, PC, PS/2, RT, 3820 Page Printer, and others.

Despite this widespread support which has been available for some time, the use of LU 6.2 is still somewhat limited, especially in comparison to 3270 LU 2 usage. For a long time, IBM's Distributed Office Support System (DISOSS) was the only mainframe-based application that supported LU 6.2 connections. Now, there are several that do so. One is OfficeVision, one of IBM's SAA Common Applications, as discussed in Chapter 6, although the first release of OfficeVision used DISOSS for this support.

The lack of turnkey LU 6.2–based applications has been a limiting factor in the use of LU 6.2. Users are only recently beginning to develop their next generation of distributed processing transaction programs based on LU 6.2. To date, there are relatively few such applications actually up and running. This, coupled with the lack of turnkey LU 6.2 applications from IBM or other vendors, has kept LU 6.2 use to a minimum.

One reason for the lack of LU 6.2 mainframe applications is that until the end of the 1980s, VTAM did not provide full support for LU 6.2. Therefore, it was up to individual subsystems and applications to implement higher-level LU 6.2 protocol processing in order to support LU 6.2 conversations. A brief description of SNA LU processing will aid in understanding this.

LU session support actually spans VTAM and its applications, which are either IBM subsystems such as CICS and TSO or user-written applications. For most LU processing, VTAM provides support for the lower session layers, primarily Transmission Control and checking of the Data Flow Control protocols. VTAM provided an API (not an LU 6.2 API) that allowed applications to send and receive SNA commands and control SNA session-level protocols. The applications implemented the higher session-level protocols including implementing DFC commands and controlling protocols such as bracketing and chaining. In addition, the applications provided the Presentation Services processing and any Transaction Services processing.

LU types differ the most in the handling of these higher-layer protocols and functions. A VTAM application must implement the particular subset of session-level commands, protocols, and functions defined by a particular LU type in order to support that type of LU connection. Therefore, support for LU 2, LU 6.2, and other LU types is built into the applications themselves, with VTAM providing the lower-level session support. Part of the LU implementation is in the application and part is in VTAM.

CICS was, for a long time, the only IBM subsystem to provide LU 6.2 support. It did this by implementing the higher-level LU 6.2 protocols and interfacing to VTAM to get support for the lower-level protocols. In addition, CICS provides an LU 6.2 API that can be used by its transaction programs in order to engage in LU 6.2 conversations with remote transaction programs. The only two IBM CICS transaction programs that made use of this LU 6.2 support were DISOSS and DDM or user-written transactions.

Other IBM mainframe subsystems such as TSO and IMS had not implemented the higher-level LU 6.2 support. This meant that LU 6.2 support on the IBM mainframe was limited to a CICS environment. It was further limited to those CICS transactions that chose to use the CICS LU 6.2 API such as DISOSS and DDM.

This situation has changed. VTAM now provides more complete LU 6.2 support and an LU 6.2 API that applications and subsystems can use for communicating with other LU 6.2 systems. This means that most of the Type 6.2 LU processing is implemented in VTAM. VTAM applications will not have to implement the higher-level LU 6.2 SNA protocols directly, but rather can use the VTAM LU 6.2 API calls. This should allow them to implement LU 6.2 support more quickly.

As a short-term effort, IBM provided an LU 6.2 application that converts LU 6.2 protocols to LU 6.1 protocols to provide indirect LU 6.2 support for the Information Management System (IMS). This program is called the IMS LU 6.1

Adapter for LU 6.2 Applications Program Offering. It is a separate VTAM application that implements LU 6.2 protocols for communicating with remote LU 6.2 systems. It then converts the LU 6.2 protocols to LU 6.1 protocols to allow these remote systems to interface with IMS (IMS uses LU 6.1 sessions today for intersystem communication with other IMS or CICS systems on other mainframes). This application acts like a protocol converter between LU 6.2 and LU 6.1. The IMS/ESA Transaction Manager will now provide direct support for LU 6.2.

The availability of LU 6.2 support in these different subsystems, applications, and mainframe environments should accelerate the use of and demand for LU 6.2 support in systems of all kinds. Also, LU 6.2–based VTAM applications are becoming available from non-IBM vendors as well.

Almost all of IBM's departmental systems support LU 6.2. This includes the System/36, System/38, AS/400, Series/1, 5520, System/88, and 8100. The system of most concern for the SAA environment is the AS/400. LU 6.2 support is provided in the APPC subsystem of the System/36's System Support Program (SSP), the System/38's Control Program Facility (CPF), and the AS/400's OS/400 operating system. These systems also provide Node Type 2.1 support. The Personal Services products (PS/36 and PS/38) and the OfficeVision/400 (AS/400 Office) products make use of LU 6.2. PS/36, PS/38, and OfficeVision/400 are used in conjunction with DISOSS and the OfficeVision/MVS products to provide electronic mail and document interchange facilities to midrange systems users.

On the System/36, PS/36 implements both DIA and SNA/DS support as does OS/400. PS/38 on the System/38 implements DIA with SNA/DS support provided as a separate subsystem. SNA/DS is used over LU 6.2 sessions to communicate between System/36, System/38, or AS/400 systems and DISOSS or between peer-coupled System/36s, System/38s, or AS/400s.

The System/36, System/38, and AS/400 also support Distributed Data Management (DDM). DDM commands and protocols are used over LU 6.2 sessions to provide remote access to data distributed across System/36, System/38, AS/400, and S/370 systems. In addition, the System/36's and AS/400's Advanced Peer-to-Peer Networking (APPN) features provides dynamic networking of peer-coupled System/36s and AS/400s making use of LU 6.2 sessions over Node Type 2.1 connections.

For personal computer systems, LU 6.2 support is provided by the APPC/PC program product for the DOS environment and by the Communications Manager of the OS/2 Extended Edition operating system. The DOS-based DDM/PC program product uses the APPC/PC subsystem to send DDM requests over LU 6.2 sessions to other System/36, System/38, AS/400, and System/370 systems. APPC/PC also provides Node Type 2.1 support as does the OS/2 Communications Manager.

IBM's NetView/PC product also provides LU 6.2 support for sending files from NetView/PC applications to DDM under CICS on S/370 MVS hosts. The NetView/PC product provides its own communications API that allows user-written applications to use LU 6.2 sessions for such file transfer operations.

It should be clear that LU 6.2 already exists on most IBM systems, including their major strategic systems. It is supported on mainframes, midrange systems, and personal computer systems—the major SAA platforms. IBM will be providing more and more turnkey applications that make use of LU 6.2 for their distributed program-to-program communications, such as their OfficeVision products.

RELATED TECHNOLOGIES

LU 6.2 is not a turnkey technology in itself. It does not provide a complete end-to-end function. It provides the program-to-program communications facilities to allow distributed transaction programs to communicate intelligently with one another. It is up to the transaction programs to provide whatever functionality for which they were designed. LU 6.2, therefore, requires transaction programs (applications) to sit on top of it.

Transaction-processing technologies, networking technologies, and connectivity technologies are all either directly or indirectly related to LU 6.2. As the only LU type included under SAA today, LU 6.2 serves as a funnel into which all higher-level transaction technologies will flow, and underneath LU 6.2 will sit networking technologies. Type 2.1 node capabilities including Low Entry Networking (LEN) and Advanced Peer-to-Peer Networking (APPN) end node support, which are based on LU 6.2, are included under SAA today.

Indirectly related to LU 6.2 are the connectivity technologies over which LU 6.2 sessions may be established. These currently include remote SDLC connections, LAN connections, and X.25 connections. LU 6.2 use over other types of connections is expected in the future.

There are already a number of IBM architectures and technologies that are designed to be used on top of LU 6.2 sessions to provide various types of distributed transaction processing capabilitites. These include DIA, SNA/DS, and APPN. The relationship of these architectures to LU 6.2 is shown in Figure 7-6. Also shown is the relationship of LU 6.2 to various connectivity technologies.

Each of these architectures is designed for a different set of distributed transaction processing functions. For example, DIA provides a range of document-oriented library and distribution services, SNA/DS provides a generalized store-and-forward delivery capability, and APPN provides dynamic networking capabilities for peer-coupled peripheral nodes. Other user applications have been developed for a variety of transaction processing applications including simple file transfers. All these different functions are supported because of the generalized nature of the program-to-program communications capability provided with LU 6.2.

Support should be provided for concurrent LU 6.2 and 3270 (LU 1, 2, 3) communications. This is because it is important to provide users access both to new LU 6.2 applications and to existing 3270 applications. LU 6.2 will not replace 3270 communications as the predominant means of IBM communications for a long time. There is too large an installed base of 3270 systems and applications written to support 3270 connections.

New distributed applications, though, are being developed to support LU 6.2 rather than 3270 connections. These applications will coexist with 3270 applications. Personal computer and departmental processor users will want and need access to both types of applications. No system should support one type of access to the exclusion of another type.

The concurrent support for LU 6.2 and 3270 connections should be implemented in a manner that allows the user to switch easily between these types of connections. This can be done by building the LU 6.2 support on top of the same base SNA support used also to support LU 1, 2, and 3 3270 connections.

Providing an LU 6.2 API will also be an important requirement for non-IBM systems. Such an API would allow users to develop their own applications that can make use of LU 6.2 connections. This API should conform closely to the generic LU 6.2 verbs and the Common Programming Interface for Communications (CPIC) that IBM will be using in its own products. This would provide customers with a consistent LU 6.2 API and put the product more directly in the mainstream of SAA specifications.

One of the complexities in implementing LU 6.2 support is that LU 6.2 is more closely tied to the operating system than is support for other LU types. LU 6.2 facilities such as invoking transaction programs, allocating memory and other system resources, and others imply an integration with the operating system. When used with transaction programs such as DDM, closer integration with the file management and database management systems is also implied.

To keep in line with SAA, Node Type 2.1 support must be provided in addition to LU 6.2 support. With Node Type 2.1 support, both hierarchical and peer-to-peer connections are supported. Both primary and secondary SDLC support should be provided as well as primary and secondary LU support. In addition, parallel sessions should be supported.

The LU 6.2 support provided should be independent of the underlying connectivity options supported. LU 6.2 sessions should be usable over both wide area and local area network connections. To support the full range of SAA connectivity options would require support for SDLC, Token-Ring, and X.25 connections. The LU 6.2 support should be usable by a wide range of transaction programs. For SAA, this support should include DIA, SNA/DS, and DDM.

IBM will continue to add transaction programs that use LU 6.2 as their vehicle for program-to-program communications and will also continue to add support for different types of physical connections over which LU 6.2 sessions may be used. LU 6.2 support on any non-IBM system should be capable of being extended to such future LU 6.2 usage.

SUMMARY

APPC/LU 6.2 has importance in two major SAA areas. For the Common Communications Support element of SAA, LU 6.2 is the only SNA LU type currently included. This raises LU 6.2 to a level of strategic importance and means that LU 6.2 is a requirement for any system that is to be SAA-compatible. As part of SAA,

LU 6.2 will be supported by IBM in a consistent manner in each of their SAA environments, including MVS/ESA and VM/ESA for System/370 and System/390 mainframes, OS/400 for AS/400 systems, and the OS/2 Extended Edition operating system for PS/2 systems.

The Common Communications Support element of SAA addresses the connectivity between SAA systems and the ability to do cooperative processing across these systems. In order to accomplish this, a consistent, compatible means of program-to-program communications facilities are required on each system. LU 6.2 is the SAA choice for the SNA program-to-program communications protocols providing such a capability.

LU 6.2 also has an impact in the Common Programming Interface element of SAA. IBM has added an SAA communications programming interface to this element, which is based on LU 6.2 and allows application programs to request LU 6.2 services. This programming interface will be supported in a consistent manner in each of the SAA environments. This will allow application programs that make use of such communications to be ported across SAA systems.

The SAA communications programming interface standardizes the LU 6.2 interface and solves the problem of the incompatibilities that exist with LU 6.2 APIs on IBM systems today. Without such a common interface, developing cooperative processing applications that span systems is a problem. Again, as part of SAA, it will be a requirement for any system that is to be SAA-compatible to support this standard LU 6.2 programming interface.

Although LU 6.2 is IBM's most strategic SNA LU type, 3270 LU 2 communications will still remain the most dominant form of communications within IBM networks for some time. This is due to the extremely large installed base of 3270 applications and products and the lack of LU 6.2 applications available today. SAA will provide a migration path from 3270 to LU 6.2 communications. The next generation of distributed transaction processing systems, linked together via both wide area and local area networks, will be based on LU 6.2.

8

SAA Networking Requirements

The level of networking support required on SAA platforms is defined by SAA's Common Communications Support (CCS) element. Specifically, this networking support is defined by the components included under the Network category of CCS. Actually, there are two levels of capability included under CCS's Network category today, as indicated in Figure 8-1. These components are Low Entry Networking (LEN) and a subset of Advanced Peer-to-Peer Networking (APPN) as implemented in SNA Type 2.1 Nodes.

NODE TYPE 2.1 VS. LEN

The relationship of Node Type 2.1 and Low Entry Networking (LEN) is similar to the relationship between LU 6.2 and Advanced Program-to-Program Communications (APPC). The peer-to-peer connectivity described as LEN, which will be discussed below, is implemented in an SNA Node Type 2.1 just as the program-to-program communications facilities described as APPC are implemented in an LU 6.2.

Another way to look at the relationship of these pairs is from a marketing vs. a technical perspective. APPC is the marketing term for the program-to-program communications protocols provided by LU 6.2, which is the SNA technical term for these capabilities. LEN is the marketing term for the peer-to-peer connectivity provided by Node Type 2.1, the SNA technical (architectural) definition for these capabilities. The marketing/technical terms are very often used interchangeably.

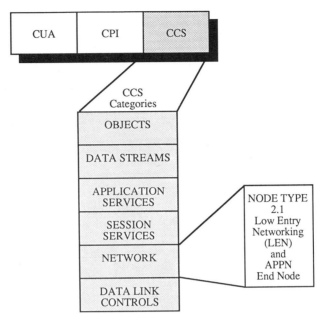

Figure 8-1. *Node Type 2.1 is the single SNA-based component in the Networking category of CCS.*

There is a close relationship between Node Type 2.1/LEN and LU 6.2/APPC, which we will discuss in detail below. LEN is also related to a newer SNA-based networking technology called Advanced Peer-to-Peer Networking (APPN). A subset of APPN has been included in SAA and will be discussed in detail later in this chapter.

Let's start by describing the capabilities defined by the Node Type 2.1 architecture. This should clarify any misconceptions about the level of networking support provided by Type 2.1 Nodes and, therefore, required of SAA platforms.

NODE TYPE 2.1 AND LOW ENTRY NETWORKING

Node Type 2.1 is the SNA node type that supports peer-to-peer connections between adjacent nodes and also provides full LU 6.2 function support. Other LU types (e.g., LU 1, 2, and 3) are also supported within Type 2.1 Nodes. We will look at this LU session support in more detail below. But first, let's look at the capabilities of Type 2.1 Nodes.

A Type 2.1 Node can be directly peer-connected to another adjacent Type 2.1 Node, as shown in Figure 8-2. This peer connectivity between adjacent Type 2.1 Nodes is called Low Entry Networking (LEN). Do not be fooled by the "Networking" part of Low Entry Networking. It is not really networking at all. Instead it is limited to the peer *connectivity* between adjacent Type 2.1 Nodes, as Figure 8-2 illustrates.

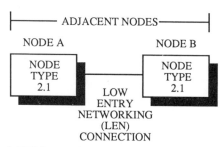

Figure 8-2. *A LEN connection between adjacent Type 2.1 Nodes.*

Some background information will help clarify this and indicate why there has been such confusion as to the capabilities provided by Node Type 2.1/LEN. In 1985, IBM published a technical bulletin titled "SNA Networks of Small Systems." This document described a set of networking facilities which allowed a network of peripheral nodes (Type 2.1 Nodes) to be networked together without any System/370 host in the network. IBM referred to this networking capability as SNA/LEN. Since then IBM has limited LEN to mean the adjacent node–to–adjacent node peer connectivity described above, thereby changing the meaning of LEN. The more complete networking capabilities described in the original SNA/LEN document are similar to the networking facilities now provided in IBM's Advanced Peer-to-Peer Networking (APPN) products available on the System/36, AS/400, and PS/2.

The first part of this chapter will concentrate on the architected Node Type 2.1/LEN support that is included under SAA. The second part of the chapter will discuss APPN which is built on top of Node Type 2.1/LEN and a subset of which is also included under SAA as indicated above.

Let's first take a look at the differences between Type 2.1 and Type 2.0 Nodes in SNA networks. This will help in appreciating both the advantages of Node Type 2.1's LEN and APPN support as well as its limitations. Examples of Type 2.0 Nodes are IBM products such as 3174 and 3274 controllers and systems such as PCs, System/36s, System/38s, AS/400s, Series/1s, or others that emulate 3270 controllers or other terminals (e.g., 3770 Remote Job Entry Terminals are also Type 2.0 Nodes). PCs, System/36s, System/38s, AS/400s, Series/1s, and other programmable systems can also function as Type 2.1 Nodes with the appropriate communications software. 3274-type controllers only function as Type 2.0 Nodes while 3174 controllers can also function as Type 2.1 Nodes.

Type 2.1 Nodes and Type 2.0 Nodes differ in two fundamental areas: type of data link support and Logical Unit (LU) session support. Both of these areas are discussed below.

Node Type 2.1 Data Link Support

A Type 2.1 Node supports multiple data links. This may not seem like much but it is one difference between a Type 2.1 Node and a Type 2.0 Node which supports only a single data link.

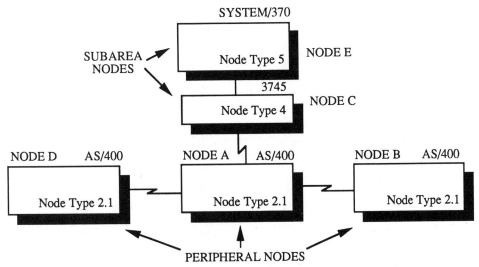

Figure 8-3. *Type 2.1 Nodes support both hierarchical and peer-to-peer connections.*

The Node Type 2.1 multiple data link support may consist of a link to a Host or Communications Controller Node (i.e., a boundary function node) or links to multiple adjacent Type 2.1 Nodes. For example, Figure 8-3 shows Node A connected to Node C (the Communications Controller boundary function node) as well as to adjacent nodes B and D. Type 2.0 Nodes, by contrast, are typically restricted to connecting to a single host in a hierarchical connection. This would be a typical connection between a 3174 controller and a System/370 host.

Type 2.1 Nodes may also be connected directly without any Host or Communications Controller acting as an intermediate node. For example, Nodes A, B, and C can be peer-connected, as shown in Figure 8-4. Node A supports multiple data links—one to adjacent Node B and one to adjacent Node C.

Node A is adjacent to Node B and it is also adjacent to Node C. Node B and Node C are not adjacent to one another since Node A sits between them. Note

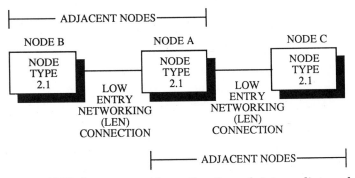

Figure 8-4. *LEN does not provide routing through intermediate nodes.*

that the connection between Node A and Node B is a LEN connection, as is the connection between Node A and Node C. LEN only addresses the connectivity between two adjacent Type 2.1 Nodes.

Nodes B and C do not have a LEN connection between themselves because they are not adjacent. The limitation with this type of LEN connectivity is that communications is supported between Node A and Node B or between Node A and Node C, but communications between Node B and Node C (through Node A) is not supported unless additional software is available in Node A that allows Node A to operate as an intermediate node. APPN is one example of software that will provide this capability. We will expand on this in the section on APPN below.

The data link between a pair of adjacent Type 2.1 Nodes can be an SDLC link, a Token-Ring LAN interface, or an X.25 link. The adjacent nodes act as link stations on the link. Each link station can assume the role of either the primary or secondary link station. These roles can be negotiated when the link is activated. The ability to dynamically negotiate link station roles reduces the data link configuration requirements for Type 2.1 Nodes.

Exchange Identification Format 3 (XID3) commands are exchanged between Type 2.1 Nodes for this type of negotiation. The information exchanged between nodes includes link station role (e.g., primary, secondary, or negotiable), node type (e.g., Node Type 2.1), the type of Transmission Header (TH) used in messages sent across the link (e.g., FID2 format), and the maximum size of messages sent across the link (e.g., maximum Basic Transmission Unit size equal to 256 bytes).

Node Type 2.1 LU Session Support

The type and level of LU session support is another distinguishing feature of a Type 2.1 Node that makes it different from a Type 2.0 Node. In order to understand fully the differences in LU session support, it is necessary to understand the difference between dependent and independent LUs.

Dependent LUs

A dependent LU has certain restrictions on the role it can play in an LU-LU session, the style of communications it supports with other LUs, and the types of connections over which it can engage in sessions with partner LUs. Let's discuss these limitations.

Dependent LUs require the support of a System Services Control Point (SSCP) residing in an attached host system. That is, a dependent LU requires an SSCP-LU session before an LU-LU session can be established with another partner LU. The SSCP-LU session is used by the SSCP to control and manage the LU and to assist in the initiation and termination of LU-LU sessions.

This means, in effect, that dependent LUs are restricted to hierarchical communications with host-based LUs, as indicated in Figure 8-5. The host system, typically a System/370-compatible processor, would contain an SSCP (implemented in VTAM) which serves as the central control point for a portion of the

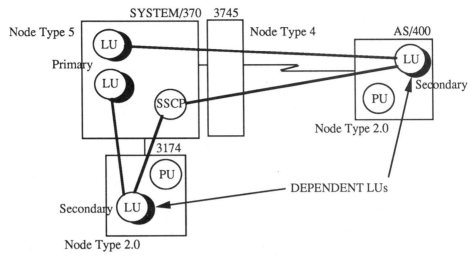

Figure 8-5. *Dependent LUs are restricted to hierarchical connections.*

SNA network (the SSCP's domain). The SSCP controls other components in the network (such as PUs and LUs) by establishing sessions with these components (e.g., SSCP-PU and SSCP-LU sessions, respectively). This is the traditional SNA hierarchical networking.

In this type of hierarchical communications, the primary LU (PLU) always resides in the host while the LUs in the remote nodes are restricted to acting as secondary LUs (SLU). A dependent LU, then, is limited to the role of a secondary LU. What does this restriction imply?

For one thing, secondary LUs cannot initiate or terminate LU-LU sessions. Only primary LUs have this capability. A primary LU initiates an LU-LU session by sending the SNA BIND command to the partner LU. The session is terminated when the PLU sends an UNBIND command to the SLU.

In the past, this restriction was less of a problem than it is with new types of distributed processing. For example, a typical SNA network consisted primarily of dumb terminals (e.g., 3270 terminals) that were connected to a centralized mainframe host. 3270 terminal users interacted with host-based application programs in order to carry out some type of functionality. In this type of arrangement, the LUs in the 3270 system functioned as secondary LUs (SLUs) while the LUs in the host representing the applications functioned as primary LUs (PLUs).

When the 3270 terminal operator wanted to communicate with a host application, he typed in a "logon" command which was sent to the host. The logon was actually a solicitation for the PLU (i.e., the host application) to initiate the LU-LU session (by sending a BIND command) so the terminal operator could exchange information with the host program.

The logon text was actually carried across the SSCP-LU session that was required to be active before the LU-LU session could be activated. Hence, the secondary LU was dependent on the SSCP. The SSCP received the logon, which identified the name of the host application desired, and then passed this request to the appropriate application program. Assuming that everything was OK (the 3270 user was authorized to logon, etc.), the host program would initiate the LU-LU session by sending the BIND command.

Because the 3270 terminals were dumb, that is, they did not have any of their own intelligence or processing capability, they had to be connected to host applications in order for any work to be carried out. Since they had to be connected that way, it was not too much of a restriction to have to solicit a session activation request from the host (via a logon) and to have only the host actually start the session.

With newer cooperative processing and distributed applications running on intelligent workstations such as personal computers, this is more of a problem. What is more desirable is for any system to be able to dynamically set up sessions with any other system based on user activity. For example, a request to access information in a database may result in the request being distributed to another system where the data resides. It would be inefficient to have to send logon requests and wait for BIND commands to come back in order to distribute the request.

Another restriction of a dependent LU is that it supports a maximum LU-LU session limit of one; this session limit is managed by the SSCP controlling the LU. This session limit means that only a single session is supported between any pair of LUs.

A dependent LU, then, is limited to acting as a secondary LU, requires an SSCP-LU session, only supports hierarchical communications with host-based primary LUs, and is limited to a single LU-LU session with any partner LU. If you are familiar with SNA LU types, you might recognize these dependent LU characteristics in many of IBM's older LU types, including the most common— the LU 1, 2, and 3 types used for 3270 communications. These are all dependent LUs that are restricted to hierarchical communications with host-based applications. On the other hand, independent LUs have none of these limitations.

Independent LUs

An independent LU is independent of a host-based SSCP. This means that an SSCP-LU session is not required for independent LUs to engage in LU-LU sessions. An independent LU is able to establish an LU-LU session with another independent LU by directly sending a BIND command without any assistance from an underlying SSCP-LU session. So, when independent LU sessions are established no Activate PU (ACTPU command which sets up an SSCP-PU session) or Activate LU (ACTLU which sets up an SSCP-LU session) commands are required.

Another additional capability of independent LUs is that they can act as either primary or secondary LUs. In fact, these roles are negotiable when the LU-LU session is established. The ability to act as a primary LU would be required if two independent LUs in Type 2.1 Nodes were communicating directly with one another without any host system involvement, as shown in Figure 8-6.

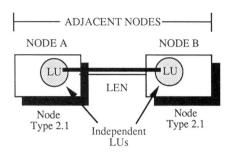

Figure 8-6. *Type 2.1 Nodes support independent LUs.*

Since there is no host (where the primary LU resides in supporting dependent LUs), one of the independent LUs in one of the Type 2.1 Nodes must assume the role of the primary LU while the other partner LU assumes the role of a secondary LU. This is a basic requirement of SNA LU-LU sessions. As with other standard LU-LU sessions, the LU that sends the BIND is the primary while the LU receiving the BIND is the secondary.

Independent LUs are not limited to the hierarchical communications described above for dependent LUs. Independent LUs in adjacent Type 2.1 Nodes can engage in peer-to-peer communications with one another. They do not have to go through host systems in order to communicate. That is, connectivity to a boundary function node is not required.

Another important aspect of independent LUs is that they support multiple, concurrent sessions with other partner independent LUs (their LU-LU session limit is not restricted to one). These multiple, concurrent sessions between a single pair of independent LUs are called parallel sessions, which are illustrated in Figure 8-7. The LUs manage the number of parallel sessions supported themselves (i.e., they manage their own session limits rather than requiring an SSCP to do this).

A major advantage of parallel sessions is the enhanced support for multiple conversations. Remember that an individual session only supports a single conversation at a time. While one conversation is active on the session, all other conversations are locked out. With parallel sessions, though, other conversations can be mapped to other parallel sessions, as shown in Figure 8-8. These sessions can be activated by the LUs on demand.

Parallel session support also minimizes network definition and configuration requirements. Compare the case where one pair of independent LUs supports

PARALLEL SESSIONS

Figure 8-7. *Independent LUs support parallel sessions.*

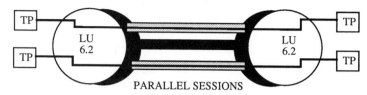

PARALLEL SESSIONS

Figure 8-8. *Multiple conversations can be active across different parallel sessions.*

parallel sessions between themselves against multiple pairs of LUs, each pair supporting just a single session, as shown in Figure 8-9. In the parallel session case, just one pair of LUs needs to be configured. In the nonparallel session case, "n" number of pairs of LUs need to be configured.

There is also less network overhead involved in activating and deactivating sessions when parallel sessions are supported. If multiple pairs of dependent LUs are used, each with a session limit of one, ACTLU (Activate Logical Unit) commands must be sent from the SSCP to every dependent LU. The primary LUs can then send BIND commands to activate the LU-LU sessions.

With independent LUs supporting parallel sessions, no ACTLU commands are required. Nor are DACTLU (Deactivate Logical Unit) commands required to

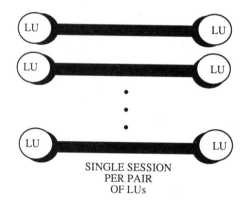

SINGLE SESSION
PER PAIR
OF LUs

PARALLEL SESSIONS

Figure 8-9. *Comparison of dependent vs. independent LU session support.*

terminate sessions. The independent LUs can send BIND/UNBIND commands for any of the parallel sessions that are dynamically activated or terminated.

The characteristics of independent LUs are those supported by LU 6.2. In fact, only an LU 6.2 can be an independent LU! This is a very important point and a major advantage of LU 6.2 over other LU types. All other SNA LU types (e.g., LU 1, 2, 3) are restricted to functioning as dependent LUs.

We see a clear distinction between the older, terminal-oriented LU types and LU 6.2 used for program-to-program communications. The older LU types are used to allow dumb terminals (or systems emulating terminals) to access host-based applications. LU 6.2 is used by distributed programs running on intelligent systems for their interprogram communications.

LU Session Support in Type 2.1 Nodes

What does this dependent and independent LU support have to do with Node Type 2.1 and Low Entry Networking? A Type 2.1 Node supports both dependent and independent LUs, as shown in Figure 8-10. A Type 2.0 Node, on the other hand, supports dependent LUs only. This provides a clear distinction in the level of communications support provided in Type 2.1 Nodes versus Type 2.0 Nodes.

Since Type 2.0 Nodes only support dependent LUs, communications are restricted to being hierarchical in nature. LU-LU sessions are not supported directly between Type 2.0 Nodes. Connectivity to a boundary function node (Host or Communications Controller) is required.

The dependent LUs supported in a Type 2.0 Node include LU 0, 1, 2, 3, as well as 6.2. Note that LU 6.2 can be used in a Type 2.0 Node. LU 6.2 does not require Node Type 2.1 as is often assumed. However, when using LU 6.2 in a

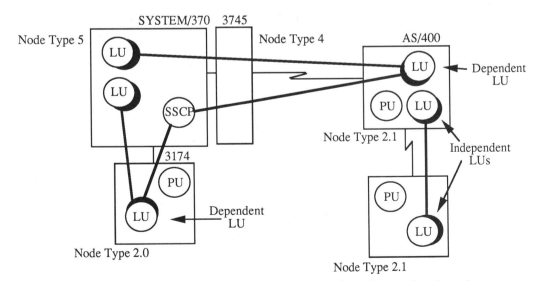

Figure 8-10. *Type 2.1 Nodes support both dependent and independent LUs while Type 2.0 Nodes support dependent LUs only.*

Type 2.0 Node, it is restricted to acting as a dependent LU. This means that it is restricted to acting as a secondary LU, only supports hierarchical communications with host-based programs, and does not support parallel sessions. All the restrictions of dependent LUs still apply.

The full use of LU 6.2 facilities (e.g., primary LU, peer-to-peer, and parallel sessions) is only supported when LU 6.2 is used in a Type 2.1 Node. This is because a Type 2.1 Node supports independent LUs as well as dependent LUs. Therefore, LU 6.2 in a Type 2.1 Node can function as an independent LU bringing to bear the full functionality of LU 6.2.

The dependent LU support provided in Type 2.1 Nodes is the same as the dependent support provided in Type 2.0 Nodes. Dependent LUs in Type 2.0 Nodes can only engage in sessions with LUs connected via boundary function nodes. SSCP-based sessions are still required. Dependent LU sessions across peer-coupled Type 2.1 Nodes are not supported.

The only type of LU sessions supported across peer-coupled Type 2.1 Nodes (i.e., Type 2.1 Nodes engaged in a LEN connection) are LU 6.2 sessions. In other words, only independent LUs can engage in LU-LU sessions across LEN connections between adjacent Type 2.1 Nodes. And, since LU 6.2 is the only type of independent LU, this is the only type of LU session that can operate using peer-to-peer communications.

Looked at in another way, this means that if LEN connections between Type 2.1 Nodes are being used, then LU 6.2 is a requirement. Other LU sessions are not supported between Type 2.1 Nodes. These other sessions are only supported between Type 2.0 or Type 2.1 Nodes (acting as Type 2.0 Nodes) and a boundary function node (Type 5 Host or Type 4 Communications Controller Node).

The consequence of this is that the relationship of Node Type 2.1 and LU 6.2 is, in a sense, opposite of what is often believed. There is a common misconception that LU 6.2 requires Node Type 2.1. We have seen that this is not the case. LU 6.2 is supported in a Type 2.0 Node but is restricted to dependent LU capabilities. However, LU 6.2 is the only independent LU session supported between peer-coupled Type 2.1 Nodes. Node Type 2.1, then, in this case requires LU 6.2.

NODE TYPE 2.1 AND SAA

The reality is that Node Type 2.1 and LU 6.2 will go hand-in-hand in most cases. One reason is that Node Type 2.1 is required to allow LU 6.2 to operate as an independent LU. With such support brings the full power of LU 6.2, including parallel session support and the ability to function as a primary LU.

Another reason Node Type 2.1 and LU 6.2 will be closely linked with one another is that Node Type 2.1 is the only SNA-based networking component included under SAA and LU 6.2 is the only SNA LU type included under SAA. This means that Node Type 2.1 support is required of all SAA platforms and the only LU types to be supported by SAA distributed application services will be LU 6.2.

SNA SUBAREA NETWORK SUPPORT FOR NODE TYPE 2.1

Up until now, we have been discussing Type 2.1 Nodes that are peer-coupled to other adjacent Type 2.1 Nodes, without any host involvement, or Type 2.1 Nodes that function as Type 2.0 Nodes when connected hierarchically to a host system. In the last few years, IBM has extended Node Type 2.1 support to their backbone SNA subarea network. This allows Type 2.1 Nodes to attach directly to the SNA subarea while acting like a Type 2.1 Node, that is, without the restriction of acting as a Type 2.0 Node.

This support for Node Type 2.1 connectivity to the backbone was introduced with VTAM Version 3 Release 2 and NCP Version 4 Release 3 (for the 3725 controller) and NCP Version 5 Release 2 (for the 3720 and 3745 controllers).

The Node Type 2.1 support provided by these and subsequent releases of the VTAM and NCP software allow peripheral Type 2.1 Nodes to communicate with each other on a peer-to-peer basis using the communications facilities of the subarea network. The Type 2.1 Nodes can also communicate with VTAM application programs running in the subarea on a peer-to-peer basis.

The crux of this support is that a Type 2.1 Node can connect to hosts in the subarea in a peer-to-peer manner—a LEN connection, as illustrated in Figure 8-11. The Type 2.1 Node is not restricted to a hierarchical connection with dependence on the SSCP. No SSCP activation of the PU or LUs in the Type 2.1 Node is required.

Prior to these releases of VTAM and NCP, peripheral nodes were restricted to connecting to the subarea as Type 2.0 Nodes. So, although LU 6.2 communications were possible between remote nodes and hosts, only dependent LU capabilities were possible, as discussed above. Even Type 2.1 Nodes, which had peer-to-peer capability, were limited to functioning as a Type 2.0 Node when connecting to the subarea.

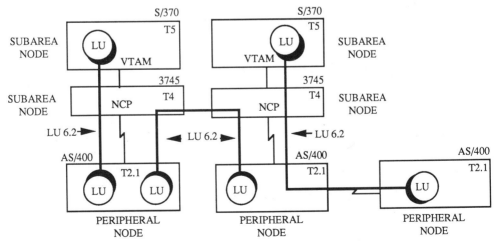

Figure 8-11. *Peer-to-peer communications across subarea nodes.*

With the releases of VTAM and NCP mentioned above, this all changed. Now, VTAM and NCP in conjunction with one another appear as a peer Type 2.1 Node to other Type 2.1 Nodes that are attached to the subarea network. NCP provides physical and logical connectivity support while VTAM provides directory services (e.g., locating the partner LU identified in the session-initiation request) and also aids in starting up the session, among other things.

One major advantage of the subarea Node Type 2.1 support is that it allows Type 2.1 Nodes that are physically connected to the subarea (but not to each other) to communicate on a peer-to-peer basis. Remember we indicated that peer-to-peer LEN connections were restricted to adjacent nodes? Well the VTAM/NCP Type 2.1 Node support allows Type 2.1 Nodes that are not physically adjacent (i.e., not directly connected via a communications link) to appear to be logically adjacent, as shown in Figure 8-11.

For example, a user may have multiple peripheral nodes that are connected via separate communications lines to the backbone subarea network. Prior to the newer releases of VTAM/NCP, these peripheral nodes were restricted to functioning as Type 2.0 Nodes. The only way communications was supported between these nodes was via a message-switch application in the host. Now, however, these nodes can connect as Type 2.1 Nodes and engage in peer-to-peer communications between themselves. They appear to be adjacent to one another. This allows them to take advantage of the in-place physical communications facilities and conduct peer-to-peer communications across the backbone without having to install direct links between the peripheral nodes themselves. Obviously there is a potential cost savings in communications facilities required to support peer-to-peer communications.

With the ability to attach as a Type 2.1 Node in a native LEN connection, full usage of LU 6.2 facilities became possible when communicating with host applications. This includes the ability to use parallel sessions and the ability for the LUs in the peripheral nodes to function as primary LUs (outboard PLU capability).

Low Entry Networking and complete LU 6.2 support within SNA subarea nodes lays the foundation for evolving SNA networks from strictly hierarchical to peer-oriented. More and more peer-oriented network facilities will be added to SNA over time, driven by the needs of local area networks and cooperative processing.

ADVANCED PEER-TO-PEER NETWORKING

As we mentioned earlier in this chapter, APPN is the newest addition to SAA networking. APPN is built on two of SAA's key communications components— LU 6.2 and Node Type 2.1. Therefore, it fits right into the mainstream of SAA's Common Communications Support. Coupled with the high desirability of APPN features in SAA environments, it is easy to see why it was finally included in SAA.

What APPN adds that makes it so important is a number of advanced networking capabilities which we will discuss. For one, APPN can be used to set up a network of peer-coupled Type 2.1 Nodes without requiring a mainframe host to control the network as would be required in a traditional SNA network. In an APPN network, control is decentralized. So, APPN provides true peer-networking of SNA peripheral nodes. This does not mean that a System/370-type system, which typically acts as a host in an SNA network, cannot participate in an APPN network; it can, but its role is restricted.

Mainframe connectivity to an APPN network is provided via the VTAM/NCP Node Type 2.1 support discussed earlier. This software does not implement the APPN networking facilities that will be discussed but allows the mainframe to participate as an end node, allowing information exchange between users on the mainframe and users on other systems supported by the APPN network.

Another major benefit of APPN is that it supports LU 6.2 sessions between Type 2.1 Nodes that are not physically adjacent to one another. This is in contrast to Node Type 2.1's support for LU 6.2 which required that the pair of LUs engaged in the session were in adjacent Type 2.1 Nodes attached via a LEN connection.

With APPN, Type 2.1 Nodes that are not directly adjacent, that is, they are not directly physically linked (there may be one or more intermediate nodes in between), are made to appear to be logically adjacent. The big advantage to this is that it makes it transparent to the LU 6.2 sessions as to how the Type 2.1 Nodes in which the LUs are executing are physically connected. No change is required of the LU 6.2 support in these nodes even though the connection may change from a LEN connection between two physically adjacent Type 2.1 Nodes to two nodes that are connected across an APPN network involving several intermediate routing nodes.

Another major benefit of APPN is the dynamic networking facilities provided. The topology of an APPN network may change because new nodes are added to the network or nodes are removed from the network, but manual reconfigurations of any of the nodes are not required. The APPN networking software will dynamically reconfigure itself and propagate these changes throughout the network. This is certainly a big improvement over the more static SNA backbone networks where network reconfigurations are a major chore.

Another type of dynamic capability supported by APPN is the ability to dynamically locate users in the network. For example, users may change locations in the network, but rather than have to reconfigure any systems to reflect the new locations, these users can be dynamically located when needed.

These dynamic networking capabilities are especially desirable in local area network (LAN) environments which are by nature more dynamic than traditional SNA networks. It is much easier to add PCs to a LAN and it is common for users to move from one location to another on a LAN. It would be a major drawback to have to reconfigure the systems every time one of these changes occurs.

APPN NODE TYPES

There are three different types of nodes that can coexist in an APPN network. Note that APPN defines its own node types which are different from the types of nodes defined as part of the SNA architecture. These APPN node types are:

> Low Entry Networking (LEN) End Node
> APPN End Node (EN)
> APPN Network Node (NN)

These nodes fall into two categories: network nodes which implement the full set of APPN networking facilities and end nodes which do not implement full APPN networking facilities. The end nodes are limited to being the source or destination of SNA sessions (i.e., the end points of the network). The network nodes support the end nodes by acting as network node servers, providing such functions as directory services, route selection services, and intermediate node services.

The node types within each category are listed below.

End Node	Network Node
LEN End Node	APPN Network Node
APPN End Node	

The table above indicates that there are two different types of end nodes (LEN and APPN End Nodes) and one type of network node (APPN Network Node). Each node type supports a different level of functionality and assumes a different role in an APPN network, as will be discussed below.

All these nodes are standard SNA Type 2.1 Nodes supporting Low Entry Networking (LEN) connections with other adjacent nodes. These nodes also support LU 6.2 sessions across the LEN connections. As the names imply, two nodes are more directly related to APPN (APPN End Node and APPN Network Node) while the third node type (LEN End Node) is not actually a "real" APPN node but is simply a standard Type 2.1 Node with no additional APPN support.

LEN End Node

A LEN End Node is a standard SNA Type 2.1 Node that implements support for the Node Type 2.1/LEN architecture described earlier in this chapter. This type of node does not implement any of the APPN facilities described in the APPN architecture nor implemented in the APPN software on the System/36 or AS/400. Since it does not itself implement any APPN functions, a LEN End Node is limited to being an end node in an APPN network. This means it can be the source or destination of LU 6.2 sessions but cannot perform any intermediate node functions.

As an end node, it must be attached to the APPN network via an adjacent APPN Network Node that will be described below. The APPN Network Node acts as a server for the LEN End Node. Users in the LEN End Node (represented by LUs) can communicate with users in other nodes in the network by making use of the services of the APPN Network Nodes. However, all remote users to which communications are desired must be configured in the LEN End Node as if these remote users all resided at the APPN Network Node server to which the LEN End Node is attached.

IBM systems that can function as LEN End Nodes are those systems that include Node Type 2.1/LEN support. These include the PC, PS/2, System/36 (without APPN), System/38, and AS/400 (without APPN), and System/370 hosts (via 3745 Communications Controller). These systems function as LEN Nodes due to the following software on these systems which implements Node Type 2.1/LEN support:

System	Software
PC	APPC/PC (DOS)
PS/2	Communications Manager (OS/2 EE)
System/36	System Support Program (SSP)
System/38	Control Program Facility (CPF)
AS/400	OS/400

APPN End Node

An APPN End Node, like a LEN End Node, is also limited to functioning as an end node in an APPN network. Again, this means that sessions can originate or terminate at these nodes. They do not support intermediate routing, though, and are therefore limited to existing at the "ends" of an APPN network, requiring attachment to APPN Network Nodes in order to communicate across the APPN network.

Unlike a LEN End Node, an APPN End Node does include some additional functionality that enhances its usage in an APPN network. The APPN End Node does not implement APPN networking facilities so it cannot function as a network node server or intermediate routing node, but it is an enhancement of a LEN Node.

One additional feature in the APPN End Node is that users, represented by LUs, can be dynamically registered with a network node server to which it is attached. The LUs do not have to be manually predefined as required for LEN End Nodes. This reduces system definition and configuration requirements in APPN End Nodes.

Another related feature is that an APPN End Node includes support that allows it to be searched by a network node for LUs that it did not register. Again, this reduces system definition requirements and provides for more dynamic operation.

AS/400 and PS/2 systems can function as APPN End Nodes. This is an enhancement in the APPN support that is not available with the System/36's APPN support. The implementation of the APPN End Node is listed below.

System	Software
AS/400	OS/400—APPC/APPN subsystem
PS/2	SAA Networking Services/2

APPN Network Node

An APPN Network Node provides the full range of APPN networking capabilities that will be described below. This includes intermediate routing, distributed-directory services, dynamic-reconfiguration services, route-selection services, resource-registration services, and others.

An APPN Network Node is a "complete" APPN node. It provides the widest range of APPN support and is the only type of node that can function as an intermediate routing node and as a network node server in an APPN network. However, APPN Network Node capability is not part of SAA. Only LEN End Node and APPN End Node support is included in SAA.

System/36s, AS/400s, PS/2s, and 3174s can function as APPN Network Nodes since these are the only IBM systems that currently have APPN software. The System/36 was the first system on which IBM provided APPN support and was used as the prototype system for APPN development. Subsequently, IBM implemented APPN on the AS/400 and more recently on the 3174 and PS/2.

The AS/400 APPN software is an enhanced, more up-to-date version of APPN than is available on the System/36. There are APPN features implemented on the AS/400 that are not supported by the System/36's APPN software. These include the APPN End Node capabilities.

The following SAA systems with their corresponding software can function as APPN Network Nodes:

System	Software
PS/2	SAA Networking Services/2
AS/400	OS/400 with APPC/APPN Subsystem

APPN VS. LEN

Earlier in this chapter we described Low Entry Networking (LEN) and indicated that it provided peer-to-peer connectivity between adjacent Type 2.1 Nodes. In Figure 8-12, two LEN connections are represented between two pairs of adjacent nodes (A-B, A-C). In this configuration, users in Node A could communicate with users in Node B and users in Node A could communicate with users in Node C. However, without additional software in Node A, users in Node B could not communicate with users in Node C (since Nodes B and C are not adjacent).

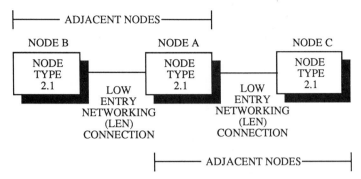

Figure 8-12. *Adjacent pairs of Type 2.1 Nodes connected via LEN connections.*

As Figure 8-13 illustrates, APPN software in Node A would allow that node to function as an intermediate node, thereby allowing communications between users on Node B and Node C. The user communications we have been discussing would involve LU 6.2 sessions since LU 6.2 sessions are the only type of LU sessions supported between peer-coupled (i.e., LEN-connected) Type 2.1 Nodes.

One major benefit of APPN, then, is to permit end-to-end LU 6.2 sessions between nodes that are not physically adjacent. The APPN software in intermediate nodes in the network make the end nodes appear to be logically adjacent. Let's look at how this works.

In the case where APPN software is not available in Node A, two independent LU 6.2 sessions must be established in order to provide communications between a user in Node B and a user in Node C, as shown in Figure 8-14.

With APPN software in Node A, only a single end-to-end LU 6.2 session is

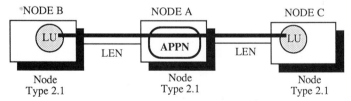

Figure 8-13. *APPN provides intermediate routing through Type 2.1 Nodes.*

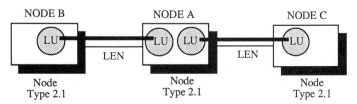

Figure 8-14. *Without APPN, multiple LU 6.2 sessions are required to support communications between users in nonadjacent nodes.*

necessary, as indicated in Figure 8-13. There are a few benefits to this support. For one, it becomes transparent to the LUs that the session may span multiple intermediate routing nodes. Secondly, there is no need for an additional application program (an LU 6.2 Transaction Program) to run in the intermediate node. This not only simplifies implementation but also eliminates any additional overhead in the intermediate nodes. Another benefit is that routing tables do not have to be configured in the intermediate nodes. The example later in the text of how APPN dynamically locates users in the network will illustrate how this is possible.

APPN SERVICES

There are a number of different categories of services provided by APPN software. These services are not formally published so we can only discuss them generically. There are differences in implementation of these services and the names used to describe them on the System/36 and AS/400.

In general, APPN implementations provide the following types of services:

>
> Connectivity services
> Directory services
> Route selection services
> Session activation services
> Data transport services

We will discuss each of these services briefly and then show some examples of how they are used.

Connectivity services are invoked when changes to the network topology occur. This happens when new nodes are added to the network and when nodes are deleted from the network. It is the responsibility of connectivity services in each of the network nodes to ensure that changes to the topology that are detected at any network node are dynamically propagated to all other network nodes in the network.

Directory services are used to locate the node containing or supporting the user to which a session has been requested. Directory services will map a symbolic name to a location in the network where that user actually resides.

Route selection services are used to determine the path through the network (i.e., the route) over which data to be exchanged between communicating end users will flow. In the AS/400 implementation of APPN, class of service support is provided, allowing selection of the most preferred path based on various criteria such as security requirements.

Session activation services provide support for activating an end-to-end session across the network between a pair of LUs. These sessions are standard LU 6.2 LU-LU sessions. They are activated and deactivated using the standard SNA session activation and session deactivation commands—BIND and UNBIND, respectively.

Data transport services provide the support to actually send end-user data over the LU-LU session. Data may flow through one or more intermediate network nodes when flowing end-to-end across the network. It is transparent to the users as to how the data flows across the network.

DYNAMIC NETWORK RECONFIGURATION

An example of how APPN allows dynamic reconfiguration of networks will show why APPN facilities are highly desirable. The APPN network represented in Figure 8-15 includes three APPN Network Nodes (NN1, NN2, and NN3), an APPN End Node (AEN1), and a LEN Node (EN1). Users in these nodes are represented by LUs with symbolic names beginning with "LU" (e.g., LU a, LU b, etc.).

The APPN Network Nodes are interconnected via data links (Linka, Linkb). All of the APPN Network Nodes, APPN End Nodes, and LEN Nodes are Type 2.1 Nodes. The connections between adjacent pairs of nodes are LEN connections.

The configuration of this network changes when a new APPN Network Node is added to the network. The new configuration is shown in Figure 8-16, the new APPN Network Node identified as NN4.

NN4 is added to the network by establishing a physical data link connection to one of the existing network nodes. In this example, NN4 establishes a link (Linkc) to the existing network node NN3. This data link between NN4 and NN3 may be an SDLC link (it may be a switched or leased communications line), or it may be a Token-Ring LAN connection, or it may be an X.25 network connecting the two nodes.

NN4, the new network node, is a Type 2.1 Node just as are all the other nodes

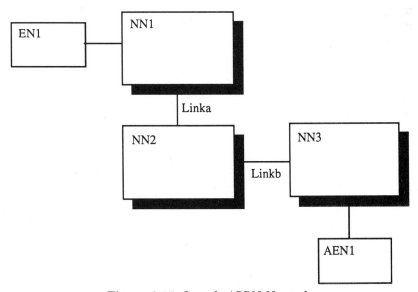

Figure 8-15. *Sample APPN Network.*

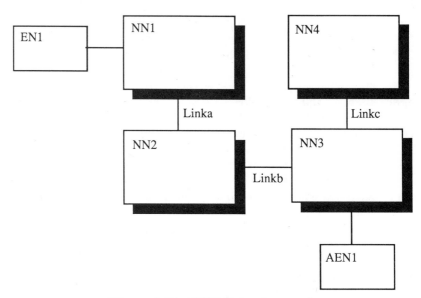

Figure 8-16. *APPN Network example.*

in the network. Linkc, connecting NN4 and NN3, is activated by the nodes first exchanging XID3 commands. Once the XID exchange is completed the data link is activated and standard protocols are exchanged across the link.

NN4 and NN3 are connected in a LEN connection. Once the link is activated, the Control Points in NN4 and NN3 establish an LU 6.2 session with one another. They then exchange their topology databases. At this time, NN4's topology database consists only of itself (since NN4 is new to the network it does not yet know about the other network nodes). NN3's topology database, on the other hand, consists of all the network nodes and their interconnections. In other words, it contains the full topology of the backbone APPN network.

The result of this topology database exchange is that both NN4 and NN3 now have an updated topology database reflecting the current topology of the network. It is next the responsibility of NN3 to propagate the changes made to the topology database to all other network nodes to which it is adjacent. In our example, the only adjacent network node is NN2. The result of NN3 sending topology database change information to NN2 is that now NN2 also has a new, updated topology database that includes the new network node, NN4, that was added to the network.

NN2, and all other network nodes in turn, will propagate the topology changes to all other adjacent network nodes. The result is that all network nodes in the network eventually will have updated topology databases reflecting the new topology of the network.

The reconfiguration of the network was done dynamically without any manual reconfigurations required of any nodes in the network.

DYNAMICALLY LOCATING USERS

Another feature of APPN is the ability to dynamically locate users in the network. This means that a user can change locations in the network and the network will dynamically determine the user's new location when subsequent access to that user is requested. The user's location does not have to be predefined nor do any systems in the network have to be reconfigured when the user changes locations. Let's show how this is accomplished.

In our example, the user represented by LU a in Figure 8-17 requests access to the user represented by LU f. LU a sends a session activation request to its adjacent node (NN1 in this case). The APPN software in NN1 searches its local directory for LU f. If there had been an entry in the local directory for LU f, it would have indicated LU f was a local user. By local it means LU f could either have been locally resident within NN1 itself or resident in another adjacent LEN Node or APPN End Node supported by NN1.

In our example, though, no entry for LU f is found in the local directory since LU f is not local, but is located at NN4. Since LU f was not found in the local directory search, NN1 then conducts a search of its local cache directory. The local cache contains the locations of the most recently accessed users. It is used as a quick means to get to users who have already been located.

The example assumes, however, that this is the first time a request to locate LU f has been initiated. Therefore, no entry for LU f is found in the cache directory. NN1 then initiates an "undirected search" throughout the network to locate LU f. This is done by NN1 sending a search request to all its adjacent network nodes. In this example, NN2 is the only network node adjacent to NN1 so the request is sent initially from NN1 to NN2 only.

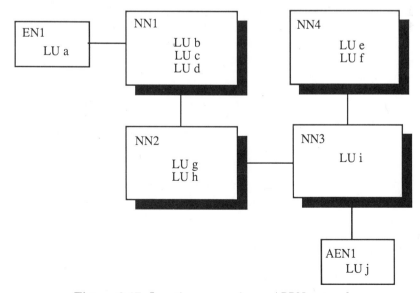

Figure 8-17. *Locating a user in an APPN network.*

When NN2 receives the request, it searches its local directory to determine if LU f is locally supported by that node. If so, a positive indication would be sent back to NN1. If not, a negative indication is returned.

NN2 must then send the request to all its adjacent network nodes, which would be NN3 in our example. NN3 (and any other adjacent network nodes if there were others) must, in turn, send the request to its adjacent network nodes. In this way, the request to locate LU f propagates throughout all network nodes in the network.

Eventually, one of the network nodes will return a positive indication that LU f is locally supported by that network node. In our example, this indication would come from NN4.

When the response from NN4 comes back, NN1 will find NN4 in its topology database. The topology database contains a layout of all the network nodes and their interconnections. In other words, it is a picture of the backbone APPN network. Each network node is responsible for maintaining a topology database and is dynamically updated when the network topology changes, as we indicated in the earlier example.

From the topology database, which is a rooted-tree database, NN1 would determine the preferred path through the network to NN4 where LU f is located. This path information is passed back to LU a, the originator of the request.

LU a would add this path information to the parameters of the SNA BIND command that it is going to send in order to establish a session with LU f. The BIND command is sent by LU a to NN1. NN1 looks at the path information in the BIND and uses it to determine the link to the next network node in the path over which it must pass the BIND command. As NN1 does this, it leaves behind session connectors which logically associate this session with a link into and out of the node. In effect, it has established a path through the node for this particular session.

Every network node in the path will perform a similar procedure. The path information in the BIND will be used to determine the next hop and each network node will set up session connectors that will be used for the duration of this session.

Eventually the BIND command will flow through all the nodes in the path and be received by LU f. In our example, LU f accepts the BIND and sends back a positive response. The positive BIND RESPONSE flows back over the same path over which the BIND command flowed.

The receipt of the positive BIND RESPONSE by LU a will result in the establishment of the LU-LU session between LU a and LU f. This is an end-to-end LU-LU session that flows across multiple intermediate network nodes. It appears to LU a and LU f that they are adjacent.

All subsequent data exchanged between LU a and LU f will flow across the same path. When information exchange is completed the session will be terminated when LU a sends an UNBIND command to LU f.

What happens if LU f changes locations, as indicated in Figure 8-18, and LU a attempts to communicate with LU f again? Initially, the same scenario takes place. LU a sends a request to NN1 to locate LU f. NN1 searches its local

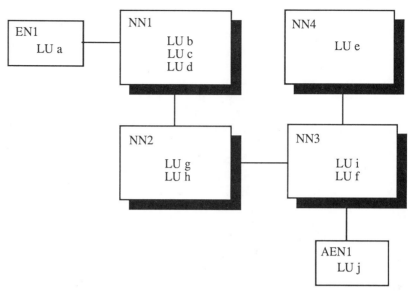

Figure 8-18. *Relocating a user that has changed location in an APPN network.*

directory but does not find an entry for LU f. NN1 then looks in its cache directory. This time, however, there is an entry for LU f since LU f was previously located. The cache entry indicates LU f is located at NN4.

NN1, however, does not automatically assume LU f is still at the same location. So, NN1 does a directed search in which it directly sends a request to NN4 (where LU f was last located) and asks NN4 if, indeed, LU f is still there. Of course, NN4 sends back a negative acknowledgement since LU f has moved.

When NN1 receives the negative acknowledgement it initiates another undirected search through the network in an attempt to relocate LU f. This new search will result in a response from NN3 (where LU f is now located) indicating that this is where LU f is now located.

Again, NN1 will use this information in conjunction with its topology database to determine the path to LU f. This information will be passed back to LU a, put into the BIND command which will then be sent back into the network and sent to LU f, just as we described earlier.

The result is that LU f was dynamically relocated without having to reconfigure any systems in the network. The fact that LU f moved and is at a different location than when first accessed is totally transparent to LU a.

The types of dynamic networking facilities we have described are obviously very beneficial. They are especially desirable in local area networks which tend to be more dynamic in nature than backbone hierarchical networks. It is very easy to add or delete users for the LAN or have users move on the LAN.

IBM will be incorporating more and more of these APPN facilities into its backbone SNA networking. Since APPN is built on top of LU 6.2 sessions and Type 2.1 Nodes, it is not surprising that it is included in SAA.

SUMMARY

LU 6.2 and Node Type 2.1 are the two IBM communications and networking technologies that provide any-to-any communications in SNA networks. They provide peer-oriented, program-to-program communications between SAA environments. Thus, they form the base for SAA cooperative processing.

LU 6.2 is a set of program-to-program communications protocols that is used by SAA Application Services such as DIA, SNA/DS, and DDM. Node Type 2.1 is the SNA node type that supports Low Entry Networking (LEN), providing peer-to-peer connectivity between adjacent Type 2.1 nodes. LU 6.2 is the only type of LU session supported across LEN connections between Type 2.1 Nodes.

Node Type 2.1 (Low Entry Networking) is the single SNA-based component included in the Network category of SAA CCS element. Therefore, Node Type 2.1 support is a requirement for SAA environments.

Advanced Peer-to-Peer Networking (APPN), some of which is part of SAA, is built on top of LU 6.2 and Node Type 2.1. APPN is a newer networking technology that allows the networking of peer-coupled Type 2.1 Nodes, without the need for a host mainframe in the network.

APPN also supports dynamic networking facilities such as dynamic network reconfiguration and the ability to dynamically locate users in the network. These capabilities greatly reduce system and network definition and configuration requirements.

Node Type 2.1 (and LU 6.2) support is provided in the mainframe, midrange, and workstation environments. VTAM and NCP provide this support in the MVS and VM environments; the APPC subsystem of OS/400 provides this support for the OS/400 environment; and the OS/2 Communications Manager provides this support for the OS/2 EE environment.

9

SAA Application Services

Application Services are the components of SAA's Common Communications Support (CCS) which implement standard application-level functions across SAA platforms. The two major functions provided are electronic mail and messaging, and remote data access. These services are implemented via software that resides in each SAA system and a set of protocols that controls the interactions of this software between SAA systems.

Each of the Application Services defines a set of commands that is sent between SAA systems to perform a specific set of application-level functions. In general, these systems interact with one another as a client-server combination. The client system requests various services which are provided by a corresponding server.

RELATIONSHIP TO OTHER CCS ARCHITECTURES

In addition to the exchange of application-level commands, usually there is also a requirement to interchange data that relates to those commands. The structure of this data is defined by the CCS Data Stream and Object Content architectures that were discussed in Chapter 5. Application Services commands that require the exchange of data will contain a data stream that is appropriate for the operation to be performed. The data stream also contains information needed to properly interpret the data being sent. Data streams can contain one or more objects that define specific types of data, such as text or graphics, which will be involved in the particular operation. Each of these objects will conform to an appropriate CCS Object Content Architecture.

The Application Services commands are carried between SAA systems on SNA Logical Unit Type 6.2 sessions. These LU 6.2 sessions in conjunction with Node Type 2.1 network layer support, provide the peer-to-peer communications required to allow any SAA system to request Application Services from any other SAA system.

APPLICATION SERVICES ARCHITECTURES

Currently, there are four IBM architectures included within CCS's Applications Services category:

Document Interchange Architecture (DIA)
SNA/Distribution Services (SNA/DS)
Distributed Data Management (DDM)
SNA/Management Services (SNA/MS)

This chapter contains a discussion of each of these architectures except for SNA/Management Services, which provides network management services for SAA networks and is therefore covered under network management in Chapter 10.

Document Interchange Architecture (DIA) provides electronic mail and document-archiving services across SAA systems. SNA/Distribution Services work with DIA to support electronic mail and, in addition, provide generalized store-and-forward networking for users of SAA systems.

The other major SAA distributed application services provide access to remote files and databases. This access is provided by the Distributed Data Management architecture (DDM).

Document Interchange Architecture

The purpose of Document Interchange Architecture (DIA) is to provide a standard method for handling documents and messages in networks of SAA systems. These documents can contain any type of information. Common examples of documents would include text documents, compound documents containing image and graphics data as well as text, and even executable programs.

The cross-system document-handling services provided by DIA include:

Document Distribution Services
Document Library Services
Application Processing Services

Document distribution includes a wide range of electronic mail and messaging services, while the document library services allow users to store documents and information about their content in centralized libraries for later retrieval. DIA's application processing services allow network users to run application programs on host computers.

The DIA Client-Server Environment

All DIA operations involve a single pair of SAA systems. In each of these interactions, one system takes on the role of a client system which requests DIA services on behalf of an end user, and a server system which is the provider of that service.

Within a DIA environment the client systems are formally known as either Source Nodes or Recipient Nodes. A Source Node, as its name implies, is capable of introducing documents and messages into the DIA network via a server (i.e., they are the source of a DIA request). A Recipient Node is capable of receiving documents and messages from a server (i.e., they are the recipients of the results of a DIA request). Most client systems are actually capable of both functions and are thus known as Source-Recipient Nodes (SRNs).

The DIA systems that act as servers are called Office System Nodes (OSNs). The OSNs are the providers of DIA services that have been requested by source nodes. They also deliver the results of these services to recipient nodes. All activity in a network that uses DIA is between pairs of Source-Recipient and Office System Nodes. The logical connections between Source-Recipient Nodes and Office System Nodes are called sessions. These are not to be confused with SNA sessions. DIA sessions logically connect DIA users while SNA sessions logically connect the SNA logical units that represent users in an SNA network. Before any DIA operation can occur, a DIA session must first be established.

DIA Protocol Subsets

Like most CCS architectures, DIA is made of subsets of functions that can be implemented as needed on SAA platforms. These DIA subsets are called function sets. Each function set identifies a group of DIA commands that performs a specific class of functions. SAA supports the following DIA function sets:

Function Set 2—supports document distribution from an Office System Node to a Recipient Node

Function Set 5—supports document distribution from a Source Node to an Office System Node

Function Set 8—document library operations

Function Set 9—application services

Function Set 10—supports management functions for DIA sessions

In addition to these SAA-supported function sets, certain other IBM products also support a DIA function set which provides file transfer capabilities.

Document Distribution Services

DIA's Document Distribution Services include the ability to exchange documents and send and receive electronic mail from a user's workstation as well as including support for mail-management functions. All these functions are performed through interaction between a Source-Recipient Node, which is typically the user's workstation, and an Office System Node, which is typically a host system. The Source-Recipient Node requests various services; the services are provided by the Office System Node. The types of services provided by DIA's Document Distribution Services include:

> Send documents to one or more recipients
> Retrieve documents from user's mailbox
> Check status of document delivery
> Cancel delivery of documents
> Check contents of user's mailboxes

Document Library Services

DIA implementations that support library services allow users to store documents in centralized libraries and to retrieve them. Libraries can be searched based on criteria that are included with the document at the time it is put into the library. DIA's Document Distribution Services can also gain access to the document libraries. Users can distribute documents from libraries to other users in the DIA network.

Application Processing Services

DIA's Application Processing Services allow a user to invoke the execution of application programs which perform functions like the conversion of document formats. Like other DIA functions, Application Processing Services are initiated by users via their workstations which are SRNs. The DIA commands that invoke the application programs are sent to an OSN where the application program will execute. The output of the application can then be returned to the user's SRN.

The Software Structure of DIA

Each SAA system that uses DIA will contain software that implements Source, Recipient, or Office System Node, or some combination of the three. This software structure is shown in Figure 9-1. Typically, low-end systems, such as personal computers, that are designed to support end users of the network will implement the Source and/or Recipient Node level of capability. Most general-purpose systems of this type will need Source-Recipient Node capability which allows users to submit documents to the network for delivery as well as retrieve documents from the network that have been sent by other users.

Systems that will act as document distribution servers and handle the delivery of documents will contain software that implements the Office System Node level of capability. Systems that implement OSN capability are usually systems that provide shared resources to network users rather than to individual workstations.

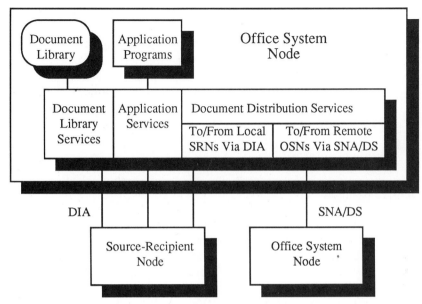

Figure 9-1. *Structure of Source-Recipient Nodes and Office System Nodes.*

Document Distribution Operations

DIA's document distribution operations typically involve combinations of Source-Recipient Nodes and Office System Nodes in a network. The Office System Nodes form the backbone of the document distribution network. There can be any number of OSNs in a network and they all communicate with one another as peers to perform document distribution functions. The users of the DIA network are represented by Source-Recipient Nodes. These SRNs provide the interface between users of the network and the OSNs that actually provide the services.

Users of the DIA network initiate the distribution operations. For example, if a user creates a document on a workstation that is to be distributed to one or more recipients, that user will request the distribution to be initiated through software running on his workstation. That software will implement the functions of a DIA Source-Recipient Node.

The SRN software on the user's workstation will build a DIA command that contains the document to be distributed along with relevant information such as the names of the intended recipients and whether the sender wants to receive a confirmation when delivery occurs. This DIA command is sent to the Office System Node which services the user's request.

The OSN that receives the document distribution command will validate and interpret that command. If the command is valid, the OSN will attempt to initiate delivery of the document. At this point the OSN must decide whether the recipients of this document are local users or remote users. A local recipient is someone whose SRN is connected to the same OSN as the sender of the document.

In the case of local users, the OSN simply puts a copy of the document into the recipient's local mailbox. The document will remain in the mailbox until it is retrieved by the recipient. The recipient, in turn, interacts with his mailbox using DIA protocols over a DIA session between his workstation, which is also an SRN, and the OSN which supports him and contains his mailbox.

In cases where the recipient(s) of a document is supported by OSNs other than the one that initiated the distribution, the delivery to the recipient's OSN is handled by another SAA Application Service called SNA/Distribution Services (SNA/DS). A discussion of SNA/DS and its relationship to DIA is included later in this chapter.

Document Library Operations

DIA document libraries reside on Office System Nodes and are accessed by network users via their workstations which act as DIA Source-Recipient Nodes. Users can add documents to the library, search the library, and retrieve one or more documents from the library.

Document libraries include not only the documents themselves, but also information that describes the content and other information about each document. This descriptive information is referenced during library search operations. The formal name for this descriptive information is the document profile. Each document in the DIA library has an associated document profile. The document profile is made up of elements called document descriptors. Various types of document descriptors contain document information such as:

> Author's name
> Creation date
> Document name
> Document type (format)
> Data of last update
> Subject

Creation of these descriptors is the responsibility of the user who files the document in the library.

DIA Protocols and Data Streams

DIA defines commands and interactions between the user's SRN and the OSN that carries out the requested operations. While many commands are defined by each of the DIA function sets, a simple document distribution operation, shown in Figure 9-2, demonstrates how DIA commands are generally used to carry out document management operations in SAA networks.

Since DIA, like all SAA Application Services architectures, uses SNA's Logical Unit Type 6.2 sessions for communications between SAA systems, an appropriate LU 6.2 session is assumed to exist between the two interacting DIA systems.

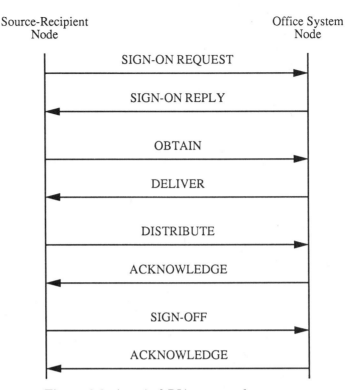

Figure 9-2. *A typical DIA command sequence.*

DIA operations are generally initiated by the user's Source-Recipient Node. Before any DIA document distribution commands can be exchanged, a DIA session must be established between the user's SRN and the Office System Node (OSN) which provides services to that user. As we said earlier in this chapter, this DIA session should not be confused with the underlying SNA LU Type 6.2 session that is a prerequisite for these DIA communications.

The DIA session is initiated by the user's SRN. The DIA SIGN-ON command initiates the session and carries information such as the user's ID and password. The receiving OSN processes the SIGN-ON request and responds by sending a SIGN-ON reply to the SRN. At this point the DIA session is established and the document distribution process can proceed.

After initiating the DIA session the user might want to retrieve from his mailbox one or more documents that have been sent by other users in the document distribution network. The user's SRN sends an OBTAIN command to the OSN where the mailbox exists. The OBTAIN command identifies the document to be retrieved. In response to the OBTAIN request, the OSN will begin sending the requested documents to the user's SRN. These documents are contained in one or more DELIVER commands. The receipt of these documents by the SRN is indicated by ACKNOWLEDGE commands which flow from the SRN to the OSN.

If the user decides to respond to one or more of the messages that have been received, the SRN will initiate these distributions by sending a DISTRIBUTE command to the OSN. Each DISTRIBUTE command will contain either the document to be distributed or a reference to a document within a DIA library that is to be sent. The OSN responds to each of these DISTRIBUTE commands with an ACKNOWLEDGE command that indicates delivery is being initiated.

Finally, when the user is finished with the document distribution operation, he can end the DIA session by causing his SRN to send a SIGN-OFF command to the OSN. This terminates the DIA session but not necessarily the underlying SNA LU 6.2 session.

Structure of DIA Commands

All DIA commands share a common structure called a Document Interchange Unit (DIU). The structure of the DIU is shown in Figure 9-3. The DIU prefix and suffix delimit the DIA and identify it as a DIA command. The command sequence contains the specific DIA command to be executed and an optional data unit contains information that supplements the command. DIA commands that carry documents will also contain one or more document units. Document units can contain either document profiles which describe document characteristics or the data which makes up the document itself.

IBM's DIA Product Support

DIA has been widely implemented in IBM office products, even prior to the introduction of SAA. On System/370/390 hosts, DIA is implemented in the OfficeVision/MVS and Distributed Office Support System (DISOSS). These System/370/390-based products support DIA's Document Distribution Services, Library Services, and Application Services. The AS/400 platform includes DIA support within the OfficeVision/400 product for electronic mail via Document Distribution Services. The OfficeVision/2 software which runs on the PS/2 platform includes DIA support for Document Distribution Services. This support across all SAA platforms makes DIA the primary SAA application service for electronic mail among the OfficeVision product lines.

SNA/Distribution Services

The store-and-forward networking services of SAA networks are provided by SNA/Distribution Services. The primary use of SNA/DS has been to provide electronic mail delivery services, but its role is expanding under SAA. New uses for SNA/DS include network management and software distribution.

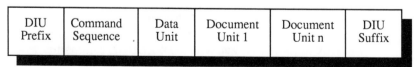

DIU Prefix	Command Sequence	Data Unit	Document Unit 1	Document Unit n	DIU Suffix

Figure 9-3. *Structure of a Document Interchange Unit.*

The network nodes that support SNA/DS operations are called Distribution Service Units (DSUs). These DSUs contain the software required to support SNA/DS store-and-forward networking. This includes support for SNA/DS routing tables and the software required to manage the queues where documents are stored as they are moved through the network.

The SNA/DS DSUs are connected to each other by SNA Logical Unit Type 6.2 sessions. These sessions use SNA's Low Entry Networking to provide the peer-to-peer connectivity between adjacent DSUs. SNA/DS provides routing tables which tie all the DSUs in a network together into a cohesive end-to-end network.

SNA/DS Naming and Routing

Every user in an SNA/DS network and every DSU in the network have a unique name. These names are used by SNA/DS to perform end-to-end routing across the SNA/DS network. Each DSU contains a user table which has the names of the DSUs where users of the network are located. DSUs also contain routing tables which describe the paths to other DSUs in the network.

In order to send a document or any other object across an SNA/DS network, an Interchange Unit is built. The Interchange Unit is the unit of data that is handled by the SNA/DS network. The Interchange Unit will typically contain an SNA/DS command which indicates the type of network operation to be performed. When a document is being distributed, the Interchange Unit will contain a DISTRIBUTE command. Also included will be the names of the network users that will receive the document along with the document itself.

The DSU that services the sender of the document is called the originating DSU. The originating DSU will determine the name of the DSU where each of the recipients of the document is located. The user table within the DSU is used to perform this operation.

Once the originating DSU knows which remote DSU the document must be sent to, it can make copies of the document which will be routed to the target DSUs. When there are recipients on multiple target DSUs, the document and the Interchange Unit that carries the document are replicated whenever the document must be sent over multiple paths to reach its destinations. This process is shown in Figure 9-4 and is known as fan-out.

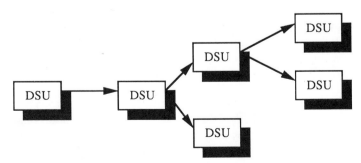

Figure 9-4. *SNA/DS fan-out processing.*

The Interchange Units carrying the documents can be routed through intermediate DSUs to reach their final destination which is known as the destination DSU. Since SNA/DS supports store-and-forward networking, Interchange Units can be stored indefinitely in intermediate DSUs.

The network shown in Figure 9-5 shows how an SNA/DS network is configured and how it performs store-and-forward networking. Each DSU in the network contains a user directory to map user names to DSU locations and a routing table to identify the connections to other DSUs in the network. The sample network contains three DSUs, each uniquely identified by the DSU names of HQTRS.OFFICE, LA.BRANCH, and BOSTON.BRANCH. The connection between the HQTRS.OFFICE and LA.BRANCH is LINKA while the link between LA.BRANCH and BOSTON.BRANCH is LINKB.

Attached to the HQTRS.OFFICE DSU are two end users, uniquely identified as MFG.JONES and PERS.DOE. Note that the DSU and user names used by SNA/DS are two-level, qualified names that can be used to logically group related DSUs and users. Both the LA.BRANCH and BOSTON.BRANCH DSUs have a single user attached—ACCT.BROWN and SALES.SMITH, respectively. Note that each DSU contains a user directory and a routing table. The user directory and routing table for the HQTRS.OFFICE DSU are shown in Figure 9-6.

If the user named MFG.JONES wanted to send a document to ACCT.BROWN, SNA/DS software in the HQTRS.OFFICE and LA.BRANCH

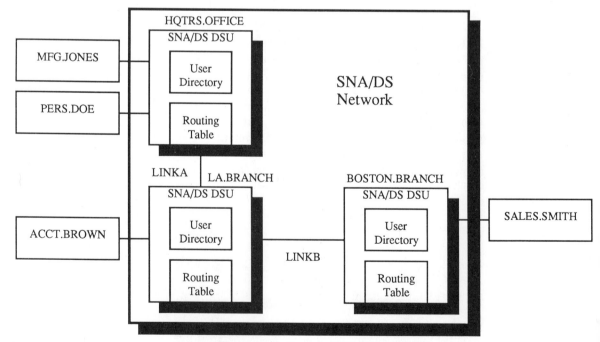

Figure 9-5. *Sample SNA/DS network.*

Destination User Name	Destination DSU Name
MFG.JONES ACCT.BROWN SALES.SMITH PERS.DOE	Local LA.BRANCH BOSTON.BRANCH Local

Destination DSU Name	Link to next DSU
LA.BRANCH	LINKA
BOSTON.BRANCH	LINKB

User Directory   Routing Table

Figure 9-6. *SNA/DS user directory and routing table.*

DSUs would use their user directories and routing tables to locate ACCT.BROWN and determine the path to get the document to ACCT.BROWN. The user directory at HQTRS.OFFICE indicates that ACCT.BROWN is located at the LA.BRANCH DSU. Next, the routing table is searched and it shows that LINKA should be used to route the document to the LA.BRANCH DSU. ACCT.BROWN would be a local user to the LA.BRANCH DSU. In a more complex SNA/DS network, the routing could involve multiple intermediate DSUs, each performing the routing table lookup operation and forwarding the document to the next DSU in the route.

Proper operation of SNA/DS networks require that the user tables and routing tables in each DSU be kept up-to-date. This requires network management or administrative support at the location of each DSU. These individual administrative functions must also be coordinated across the entire SNA/DS network. The maintenance of these tables imposes another level of network management over and above that required to maintain the underlying SNA network.

SNA/DS Implementation in IBM Products

SNA/DS is generally implemented on systems that handle a high volume of electronic mail and messaging traffic on behalf of other users of the network. The key SAA platforms that support SNA/DS are the System/370/390 processors and the AS/400. The PS/2, which generally supports a single user, currently implements only DIA's electronic mail services.

On the System/370/390 processors, SNA/DS is implemented by the Distributed Office Support System (DISOSS). The SNA/DS implementation on the AS/400 is actually a component of the OS/400 operating system and its services support the electronic mail functions of the OfficeVision/400 program product. The SNA/DS services provided by the OS/400 operating systems can also be used for purposes other than electronic mail since it is a generalized store-and-forward networking product.

Distributed Data Management

Remote file and database access is supported by Distributed Data Management (DDM). DDM defines a product-independent, distributed file management and database system. In SAA systems, DDM is implemented as a part of the product's file management system or relational database manager.

In order to support distributed file access, DDM defines a generic, product-independent model for file I/O. This model includes several widely used methods for organizing files. One category of files supported by DDM are the record-oriented files commonly used on IBM mainframe and midrange systems. These files can be organized and accessed in several ways: sequential access, direct access, and keyed access.

The other major types of file I/O supported by DDM are the byte stream files that are widely used on personal computers and systems that use the UNIX operating system. In addition to file access, DDM supports access to distributed databases. The remote database access support included within DDM is designed to provide access to distributed databases.

DDM File Access Methods

There are many different ways in which data can be accessed from a file. The way data is stored and retrieved is called an access method. Different data management systems support different types of access methods. Some access methods are more appropriate for some types of files than for other types. Some access methods are not appropriate for some file types.

To bring some consistency and standardization to the way in which data is stored and accessed on different systems, DDM defines its own generic access methods. As with the DDM file models, the DDM access methods exist as models only. The DDM access methods have to be mapped to the actual access methods used by particular data management systems on a given product. The DDM architecture defines the following access methods:

> Relative by record number
> Random by record number
> Combined relative and random by record number
> Relative by key
> Random by key
> Combined relative and random by key
> Combined relative and random access by record number and key

These access methods group along file model lines. There are access methods for the record-number-oriented file models (sequential and direct), access methods for the key-oriented file models (keyed and alternate index), and an access method that is a combination of all types of access.

Not every access method can be used with every file model. The choice of file model and access method support is up to the developers of the DDM software for a particular product. Usually the choice is based on the type of file support already existing on the system.

If a system supports sequential or keyed files, it may be relatively easy to map the generic DDM access methods and file models to those used on the system. In theory, any type of file organization and access method can be supported as long as it is possible to map to one or more of the standard, architected DDM file models and access methods.

Overview of DDM Operations

The general operation of DDM is the same regardless of whether it is being used for remote file access or remote relational database access. All DDM operations are structured as client-server processes. Figure 9-7 shows the software structure of a DDM client-server combination.

The client system, which is called the DDM Source system, makes requests for data on behalf of local users or application programs. The request is then sent by the DDM Source system to the server, which is called the DDM Target system. The Target system accesses the requested data and sends it back to the client system.

When implemented in SAA products, DDM software is integrated with the file management system of the local operating system or relational database

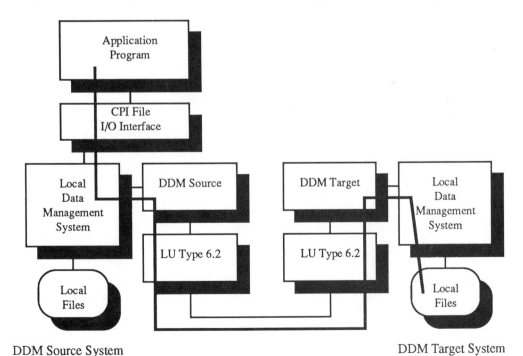

DDM Source System   DDM Target System

Figure 9-7. *DDM Source and Target systems.*

manager. Application programs running on the Source system are not aware of the physical location of the data they are accessing. Applications simply issue the file I/O requests, such as OPEN, CLOSE, READ, and WRITE, that would normally be used to access local files. If the requested file is not found to reside on the local system, the request is turned over to the software that implements the DDM Source system capability. The DDM Source software then attempts to find the requested file in a list of remote resources that DDM has access to.

If the file is determined to be on a remote DDM target system, the local DDM Source software converts the file I/O request into a product-independent I/O command that is defined by DDM. This command is sent to the DDM Target system via an SNA Logical Unit Type 6.2 session.

The Target DDM system converts the generic DDM file I/O command into the corresponding command which is defined by the file I/O system on the Target system. The file I/O system on the Target system is then used to perform the requested operation. The results of the operation on the Target system are then converted into the generic DDM format and sent back to the source system via the LU Type 6.2 session.

The application program that issued the original request is then notified of completion by the file I/O software on the DDM Source system. The application program is not aware of whether its I/O request was processed locally or handled, as in this case, by a remote DDM Target system. All DDM operations, whether they are targeted at remote files or remote databases, operate in this same general way.

IBM's DDM Product Implementations

DDM is currently implemented on the SAA System/370/390 and AS/400 platforms. The System/370/390 implementation is a program product called DDM/CICS which, as its name implies, runs under the CICS operating environment. The AS/400 DDM support is included in the OS/400 operating system.

The DDM/CICS program product supports only DDM Target capability while the AS/400 implementation supports both Source and Target systems.

Distributed Relational Database Support

In order to provide support for remote relational database access, IBM has created its Distributed Relational Database Architecture (DRDA). This architecture, which is a part of SAA, includes the DDM Level 3 extensions needed to support distributed relational databases. DRDA also includes the Formatted Data Object Content Architecture (FDOCA) which defines a standard format for the interchange of tabular data such as that contained in relational databases. DRDA also uses IBM's FDOCA to represent the tables of information that are interchanged among databases. The conversion of internal data formats which might differ from system to system is handled by IBM's Character Data Representation Architecture (CDRA).

From an application programming point-of-view, SAA database support is provided through the SQL interface defined by SAA's Common Programming Interface (CPI). DDM provides the application-level protocols which integrate the operations of multiple database managers across a network.

IBM has committed to support two levels of distributed database access in SAA networks: remote unit of work and distributed unit of work.

A unit of work relates to the operations that the application programs are performing. In order to maintain the integrity of databases, application programmers must be able to logically group several related database updates into units of work that must either be completed in their entirety or backed-out to restore the original state of the databases.

For example, a banking transaction might transfer funds by debiting one account and crediting another. If some exception condition occurs during these updates the application must be able to back-out any partially completed updates.

Remote Unit of Work   The remote unit of work capability will control the update of a single remote database. Multiple SQL statements issued by an application program can be grouped together into a single unit of work. The application can then decide to commit any group of database updates upon completion of a transaction or to back-out all the changes in the event of an exception condition.

Distributed Unit of Work   The distributed unit of work extends the unit of work concept across multiple databases. The application program can issue multiple SQL statements within a distributed unit of work, but each SQL statement must reference a single database.

In order to support the distributed unit of work, the SNA LU 6.2 sessions that carry the DDM commands between distributed databases must support the two-stage commit capability. The two-stage commit capability provides the required synchronization of communications among the distributed database managers.

SNA/Management Services

Network management is also a function of CCS's Application Services. The protocols used for network management are defined by SNA's SNA/Management Services (SNA/MS). The complex topic of SAA network management is discussed separately in Chapter 10.

SAA ELECTRONIC MAIL SERVICES: DIA AND SNA/DS VS. X.400

We have discussed IBM's electronic mail architectures, DIA and SNA/DS, which are part of the SNA-based protocol stack used by SAA. SAA users can also choose to base their communications on the OSI protocol stack within networks of SAA systems. These OSI users will use X.400 protocols to provide their electronic mail services.

Since X.400 is probably the most widely used OSI application service in current use on IBM platforms, a comparison between X.400 and IBM's DIA and SNA/DS protocols is useful.

Different Design Objectives

In the world of international standards, electronic mail functions and protocols are defined by a series of standards known as X.400. Even though X.400 and DIA/SNADS are both electronic mail protocols, it is an apples and oranges comparison to some extent because of very different design objectives. IBM protocols are designed to support homogeneous networks of IBM and IBM-compatible products within a single organization. X.400 protocols, on the other hand, were designed from the perspective of public networks that provide electronic mail services throughout a country and even across international borders.

The X.400 Series of Standards

When most people talk about X.400 they are actually referring to a series of electronic mail standards designated X.400 thru X.430. These standards have been established by the Consultative Committee for International Telephony and Telegraphy (CCITT).

X.400—describes the system model and the services provided
X.401—specifies required and optional features
X.408—specifies conversion rules between dissimilar document formats
X.409—specifies a machine-independent encoding scheme for data interchange
X.410—describes the reliable transfer mechanism used to deliver documents
X.411—defines the Message Transfer Layer services responsible for delivery of messages
X.420—defines message formats and protocols required to exchange messages among network users
X.430—describes how Teletex terminals access the electronic mail network

The X.400 series of standards is designed to operate within the OSI Reference Model at the Application Layer (Layer 7). CCITT refers to electronic mail systems as message handling systems. The X.400 standard itself is the cornerstone for the series of electronic mail standards because it defines the message handling system model, addressing scheme, and the services provided to network users.

An X.400 Network vs. a DIA/SNADS Network

Despite the differences in design objectives between X.400 and DIA/SNADS, it is interesting to note the similarities of design approach. An example of these similarities is shown by comparing the network components and services from an architectural point of view.

Within both architectures, the task of sending mail is partitioned into two parts, an interactive protocol used to submit and retrieve messages to be delivered by the network, and a store-and-forward protocol that moves the mail through the network. Figure 9-8 shows a network that implements IBM's version of electronic mail.

The IBM office network in this diagram is made up of Source-Recipient Nodes (SRN) which interface with the end users of the network and handle the interactive dialog with the components of the network that actually provide the services. These service providers are the Office System Nodes (OSN). The interactive protocol used by the SRNs to submit requests for network services is Document Interchange Architecture (DIA) which also acts as an envelope to

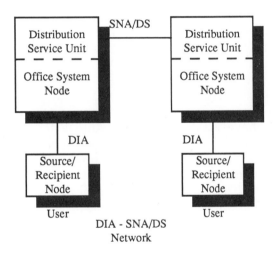

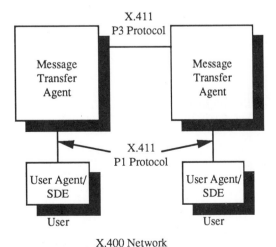

Figure 9-8. *SNA vs. OSI electronic mail.*

carry the messages. Most products that support OSN capabilities also contain an SNA/DS Distribution Service Unit (DSU) which is the vehicle used for store-and-forward delivery of messages across multiple intermediate network nodes.

Figure 9-8 also shows essentially the same network, but this is the X.400 approach to electronic mail. The X.400 network is made up of components called User Agents (UA) which interface with the end users of the network. The UAs submit requests for services to the network's service providers, called the Message Transfer Agents (MTA), on behalf of the users via an interactive protocol. If the UAs are not located on the same processors as the MTAs, the interaction is carried out through a Submission and Delivery Entity (SDE) which uses a protocol defined within the X.411 standard called the P3 protocol.

The delivery of the message through the X.400 network is handled by the MTAs which interact at a peer level using the P1 protocol which is also defined within the X.411 standard. In addition to the P1 and P3 protocols shown in this diagram, there is also an end-to-end protocol between the UAs which is known as the P2 protocol. The P2 protocol is defined in the X.420 standard and describes the specific operations and options requested by the user that originated the request for service.

Other X.400/IBM Differences

As we have shown, there are quite a few similarities between the general structures of X.400 and IBM's electronic mail technologies, but there are differences that these diagrams do not reveal. The differences are important because they are one factor involved in making a choice between the use of X.400 or IBM protocols. They also affect the level of performance that can be achieved by gateways between the two technologies.

The list of features that are available to network users is one area of difference between X.400 and the IBM architectures. The following table of some of these features shows their availability to both X.400 and DIA/SNADS users. It should be noted that these are architected features that are not necessarily available in all product implementations.

Feature	X.400	DIA/SNADS
Deliver Priority Levels	X	X
Delivery Confirmation	X	X
Personal/Public	X	X
Expiration Date of Document	X	
Obsolete Previous Message	X	
Mark as Reply to Previous Message	X	
Cross Reference to Another Message	X	

At least from an architectural point of view, the table above shows that X.400 is more "feature rich" than IBM's technologies. This is due in part to the fact that X.400 was designed to satisfy the requirements of a broad range of electronic mail users, while IBM's design objectives were limited to its more narrowly defined customer base. However, as we said earlier, implementation is frequently another matter and most of the features listed under X.400 are designated as optional.

Another area of difference between the two technologies that is not shown in the table above but needs to be considered is the fact that the naming and addressing schemes used by the two technologies are very different from one another and they support different document-formatting schemes. Gateways between the two technologies will have to provide name/address mapping and document-conversion capabilities. Because of all these differences the gateways will only be able to deal with the lowest common denominator of functionality.

FTAM FILE SERVICES

Users of SAA's OSI-compatible protocol stack can use File Transfer, Access, and Management (FTAM) protocols to access remote files. FTAM is in many respects the OSI counterpart of the Distributed Data Management (DDM) protocols which are available to users of SAA's SNA protocol stack. While FTAM, in general, is capable of supporting the type of record level access that is provided by DDM, the current implementation of FTAM in IBM's SAA products supports access and file management only at the file level.

Current FTAM servers fall into two categories—Transfer and Management. Files can be transferred in their entirety from one platform to another using FTAM. The FTAM Management Services include the ability to create and delete files on remote systems. It is also possible to read the attributes of files on remote systems and to change those attributes.

SUMMARY

CCS's Application Services provides the essential cross-platform services required for almost all cooperative processing applications. These services include electronic mail and messaging, and remote data access.

The DIA and SNA/DS protocols support electronic mail and messaging. DIA is used to allow individual users to access the mail services of an SAA network. DIA also supports additional services such as document libraries and the ability to execute application programs on office servers. SNA/DS provides a store-and-forward delivery system that forms the backbone of the SAA electronic mail network. SNA/DS can also be used for generalized store-and-forward networking with certain IBM products.

The cross-platform data sharing provided by Distributed Data Management supports both distributed files and distributed databases. In most cases, the use of DDM to access remote data is transparent to the requesting system. DDM is usually implemented as a part of the file systems or database managers running on SAA platforms.

Users of OSI communications protocols also have access to generic electronic mail and remote file access services in SAA networks. While the corresponding OSI applications protocols, X.400 and FTAM, are not yet widely implemented on SAA platforms, they will provide a parallel set of services for OSI network users.

10

Network Management Requirements

Network management is becoming increasingly important as corporate networks continue to grow in size and complexity. The distribution of programs and data across networks adds new requirements for managing these resources. Network Management is an important enough issue that IBM has included it under its SAA umbrella. Specifically, the SNA/Management Services (SNA/MS) architecture is one of the Application Services components in SAA's Common Communications Support (CCS) element, as shown in Figure 10-1.

Every SAA environment must support SNA/MS although the level of support provided is different in different environments. For example, the mainframe environments include a greater level of management services support than does the workstation SAA environment. This is because of the way IBM has chosen to position their various systems and how they have implemented network management services in the different environments.

IBM has identified several major categories of management services:

> Problem management
> Performance and accounting management
> Configuration management
> Change management

Problem management deals with the detection, isolation, and resolution of problems that occur in a network. Performance and accounting management deals with measuring, reporting, and controlling things such as usage charges, component utilization, and availability of components. Configuration management deals with the physical and logical configurations of networks, that is, how the

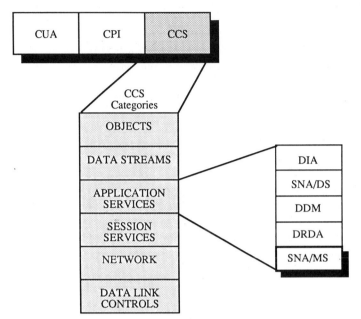

Figure 10-1. *SNA/MS is one of the Application Services components of SAA's CCS element.*

network looks at a given point in time. Change management, which is closely related to configuration management, addresses additions, deletions, and modifications to the network configuration.

Support for these various categories of network management services are implemented in a variety of network management products. Problem management is the area specifically included as part of SAA's CCS element.

IBM'S NETWORK MANAGEMENT APPROACH

IBM's network management strategy is based on centralized management and control with distributed network management intelligence. With this strategy, individual nodes in the network include support for some level of network management intelligence. For example, a node has the ability to detect errors that occur at the node. Network management support, therefore, is distributed throughout the network.

The actual management of the network, however, is provided at centralized control points in the network. As an example, an IBM mainframe running NetView, an IBM network management product, acts as a centralized management node in an SNA network. The management node collects information from the other nodes in the network and provides network management services for these nodes.

IBM mainframes play an important role in this strategy. As we said above, mainframes running NetView are *the* centralized control points of a network. In some cases, a single mainframe is being entirely dedicated to managing a network. In order for all systems and devices in the network to be managed from these centralized hosts, they must be able to send network management information to the host(s).

This also implies that each system or device in the network has the ability to perform some level of network management processing, or other systems in the network must perform this function for those systems or devices that may not have this capability. This is, in fact, the case. Let's see how this fits into IBM's architected network management approach.

SNA/MS ARCHITECTURE

The SNA/MS architecture describes three different types of components which may exist in a network, as shown in Figure 10-2. IBM refers to these components as "points" in the network. They are focal point, entry point, and service point. Each of these components has a different network management role.

Focal Point

A focal point is a centralized location in the network where network management services are provided. A focal point can monitor and control other nodes in the network. Other entry point and service point nodes send network management information that has been collected at these nodes to a focal point for processing.

IBM's major focal point product is NetView, as indicated in Figure 10-3. NetView, which runs on IBM mainframes under the MVS and VM environments, provides centralized network management services for SNA networks. In other words, NetView implements focal point services; it acts as a focal point in the network.

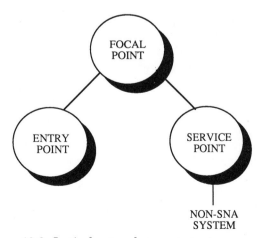

Figure 10-2. *Logical network management components.*

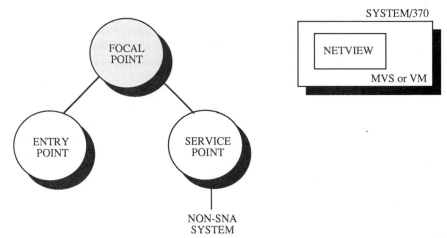

Figure 10-3. *NetView is a network management focal point product.*

Entry Point

An entry point is a standard SNA node that provides its own network management support. This means that it implements a level of network management services that allows it to collect information about the node (e.g., error conditions, performance statistics, etc.). This information is sent from the entry point to a focal point in the network where it is actually processed.

IBM's midrange and workstation systems function as entry points in the network, as shown in Figure 10-4 (using the System/36 as an example). Entry points all provide the required level of SNA/MS support and are able to send

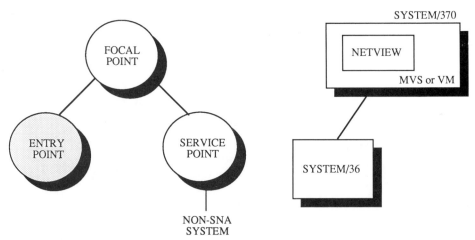

Figure 10-4. *Standard IBM SNA-based systems such as the System/36 are network management entry point products.*

network management information to NetView, the focal point. Entry point systems include the AS/400, System/36, System/38, Series/1, PC, PS/2, 3274 and 3174 controllers, and others. These are standard IBM SNA-based products.

Service Point

The role of a service point is to provide network management support for a device or system that does not have its own network management support—that is, a system that cannot function as a focal point or entry point. This kind of system may be a non-SNA device such as CBX or it may be a non-IBM system that does not have support for SNA/MS. It might also be a telecommunications product such as a modem or multiplexer/concentrator. These products do not typically include integrated SNA support.

IBM's NetView/PC product is an example of a service point, as indicated in Figure 10-5. A service point interacts with the non-SNA device it is supporting in order to monitor this device and/or to collect network management information from it. The service point will then provide the necessary communications support to allow this information to be sent to a focal point product such as NetView.

A service point acts like a network management protocol converter or gateway for non-IBM devices. It is used to bring these non-SNA devices under the control of focal point products such as NetView. This allows management of a network that includes a mixture of SNA and non-SNA devices and systems.

A key to using a service point product such as NetView/PC is that an application must reside at the service point in order to interact with the non-SNA device being supported. This application could be either an IBM-supplied, a customer-written, or a third-party-developed application. The application would

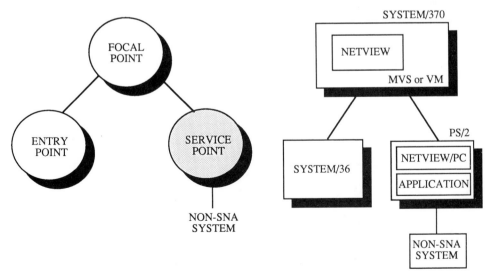

Figure 10-5. *NetView/PC is a network management service point product that provides network management support for non-SNA systems.*

be written specifically to interact with the non-SNA device. It would use the services of the service point to communicate with the focal point.

As an example, IBM supplies NetView/PC applications that provide network management services for the ROLM CBX. One such application, the NetView/PC ROLM Alert Monitor, supports the attachment of one or more ROLM CBXs. This application, which runs in conjunction with NetView/PC on a PC or PS/2 system, periodically polls the CBXs for any errors that have been detected. The types of errors recorded by the CBX include data errors, telephony errors, and T1 link errors. If the error table has changed since the last polling, the NetView/PC application analyzes the error data and determines if it should be sent to a focal point for processing. Whether or not it needs to be sent to NetView is determined by user-defined criteria.

If a network management message, called an alert, does need to be sent, the application builds the appropriate alert message in the required Network Management Vector Transport (NMVT) format. The application then passes the NMVT to the NetView/PC Alert Manager via the API provided by NetView/PC. NetView/PC's Alert Manager will then send the NMVT over its SSCP-PU session with the host where NetView resides. This makes it appear to the Focal Point that the NMVT came from a standard entry point product. NetView/PC, the Service Point, emulates an entry point in order to pass the alert messages to NetView.

HIERARCHICAL NETWORK MANAGEMENT

As indicated earlier, IBM's network management approach is based primarily on hierarchical control, although this is changing. Host-based focal point products such as NetView provide centralized network management services. Other entry point systems in the network, such as midrange and personal computer systems, are under the control of the host network management software.

A brief review of SNA will help in understanding how the network management support is provided. In an SNA network there may be four different types of nodes (a node is a system that implements some portion of SNA). The node types defined by the SNA architecture are:

SNA Node Type	Associated Name
Type 5 Node	Host
Type 4 Node	Communications Controller
Type 2.0 Node	Peripheral Node
Type 2.1 Node	Peripheral Node

These different node types are illustrated in Figure 10-6. A Type 5 (Host) Node is distinguished from other nodes because it includes a component called the System Services Control Point (SSCP). An SSCP is responsible for controlling and managing other nodes under its control (within its domain).

An SNA network can include multiple Type 5 Nodes (i.e., multiple Hosts

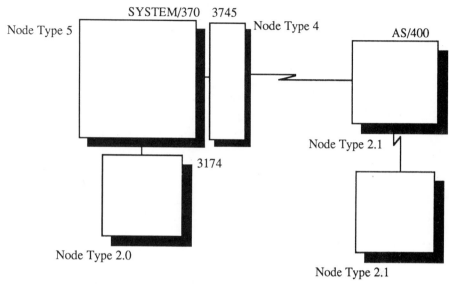

Figure 10-6. *Different types of nodes can exist in an SNA network.*

which are typically IBM mainframe systems). Each Host would have its own SSCP. The SSCPs on the different Hosts in the network cooperate with one another in controlling the network.

VTAM implements the functions of a Type 5 Node, including the functions of an SSCP. It is VTAM, then, that allows a System/370 or System/390 mainframe to act as a Type 5 Host node in an SNA network.

The role of a Type 4 (Communications Controller) Node is to act as a "pure" communications processor. It is responsible for handling communications with other remote nodes or nodes connected via an LAN. It provides support for physical data link connections such as SDLC links or Token-Ring LANs. It also provides network routing functions.

The functions of a Type 4 Node are provided by the Network Control Program (NCP) that runs in an IBM 37XX Communications Controller (e.g., 3745). Type 5 and Type 4 Nodes are collectively referred to as subarea nodes. Each of these nodes defines a different subarea (portion) of an SNA network. Together, they provide the backbone SNA network routing.

There are two types of peripheral nodes—Type 2.0 Nodes and Type 2.1 Nodes. One difference between these nodes is that a Type 2.0 Node is restricted to a hierarchical connection. That is, it must connect to a subarea node. Type 2.1 Nodes, on the other hand, can either be connected hierarchically to a subarea node, or they can be peer-connected to other adjacent Type 2.1 Nodes.

All these different types of nodes contain a component called a Physical Unit (PU). The PU in a node is responsible for managing that node's resources such as the data links attached to the node.

Network management services are provided by control points within these nodes. The centralized control point in a host node is the SSCP while the control points in other nodes are the PUs which provide a small subset of the SSCP control point services.

An SSCP, residing in a host system, manages other nodes by establishing a session with the PU in each of these nodes. This session is called an SSCP-PU session, as indicated in Figure 10-7. One of the functions for which this session is used is to exchange network management information.

Remember we said that the SSCP is actually implemented in VTAM. NetView, which is a network management focal point product, is a VTAM application. NetView collects network management information from the nodes in the network via the SSCP-PU sessions maintained by VTAM.

ALERTS

The network management information that flows across the SSCP-PU session is a specially formatted SNA request unit (RU) called a Network Management Vector Transport (NMVT). A Network Services (NS) header at the beginning of the RU indicates this is an NMVT that contains network management information. Nodes in the network can send these types of "alert" messages to NetView when problems are detected at the node. The alert will be displayed on the operator's console and logged in a database.

Alerts are sent automatically and unsolicited from the node where the problem was detected to a NetView host. The alert notifies the network operator that a problem has occurred. In addition, the alert contains other information that is required or useful in handling the problem.

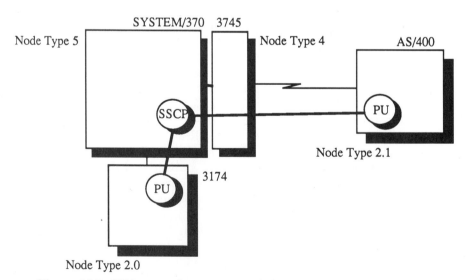

Figure 10-7. *SNA network management information is exchanged across SSCP-PU sessions.*

LU 6.2–BASED NETWORK MANAGEMENT

In September 1990, IBM announced support for LU 6.2 in NetView. This LU 6.2 transport capability allows alerts, commands, and data to be routed between NetView and other applications that support the same level of LU 6.2 management services transport architecture. The other applications could be other Net-View programs or any other non-NetView applications.

The LU 6.2 support is in addition to the SSCP-PU support we have been discussing. This support is the first step towards moving NetView beyond strictly hierarchical network management. LU 6.2, which is discussed in detail in Chapter 7, allows for cooperative processing–based network management. LU 6.2 can be used for peer-to-peer communications between both host and nonhost systems. The significance of moving SNA network management from being SSCP-based to LU 6.2–based is explored more fully below in the section on AS/400 network management.

NETVIEW

NetView is IBM's primary host-based network management product. NetView runs under the MVS and VM operating systems. It is an integrated network management product that originally integrated the functions provided by other IBM network management products. These earlier products included the Network Communications Control Facility (NCCF), Network Problem Determination Aid (NPDA), and Network Logical Data Manager (NLDM).

Some of IBM's goals in combining these separate products into a single NetView package were to provide a more consistent user interface for all network management functions (each product had its own interface), make it easier to move from product to product, and provide better integration of functions and ensure that all are at equivalent levels of support.

NetView consists of a number of "facilities" that address different aspects and requirements for network management. The NetView facilities include:

> Command Facility
> Session Monitor Facility
> Hardware Monitor Facility
> Status Monitor Facility
> Help Desk Facility
> Browse Facility
> Service Point Command Service Facility
> Graphic Monitor Facility

NetView's Command Facility was an enhanced version of the older NCCF product. It included all NCCF's functions plus additional support that IBM added. The Command Facility provides the base support for other NetView facilities and also provides network operator support. Some services provided by the Command

Facility are logging and routing of messages, display of messages, database access, and operator command interface.

The Session Monitor Facility provides SNA response time monitoring, session configuration, and session-level diagnostic services. It was an enhancement to the NLDM product. With this facility, information about SNA sessions can be collected which aid in identifying session-level problems such as sessions that are hung or messages that are lost.

NetView's Hardware Monitor Facility is an enhanced version of NPDA. It is used to collect and interpret information about errors that have been detected in the network and it can be used to collect statistical information as well. This information can come from hardware or software components in the network. The Hardware Monitor also provides an alert management facility. This facility monitors alert messages and automatically notifies the network operator when error thresholds are exceeded. The Hardware Monitor Facility also provides recommended actions to find and fix problems in the network.

The NetView Status Monitor Facility can be used to display the status of components in the network. It can present a full-screen panel display of the status of a domain under the control of a network operator. It can also provide a view of the status of various groups of network resources in a hierarchical panel structure. For example, the operator can view all NCPs in the domain, followed by a view of all lines on a specific NCP, followed by all PUs on a particular line, and so on. Automatic updating of status changes is provided.

A critical message monitor relieves the operator of having to monitor all network messages continuously. The Status Monitor can filter all messages and highlight those that are critical. An indication can then be given to the operator that a critical message is pending.

The Help Desk Facility provides an easy-to-use, step-by-step method of isolating problems in the network. It guides network help desk operators in a structured manner to assist them better in diagnosing and solving problems reported by users in the network. Customizing facilities allow the Help Desk to be customized to a user's particular requirements. It provides support for problems associated with terminals not working, transactions or applications not working, slow response time, and others.

The Browse Facility allows operators to browse through message logs, installation files, CLISTS, and other information.

The Service Point Command Service Facility allows network management commands to be sent to service points in the network. For example, network management commands can be sent from NetView, a focal point, to a service point such as NetView/PC.

NetView's Graphic Monitor Facility provides a graphics-oriented user interface to NetView. Multilevel or hierarchical view sets of the network are supported. Network operators can navigate down from global views of the entire network, to different segments of the network (e.g., regions or sites), to individual NCPs and peripheral node PU type resources.

The Graphic Monitor Facility is a cooperative processing application that requires an OS/2 EE-based PS/2 workstation. Workstation users using the graphics views augmented with color-coded status can see the "network-at-a-glance." Real-time events can be detected and correlated with associated resources.

The NetView Installation Facility provides an interactive dialog capability that can be used to define network parameters and execute NetView installation jobs. Its use will reduce the time it takes to install NetView on a system.

NetView is an SAA product participant. It implements support for the SNA/MS component of SAA's CCS element in the SAA MVS and VM operating environments. In particular, NetView implements many of the focal point facilities defined by the network management architecture. NetView, therefore, is IBM's primary network management focal point product for the mainframe SAA environments.

DECENTRALIZED NETWORK MANAGEMENT

Almost all discussions about SNA network management seem to assume the presence of an IBM mainframe running IBM's NetView software. While the mainframe is and will continue to be the primary network management platform in very large SNA networks, there is a growing need to provide more sophisticated management capabilities in networks that support personal computers and midrange multi-user systems. These distributed networks may not have any need for an IBM mainframe, but they certainly do need a comprehensive network management system.

IBM's leading-edge solution to this problem is the AS/400 and its network management support. The network management support provided on the AS/400, which is one of the major SAA platforms, may be a good indication of IBM's future direction in managing highly distributed networks.

While the network management support provided by NetView still reflects much of its mainframe-oriented, hierarchical heritage, the network management software on the AS/400 was designed from the ground up to support truly distributed networking of intelligent systems. For this reason, the current implementation of network management on the AS/400 gives some clues as to how IBM's network management strategy will evolve to support the evolutionary migration from hierarchical to distributed SNA networking.

THE EVOLUTION OF SNA'S NETWORK MANAGEMENT ENVIRONMENT

For most of its history, the configuration of SNA networks has revolved around IBM mainframe computers. These networks were designed for a single purpose—to connect dumb terminals (usually 3270s or lookalikes) to mainframes. These dumb terminals relied totally on the mainframe for application processing power. Since the presence of a mainframe was a given in these networks, it made sense to position the mainframe as the source for network management services. IBM's strategic mainframe-based network management software continues to be Net-View and its associated software products.

Over the years, however, IBM's customers began to distribute the application processing power from the mainframe to intelligent remote systems like multi-user departmental processors and personal computers. Virtually all large SNA networks still have one or more mainframes that provide application processing and database services to the distributed systems, but the trend is clearly toward more and more independence from the mainframe. The question is—how is IBM addressing these changing requirements within NetView and other products that do not reside on IBM mainframes?

NEW NETWORK MANAGEMENT REQUIREMENTS
FOR DISTRIBUTED NETWORKS

Let's look at some areas in which SNA's hierarchical network management approach is deficient for more distributed networks. The original concept of centralized network control revolved around SNA's System Services Control Point (SSCP), as indicated earlier. The SSCP is the element of a hierarchical SNA network that supports the network management software.

The mainframe software, like NetView, that implements network management services controls network resources by communicating with remote systems through the SSCP. Figure 10-8 shows how the SSCP is logically connected to the remote systems it controls.

The SSCP communicates with Logical Units (LUs) and Physical Units (PUs) in each of the distributed systems it controls. The SSCP-LU sessions support the

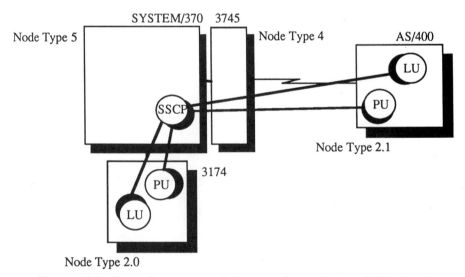

Figure 10-8. *Network management data is exchanged across SSCP-based sessions.*

connection of end users to host-based applications via logon and logoff procedures. The SSCP-PU sessions are the conduits through which network management commands like alerts and resource activation commands are exchanged. These SSCP sessions form a data transport network within the overall SNA network which is dedicated to network management functions. While these SSCP sessions are used to support network mangement functions, end users of the SNA network communicate via Logical Unit–to–Logical Unit sessions. This structure has been used for all host-connected SNA devices like 3270s.

This scheme works for networks where cluster controllers are directly connected to SNA hosts, but it breaks down as cluster controllers are connected with each other in peer-to-peer configurations. The problem is that these SSCP sessions were never designed to allow routing through intermediate cluster controller nodes which is a requirement in many peer-coupled networks. As indicated above, NetView's LU 6.2 support is the first step towards solving this problem.

The SNA host-oriented network management approach also, obviously, breaks down in peer-coupled networks where there is no SNA host present—no mainframe. The static definitions of network resources that have traditionally been supported by mainframe SNA software like VTAM also become a problem in decentralized networks where reconfiguration is a daily occurrence.

IBM's general solution to these problems, which is currently implemented on the AS/400 system, is to exploit SNA technologies that are more suited to functioning in a peer-coupled network. These technologies are:

> Advanced Program-to-Program Communication (APPC) (Logical Unit Type 6.2)
> Advanced Peer-to-Peer Networking (APPN)

These, of course, are the same technologies being used to support end-user–to–end-user communications in peer-coupled SNA networks. APPC (Logical Unit Type 6.2) provides peer-to-peer session-level connections between network users, while APPN provides the network routing and dynamic reconfiguration capabilities required to support networks of peer-coupled systems. APPC/LU 6.2, which is a key SAA component, is discussed in detail in Chapter 7 while APPN, which is built on LU 6.2 and Node Type 2.1 (another key SAA component), is discussed in detail along with Node Type 2.1 in Chapter 8.

One of the key advantages of IBM's APPN networking technology is its ability to perform true, dynamic network reconfiguration. This capability becomes more important every day. New technologies like local area networks and personal computers promote easy reconfiguration of the physical network, while APPN adds the same flexibility to the logical configuration of the network.

One piece of the dynamic networking puzzle that has been missing is network management—more specifically, the issues of how network management systems can keep up with networks whose configurations may change, literally, minute-by-minute. In order to provide network management data flows that are as dynamic as end-user connections, IBM is adopting the APPC and APPN technologies to form the foundation of the network management system.

The AS/400 uses Logical Unit Type 6.2/APPC sessions for both end-user–to–end-user communications as well as network management functions. Figure 10-9 shows how the SSCP network management sessions are replaced by Logical Unit Type 6.2 sessions in networks of AS/400s.

The LU Type 6.2 sessions shown in Figure 10-9 are interconnecting components of the AS/400s, which are known as Control Points. Each AS/400 that supports APPC/APPN has a Control Point that performs network management functions. These Control Points are, in a sense, replacements for the SSCPs that were used to control hierarchical SNA networks. They are the software components of the AS/400 that create, interchange, and act on network management commands.

These Control Points exist in all AS/400s that use APPC/APPN. This results in a completely decentralized network management configuration. However, total decentralization is frequently undesirable. Most networks are designed to funnel information about errors and exception conditions to one or more network management centers that are staffed by trained network operations personnel. This ensures that these exception conditions are logged and handled properly without requiring the presence of network operators at each remote site.

Control of these AS/400 networks can be centralized to any degree required by declaring that one or more control points act as network management Focal Points. As discussed, a Focal Point is a network node to which network alerts are forwarded by the network node that detects and reports problems. The role of these Focal Points is defined by IBM's SNA/Management Services (SNA/MS) architecture, which is described above.

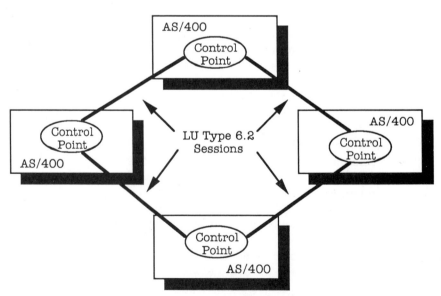

Figure 10-9. *AS/400 Control Points use LU 6.2 sessions to exchange network management data.*

ALERT HANDLING IN AS/400 NETWORKS

One of the most important network management functions in the SNA network is the handling of network alerts. Remember that an alert is an architected SNA message that provides notification of the actual or impending loss of availability of some network resource. The alerts also carry information designed to aid in the analysis and correction of the problem. This usually includes information about the probable cause of the problem and even suggested corrective measures to be taken.

In traditional hierarchical SNA networks the handling of alerts is, not surprisingly, highly hierarchical. In these networks, SNA hosts running Net-View process alerts generated by all the other hardware and software components of the network. This processing typically includes the display of the alert to network operators, logging of the alerts in NetView databases, and automatic programmed responses to the exception conditions. In short, the SNA host(s) in these hierarchical networks is always the active network manager, while all other components of the network simply report exception conditions and respond to commands from the SNA host.

How does a network of peers, like the AS/400, handle alerts? Is there centralized management with the equivalent of an SNA network management host, or is there no management hierarchy at all? The answer is that either extreme case, or anything in between, is possible. The creation of a network management hierarchy, if any, in AS/400 networks is at the discretion of the network designers and managers.

There are three general roles the AS/400 can assume in a peer-coupled network:

It can send its alerts to a Focal Point for processing.
It can act as the Focal Point for systems that are attached to it.
It can act as a nested Focal Point which relays alerts to another Focal Point (which could be NetView) in the network.

FLEXIBILITY FOR THE NETWORK DESIGNER

The network designer has various options on the AS/400 that can be used in combination with one another to engineer a network management system that is centralized, decentralized, or any combination in between. In addition, these options can be used to allow the network management system to react dynamically to changes in the configuration of the network.

These network management options for the AS/400 fall into two major categories:

Definitions of how alerts are processed on each of the individual AS/400 systems
Rules that direct the forwarding and routing of alerts from system to system within the network

By using these options, the network designer can define the locations within the network where alerts will be sent and processed, that is, the Focal Points. These AS/400 Focal Points are similar in function to NetView within hierarchical SNA networks. The AS/400 network designer can also decide how the alerts will be processed after they arrive at a Focal Point. Some Focal Points may display alerts to a local operator who will initiate corrective action while other unattended Focal Points may simply log the alerts or forward them to still other Focal Points for processing.

AS/400 ALERT PROCESSING OPTIONS

On each AS/400, the network designer can specify the following options for generating and processing network alerts:

> Create alerts to report system-detected problems.
> Log alerts that have been created by the local system or other systems in the network.
> Display alerts that have been logged in the alert database.

All AS/400 messages can optionally generate an alert which can be sent to a network Focal Point. The network designers can therefore decide which messages have significance to only the local system operator and which should be forwarded to other network nodes. There is also an option for creating alerts for certain events only when the system on which the event occurred is operating in unattended mode.

It is particularly significant that any AS/400 system message can cause an alert to be generated. This fact redefines the whole concept of network management to include not only network operation problems like line, modem, and protocol errors, but also the entire operation of distributed AS/400s. What is being supported here is a management system for geographically dispersed data center operations. This is a requirement for controlling distributed data processing.

ROUTING OF NETWORK MANAGEMENT INFORMATION

The other key to managing these new peer-coupled networks of AS/400s is to ensure that alerts are routed to their proper Focal Points for processing. This is more of a challenge in networks, like those of AS/400s, whose configurations are much more dynamic than those of the traditional mainframe-centered SNA networks.

Some of the alert routing configuration options that the AS/400 supports include:

> Send locally created alerts to a Focal Point. (Initiate transmission of an alert.)

Receive alerts created by other systems and forward them to a Focal Point. (Relay alerts generated by other AS/400s to a Focal Point.) Hold alerts until they can be forwarded to a Focal Point. (Act as a store-and-forward node.)

The network designer can control the creation of alerts on each AS/400. Any local AS/400 can be made to result in an alert. The designer can, therefore, determine the types of messages that will have only local significance and those that will be sent to a remote Focal Point.

AS/400 systems can also be configured to relay alerts that have been received from other systems to a remote Focal Point. AS/400s can also, optionally, store alerts that are to be forwarded to remote Focal Points for later transmission. The use of this feature will allow alerts to be sent to Focal Points that might not always be active or have an active communications path available. This store-and-forward capability is particularly important in networks where resources are dynamically activated and deactivated.

All these features can be used to control the routing of alerts between the originating nodes and the Focal Points that will process the alerts. But, how do the AS/400 systems determine which Focal Points the alerts should be sent to in the first place? That's the role of the AS/400's concept of sphere of control.

DEFINING SPHERES OF CONTROL FOR FOCAL POINTS

Just as the Physical Units and Logical Units of network nodes are "owned by" or in session with a host-based Focal Point (the SSCP), AS/400 systems are logically associated with their controlling Focal Point(s) by defining what are known as spheres of control. Figure 10-10 shows how spheres of control can be used to direct alerts to the proper target Focal Point for processing.

In this sample network of AS/400s, there are three spheres of control. Each sphere of control is defined by a Focal Point and all the AS/400 systems that forward their alerts to that Focal Point.

The AS/400 that contains Focal Point C has one remote AS/400 in its sphere of control, while the AS/400 that contains Focal Point B supports two downstream AS/400s. In order to designate an AS/400 as being the sphere of control of a particular Focal Point, only the Focal Point needs to be configured and it maintains a list of all remote systems within its sphere of control. This simplifies the configuration of the network because it eliminates the need to configure each individual AS/400 with information about its network management Focal Point.

Instead, the Focal Points dynamically start sessions with the remote systems in their sphere of control. The Focal Points "take control" of the systems they manage at network start-up time and whenever new remote systems are added to their sphere of control.

The systems containing Focal Points A and B are both in the same sphere of

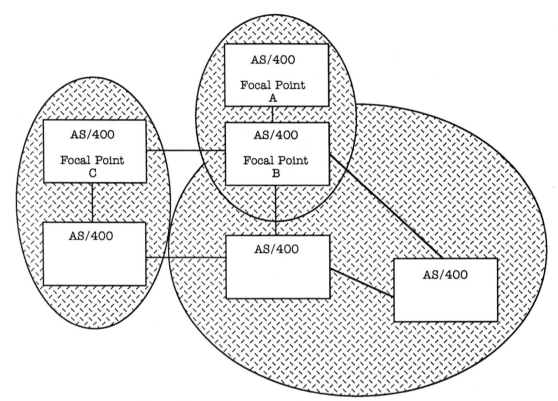

Figure 10-10. *AS/400 network management spheres of control.*

control. This is an example of nested Focal Points, where one Focal Point is in the sphere of control of another Focal Point. A nested Focal Point forwards all alerts that it has received to its Focal Point. This means the alerts received by Focal Point B are forwarded to Focal Point A because B is within A's sphere of control. Focal Point C is the final destination of alerts received because it is not in the sphere of control of any other Focal Point.

Nested Focal Points provide a vehicle for concentrating the flow of alerts within a network of AS/400s. The nesting of Focal Points has both advantages and disadvantages.

> Advantages
>> Reduces the path length between systems and their Focal Points, which results in greater reliability
>> Distributes the processing management services functions across a greater number of systems to reduce system loads
>
> Disadvantage
>> Sphere of control management involves a greater number of systems, which complicates configuration management

HOW DYNAMIC RECONFIGURATION IS ACCOMMODATED

To add further flexibility to the AS/400 network management scheme, the network designer may designate Focal Points within the network as either Primary Focal Points or Default Focal Points. These two types of Focal Points work together to support both the ability to control tightly the flow of alerts within the network and to respond to changes in network configuration dynamically, without requiring intervention from the network operations staff.

Primary Focal Points receive alerts from systems that have been explicitly defined to be in its sphere of control. A Default Focal Point receives alerts from any systems in that network that do not currently have a Primary Focal Point.

The networks, or portions of networks, whose configurations remain fairly static rely on Primary Focal Points for control. The network operations staff configures these Primary Focal Points with the explicit lists of all nodes they control. This provides a highly structured flow of network management information to the network operators that would be located at the Focal Point nodes.

What happens when a new node is connected into the network? Is it unable to forward alerts to a network management Focal Point until the Focal Point is reconfigured? This is where the Default Focal Point comes into play.

If the network is initially configured with one or more Default Focal Points, any alerts sent from network nodes that are not explicitly configured to be within the sphere of control of a Primary Focal Point will go to a Default Focal Point. The presence of a default Focal Point ensures that, even in a network that is being dynamically reconfigured, alerts will always be sent to nodes that can respond to exception conditions or, at least, write the alerts to a log file.

If a highly structured flow of network management information is desired, the network operations staff can, at some later time, reconfigure one or more of the network's Focal Points to include the newly connected nodes within their sphere of control.

Another possible network management configuration would be a situation where one of the AS/400s in the network would be designated as the Default Focal Point for the entire network. In this situation, no explicit spheres of control would need to be defined. This approach would eliminate the need to perform any manual reconfiguration for network management purposes. Any new nodes joining the network would automatically send their alert to the Default Focal Point.

THE MAINFRAME CAN STILL PARTICIPATE
IN NETWORK MANAGEMENT

The discussion up to this point has focused on the management of networks that are made up only of AS/400 systems. This does not imply that the AS/400's network management scheme and the traditional SNA NetView environment are mutually exclusive. In fact, they are likely to be used in combination with one another in large SNA networks.

In situations where a group of AS/400 systems are configured as a subnetwork with a larger mainframe-based, hierarchical SNA network, the AS/400s can be managed by a hybrid mainframe-AS/400 network management system. From an SNA architectural point of view, this would mean that Focal Points on both the AS/400s and within NetView on the SNA host would cooperate to manage the network. Some of the AS/400s within the subnetwork might be controlled by Focal Points on one or more AS/400s while others might send their alerts to NetView for processing. The routing of alerts to NetView might be accomplished through the use of nested Focal Points where AS/400 systems act as remote network management concentrators that, in turn, funnel the alerts they have received to NetView.

AS/400 DOES NOT YET PROVIDE "COMPLETE" NETWORK MANAGEMENT

One of the reasons for continuing to use NetView in conjunction with AS/400 systems is the fact that the AS/400 does not yet provide the range of network management functions that are included within NetView and its associated mainframe products.

For example, the AS/400 is not capable of providing network management functions for the kinds of mixed-technology, multivendor networks common in large organizations today. While the AS/400 is in many ways a leading-edge IBM network management product, it has severe shortcomings in its current lack of ability to manage systems other than AS/400s.

Some IBM products, like System/36s and System/38s, can be configured to send alerts into AS/400-based Focal Points, but these configurations cannot take advantage of features such as the use of Default Focal Points and they cannot be configured as a member of a Primary Focal Point's sphere of control. Each System/36 or System/38 must be individually configured to send its alerts to an AS/400 Focal Point.

The AS/400 also does not support the broad scope of network management functions present in NetView. Although it does support SNA/MS alert processing, which is the foundation of problem determination and resolution in distributed networks, alert processing is only one aspect of the total network management picture. Other key elements of network management include:

> Performance measurement
> Management of remote software and data distribution
> Operations of remote systems
> Problem tracking
> Configuration management and change management

While IBM's mainframe-based NetView software addresses all these issues, the AS/400 either does not provide equivalent support or, in some cases, it provides such support only for homogeneous networks of AS/400s and not generalized cross-product solutions.

SUMMARY OF AS/400 NETWORK MANAGEMENT TRENDS

The AS/400's network management support is important because it offers some important insights into IBM's directions in the area of network management. These directions will influence both users and manufacturers of any systems that operate in SNA networks.

The use of APPC/LU 6.2 sessions to move network management data is one of the most important directions. While SSCP sessions will continue to be used in existing products for the foreseeable future, expect to see the use of APPC/LU 6.2 sessions for network management to spread throughout the IBM product lines. An example of this is IBM's NetView Distribution Manager's use of LU 6.2 and SNA/DS to implement configuration management and software distribution for the 3174 controller.

The value of using LU 6.2 for network management data flows is multiplied by its use in conjunction with APPN. The dynamic reconfiguration capability of APPN means the network management system will have the configuration flexibility required for modern decentralized networks.

The AS/400's network management software also reflects the industry trend toward true distributed or cooperative processing, which is what SAA is all about. As indicated in the discussion on AS/400 alert processing, any or all system messages that originate on the AS/400 can generate alerts that are forwarded through the network. This means that the alert processing system is capable of handling not only traditional communications problems, but also application-related alerts. The AS/400 is focusing on the management of a geographically dispersed data center, not just networking problems. These and other networking features of the AS/400 will find their way into other IBM and non-IBM communications products.

SYSTEMVIEW

IBM has broadened its systems management strategy to encompass enterprise-wide information systems management. This is addressed by IBM's SystemView structure and a variety of SystemView conforming products. SystemView is the SAA strategy for managing enterprise information systems.

SystemView is structured into three major areas called dimensions. These dimensions define the guidelines, specifications, standards, and interfaces that will be used for integrating systems management applications. Thus, they form the framework for developing systems management applications. SystemView consists of the following dimensions: end-use dimension, application dimension, and data dimension. The end-use dimension serves a similar purpose to SAA's Common User Access (CUA) element. The end-use dimension addresses the user interface provided by systems management application programs. The intent is for such applications to provide a consistent end-user interface that is "user friendly."

The application dimension is similar to SAA's Common Programming Interface (CPI) element. It addresses the implementation and integration of systems management application programs. The application dimension consists of guidelines that developers will follow in developing systems management applications in order to bring consistency to such applications and allow them to be integrated within an enterprise.

The data dimension is targeted at standardizing data definitions and the access to this data. This will allow data to be consistently defined, exchanged, and shared among systems management applications and users.

Let's look at each of these areas in more detail.

End-Use Dimension

The primary purpose of the end-use dimension is to provide a consistent user interface in SystemView applications. This will make it easier to use and learn different SystemView applications. The result should be increased user productivity and performance. The users of different SystemView products will include operators, system administrators, analysts, system programmers, and others that may be involved in systems management tasks.

This is similar to the purpose of SAA's CUA element. In fact, the SystemView end-use dimension supports an SAA CUA Graphical Model interface on programmable workstations. With the CUA Graphical Model, applications are presented as objects and actions on those objects. Providing a consistent user interface across applications should make it easier to learn and use different SystemView applications. SystemView applications will have the same look and feel and the user interface will also provide transparent access to other systems management applications and resources in the network.

The SystemView user interface conforms to SAA CUA guidelines. It assumes a programmable workstation is being used for systems management tasks. Actually, multiple user interfaces are included as part of the end-use dimension. Developers have their choice as to the type of interface to provide in their application.

OS/2 is the workstation platform that supports the SystemView end-use dimension. OS/2's Presentation Manager and Dialog Manager are used by SystemView applications running under OS/2 to provide an end-user interface consistent with SystemView's end-use definition and SAA CUA specifications.

Application Dimension

The application dimension focuses on the development and integration of SystemView applications. It defines various interfaces and services used to support the different tasks and applications. SystemView's application dimension groups tasks into management areas called disciplines. The SystemView application definition includes the following disciplines:

> Business Management
> Change Management

Configuration Management
Operations Management
Performance Management
Problem Management

As you can see, each of these disciplines addresses a different area of systems management. Functions that fall under the Business Management discipline include business planning, financial administration, inventory management, and other enterprise-wide management services.

As its name implies, the Change Management discipline deals with changes made to the enterprise-information system. This category covers changes to plans and schedules and includes change tracking facilities.

The Configuration Management discipline addresses the physical and logical configurations of the enterprise-information system. It manages the relationships among resources such as connections and dependencies of resources.

Operations Management focuses on the operational aspects of managing the network. This includes facilities to manage the use of systems and resources to support the enterprise-information-processing workloads.

The Performance Management discipline is targeted at capacity planning, collecting performance data, and tuning the network.

The Problem Management discipline is geared towards detecting, analyzing, correcting, and tracking problems in the information systems operations.

The application dimension will also conform to existing ISO/IEC standards. These include Common Management Information Services (CMIS) (ISO/IEC 9595) and Common Management Information Protocol (CMIP) (ISO/IEC 9596).

Data Dimension

The Data Dimension is targeted at bringing consistency to data definition and access. Specifically, an objective is to allow data sharing of systems management data among various systems management applications. This will reduce duplicating the same input data by multiple applications. A goal of this dimension will be to generate input data automatically as much as possible. This will eliminate the need for manual input, which should improve efficiency and reduce errors.

The Data Dimension defines an architected set of data definitions and database facilities for systems management applications. The definitions will be for systems management resources as well as for the relationships among resources.

A SystemView Data Model will specify data definitions that represent the information-processing resources of an enterprise. IBM's intent is that this data model will be consistent with related industry standards. These include the ISO/IEC 10165-4, Guidelines for the Definition of Managed Objects, and ISO/IEC 10165-1, Management Information Model.

SystemView management data defined as part of the data dimension will be stored in a relational database using SQL, the SAA CPI Database Interface. SystemView products that support the data dimension (e.g., SAA Asset Manager, SAA Delivery Manager) will utilize the SystemView Data Model for defining management data and will use SQL for storing and retrieving this information to/from relational databases managed by SAA relational database management systems such as DB2.

The combination of modeled data and architected interfaces will allow more consistency across systems management applications and greater integration of these applications.

SYSTEMVIEW AND SAA

SystemView relates to SAA in a number of ways. Foremost is the fact that SystemView is the SAA strategy for managing enterprise-information systems. As such, SystemView applications will span the SAA operating environments. SystemView support, therefore, will be available in MVS/ESA, VM/ESA, OS/400, and OS/2 Extended Edition.

SystemView applications will conform to SAA specifications and use SAA components. As an example, these applications will provide an end-user interface that conforms to SAA's Common User Access (CUA) guidelines. The consistent user interfaces to be provided by SystemView applications will also conform to SystemView's end-use dimension, as indicated above.

SystemView applications will also use SAA CPI components and interfaces. For example, systems management data storage and retrieval will be done using the SAA CPI Database Interface, which is SQL. In addition, communication between SystemView applications will be based on SAA CCS components and protocols.

SUMMARY

The area of network management is becoming more and more of a concern to companies with large networks in place. As the networks grow in size and complexity they become increasingly more difficult to manage. As resources are distributed throughout the network, the complexity of network management grows as well.

IBM has formally architected how network management services will be provided in SNA-based networks. The SNA/Management Services (SNA/MS) architecture is included within the Application Services category of SAA's Common Communications Support (CCS) element.

IBM's approach to network management is centralized management with distributed intelligence. Most networks still make use of SSCP-to-PU sessions for network management although this will change in the future towards wider use of LU 6.2 sessions for network management.

part 4

SAA IN THE FUTURE

11

SAA Futures

SAA has been steadily evolving since its introduction in 1987. This trend will continue through the 1990s. The evolution of SAA will be driven by new technologies and the requirements of IBM's customers who are designing and implementing new SAA applications.

Another important dimension of SAA still in its infancy is SAA support on application platforms from vendors other than IBM. Just as SNA became an industry standard in the 1980s, SAA's influence will expand beyond the IBM product line in the 1990s.

EVOLUTION OF COMMON USER ACCESS

Current CUA interfaces are designed to support the workstations in widespread use today. This workstation is evolving rapidly to include new graphics capabilities including higher resolutions.

The new technology that will have the greatest impact on CUA is multimedia. As multimedia workstations and personal computers come into widespread use, CUA will be enhanced to include standards not only for still graphics, but for animation and full-motion video. These multimedia workstations will also include support for CD-ROM storage devices, as well as sound and touchscreen support to enhance the user interface.

As intelligent workstations continue to displace the nonprogrammable 3270 and 5250 terminals now widely used by IBM customers, there will be greater usage of the the CUA Graphical and Workplace models. Many applications that currently claim CUA compliance are designed to meet the requirements of CUA's low-end Entry and Text Subset models. As SAA and UNIX platforms continue to coexist in cooperative-processing networks, it will also become more common to see UNIX workstations becoming the intelligent workstations that support SAA host applications.

EVOLUTION OF THE COMMON PROGRAMMING INTERFACE

While the CPI definition already includes support for most of the popular programming languages currently used by IBM customers, it is notably lacking in support for more specialized languages. These would include languages to support artificial intelligence and knowledge-based applications.

The field of object-oriented programming is also not directly addressed by current CPI standards. Tools and languages for building object-oriented applications are required to support the iconic CUA Workplace Extensions user interface.

The problem IBM currently faces in standardizing on both artificial intelligence and object-oriented programming languages is that these areas of technology are still in their infancy and are highly fragmented. This situation makes it difficult to make a commitment to any particular language or technology. IBM is currently working with its business partners and in joint ventures in developing the next generation of technologies in these areas. A good example of such a joint effort is IBM's participation with Metaphor Computer Systems in Patriot Partners, which is designing a platform-independent environment for the development of object-oriented applications. The results of efforts like this could eventually become a part of SAA's Common Programming Interface.

EVOLUTION OF COMMON COMMUNICATIONS SUPPORT

IBM has included in SAA's CCS element OSI-based application services such as FTAM for remote file access and X.400 for electronic mail. IBM will also support the OSI transaction-processing standard. This support will provide the OSI counterpart for the APPC support that is driven by the CPI Communications interface. In fact, IBM's objective is to allow programmers to use the CPIC programming interface to communicate over either the SNA or OSI protocol stacks.

It is also likely that IBM will include new communications technologies like the FDDI standard for high-speed fiber optic LANs. The functional layering of the SAA CCS model and that of the SNA and OSI protocol stacks that implement CCS will ensure that new technologies can be adopted without disrupting the use of existing CCS technologies.

The area of network management in SAA is also evolving rapidly. In the early days of SAA, IBM relied on the network management services provided within SNA. The traditional SNA view of network management was too narrow and, therefore, IBM has introduced its SystemView architecture. SystemView broadens the scope of network management to include all the issues involved in managing networks that support cooperative processing. These include the management of the distributed resources like application programs and databases. Over the next few years IBM will have to make major product enhancements to fulfill the promise of its SystemView architecture.

DISTRIBUTED DATABASE SUPPORT

The current SAA distributed database support includes remote request and remote unit-of-work levels of access. In the future, IBM will add support for the distributed unit of work. This level of access allows an application to coordinate the update of multiple remote databases and to provide integrity in case of a failure. Within the distributed unit of work there is a one-for-one relationship between requests and remote locations.

Further down the road, IBM will support the distributed request definition, which extends flexibility by allowing a single request to act on multiple remote databases.

SUPPORT FOR EVOLVING INDUSTRY STANDARDS

In addition to its own technologies, IBM is likely to include support within SAA for significant industry standards. An example of such support that IBM is already committed to is an SAA remote procedure call capability which will be compatible with that defined by the Open Software Foundation. These types of additions to SAA will result in an increased level of interoperability between SAA and systems based on the evolving open-systems environments.

SAA ADD-ON PRODUCTS FROM VENDORS OTHER THAN IBM

While IBM can be expected to be the primary supplier of the enabling software required to implement SAA, it is likely other vendors will provide products that will add value to the SAA environment in various ways.

A current example of this type of strategy is the Easel product produced by Interactive Images, Inc. and jointly marketed with IBM. The Easel product makes it easy to implement graphic CUA interfaces for existing applications that predate SAA. The Easel software runs on personal computers and users can design new user interfaces via a high-level scripting language. Existing applications can therefore implement the SAA distributed dialog model of cooperative processing without making any changes to existing mainframe-based applications.

SAA MAY ACHIEVE SOME LEVEL OF VENDOR INDEPENDENCE

There is a possibility that SAA support will achieve the critical mass needed to make it a standard for non-IBM application platforms. This means other vendors would implement major portions of CUA, CPI, and CCS on their systems. These systems could use either proprietary operating systems or be built on industry standards such as UNIX. This would be similar to the level of support achieved by IBM SNA during the 1980s.

Whether SAA remains a standard only for IBM platforms or becomes a multivendor application platform standard, it will continue to have an important impact on the computer industry of the 1990s.

$\overline{\mathbf{A}}$

SAA Product Summary

	SAA Operating Environment			
	MVS/ESA	**VM/ESA**	**OS/400**	**OS/2 EE**
CUA				
CUA Models:				
Entry	ISPF	ISPF	OS/400	—
Graphical	—	—	—	OS/2 PM
Text Subset	ISPF	ISPF	—	—
Workplace	—	—	—	OV/2
CPI				
Languages:				
C	C/370	C/370	C/400	C/2
COBOL	VS COBOL II	VS COBOL II	COBOL/400	COBOL/2
FORTRAN	VS FORTRAN	VS FORTRAN	FORTRAN/400	FORTRAN/2
RPG	RPG/370	RPG/370	RPG/400	—
PL/I	OS PL/I	OS PL/I	AS/400 PL/I	—
Application Generator	CSP	CSP	CSP	EZ-RUN
Procedures Language	REXX	REXX	400/REXX	2/REXX
Services:				
Presentation	GDDM	GDDM	OS/400	OS/2 PM
Dialog	ISPF	ISPF	—	OS/2 DM
Database	DB 2	SQL/DS	SQL/400	OS/2 DBM
Query	QMF	QMF	—	OS/2 QM
Communications	APPC/MVS	VM/ESA	OS/400	OS/2 CM

	SAA Operating Environment			
	MVS/ESA	**VM/ESA**	**OS/400**	**OS/2 EE**
Repository	Repository Manager/MVS	—	—	—
Resource Recovery	IMS/ESA	VM/ESA	—	—
PrintManager	PrtMgr/MVS	PrtMgr/VM	PrtMgr/400	—
CCS				
Objects:				
PTOCA	DW/370	DW/370	—	—
GOCA	DW/370 GDDM	DW/370 GDDM	OS/400	OS/2 EE
IOCA	DW/370 GDDM	DW/370 GDDM	OS/400	OS/2 EE
FDOCA	DB2	SQL/DS	OS/400	OS/2 EE
FOCA	PrtMgr/MVS	—	—	—
Data Streams:				
3270 DS	TSO/E,CICS IMS, GDDM	CMS, GDDM	OS/400	OS/2 CM
RFT:DCA	OV/MVS	OV/VM	OV/400	OV/2
IPDS	GDDM, PSF	GDDM	OS/400	—
MO:DCA	ImagePlus	—	OS/400	OS/2 EE
CDRA	DB2	SQL/DS	OS/400	OS/2 DBM
SNA Application Services:				
DIA	OV/MVS	OV/VM	OV/400	OV/2
SNA/DS	DISOSS	—	OS/400	—
DDM	DDM/CICS	DDM/CICS	OS/400	—
SNA/MS	NetView VTAM	NetView VTAM	OS/400	OS/2 CM
DRDA	DB2	SQL/DS	OS/400	OS/2 DBM
SNA Session Services:				
LU 6.2	VTAM	VTAM	OS/400	OS/2 CM
SNA Network:				
LEN End Node	NCP, VTAM	NCP, VTAM	OS/400	OS/2 CM
APPN End Node			OS/400	SAA NS/2
SNA Data Link Controls:				
SDLC	NCP, VTAM	NCP, VTAM	OS/400	OS/2 CM
Token-Ring	NCP, VTAM	NCP, VTAM	OS/400	OS/2 CM
X.25	NPSI	NPSI	OS/400	OS/2 CM
OSI Application Services:				
FTAM	OSI/FS	OSI/FS	OSI FS/400	OSI FS/2
X.400	ONDS	ONDS	OSI MS/400	—

	SAA Operating Environment			
	MVS/ESA	**VM/ESA**	**OS/400**	**OS/2 EE**
OSI Session Services:				
Transport, Session, and Presentation Layer	OSI/CS	OSI/CS	OSI CS/400	OSI CS OS/2
OSI Network:				
Network Layer	OSI/CS	OSI/CS	OSI CS/400	OSI CS OS/2
OSI Data Link Controls:				
X.25	NCP/NPSI	NCP/NPSI	OS/400	OS/2 EE
ISO 8802-2 LLC	OSI/CS	OSI/CS	OSI CS/400	OSI CS/2
ISO 8802-3	OSI/CS	OSI/CS	OSI CS/400	OSI CS/2
ISO 8802-5	—	—	OSI CS/400	OSI CS/2

B

Summary of IBM SAA Publications

AIX Family Definition Overview	GC23-2002
An Introduction to APPC	GG24-1584
Architectures for Object Interchange	GG24-3296
Common User Access: Panel Design and User Interaction	SC26-4351
CUA 1989 Evaluation	GG24-3456
DDM Architecture: Implementation Planner's Guide	SC21-9528
DDM Architecture: Implementation Programmer's Guide	SC21-9529
DDM Level 2.0 Architecture: General Information Manual	GC21-9527
DDM Level 2.0 Architecture Reference	SC21-9526
DIA Interchange Document Profile Reference	SC23-0764
DIA Technical Reference	SC23-0787
DIA Transaction Programmer's Guide	SC23-6763
Document Content Architecture Revisable-Form-Text Reference	SC23-0758
Font Object Content Architecture Reference	S544-3285
Graphics Object Content Architecture Reference	SC31-6804
IBM Systems Journal, Vol. 27, No. 3, 1988	G321-0091
IBM Systems Journal, Vol. 29, No. 2, 1990	G321-0099
Image Object Content Architecture Reference	SC31-6805
Intelligent Printer Data Stream Reference	S544-3417
Introduction to IBM's Open Network Management	SC30-3431
Mixed Object Document Content Architecture Reference	SC31-6802
Office Information Architectures	GC23-0765
OSI Within Systems Application Architecture (SAA)	G511-1137
Presentation Text Object Content Architecture Reference	SC31-6803

Program-to-Program Communications in SAA Environments	GG24-3482
Repository Manager/MVS General Information	GC26-4608
SAA AD/Cycle Concepts	GC26-4531
SAA: A Guide for Evaluating Applications	G320-9803
SAA An Introduction	GC26-4341
SAA and LU 6.2 Considerations on CICS/MVS Applications	GG24-3295
SAA: A Value Guide	G320-9804
SAA Common Communications Support Primer	GG24-3483
SAA Common Communications Support Summary	GC31-6810
SAA CUA Advanced Interface Design Guide	SC26-4582
SAA CUA Basic Interface Design Guide	SC26-4583
SAA CUA Application Design Guidelines for CICS BMS	GG66-3115
SAA CPI Application Generator Reference	SC26-4355
SAA CPI C Reference	SC26-4353
SAA CPI COBOL Reference	SC26-4354
SAA CPI Communications Reference	SC26-4399
SAA CPI Database Reference	SC26-4348
SAA CPI Dialog Reference	SC26-4356
SAA CPI FORTRAN Reference	SC26-4357
SAA CPI Presentation Reference	SC26-4359
SAA CPI Procedures Language Reference	SC26-4358
SAA CPI Procedures Language Level 2 Reference	SC24-5549
SAA CPI Query Reference	SC26-4349
SAA CPI Repository Reference	SC26-4684
SAA CPI Resource Recovery Reference	SC31-6821
SAA CPI RPG Reference	SC09-1286
SAA CPI Summary	GC26-4675
SAA PL/I Reference	GC26-4381
SAA Portability Guidelines, Phase 1	GG24-3354
SAA: The Framework for an Enterprise Information System	G580-4005
SAA: The Key to Greater Productivity	G580-0853
SNA Concepts and Products	GC30-3072
SNA Distribution Services Reference	SC30-3098
SNA Format and Protocol Reference Manual: Architectural Logic	SC30-3112
SNA Formats	GA27-3136
SNA LU 6.2 Reference: Peer Protocols	SC31-6805
SNA Management Services Reference	SC30-3346
SNA Network of Small Systems	GG66-0216
SNA Format and Protocol Reference: LU Type 6.2	SC30-3269
SNA Technical Overview	GC30-3073
SNA Transaction Programmer's Reference Manual for LU Type 6.2	GC30-3084
SNA Type 2.1 Node Reference	SC30-3422
Synchronous Data Link Control Concepts	GA27-3093
The X.25–1984 Interface for Attaching SNA Nodes to Packet Switched Data Networks: General Information Manual	GA27-3761

Token-Ring Network Architecture Reference	SC30-3374
Writing Applications: A Design Guide	SC26-4362
Writing IMS SAA Applications: A Design Guide	GG24-3324
3270 Information Display System Data Stream Programmer's Reference	GA23-0059

C

Common Programming Interface for Communications (CPIC)

The Common Programming Interface for Communications (CPIC), which is also referred to as the Communications Interface (CI), is the standard application programming interface SAA applications will use to communicate with other application programs. CPIC is based on the LU 6.2 protocol boundary verbs described in Chapter 7.

What is different about CPIC and the LU 6.2 verbs? For one, IBM's architected set of LU 6.2 protocol boundary verbs are documented only as descriptions of the functions provided by LU 6.2. These descriptions are not at a level that is totally adequate for direct implementation. IBM did not go far enough in explicitly stating various aspects of the verbs (e.g., calling sequences, parameter and return-code values, options, etc.) which would provide for consistent implementations in all LU 6.2 products. The result is that there are not consistent implementations of these verbs in IBM's products.

CPIC, on the other hand, is an "exact" definition of how the programming interface for these functions will actually be implemented in every system that provides CPIC support, which includes every SAA environment. CPIC specifically defines the names of the CPIC "calls," the calling sequences, parameter sequences, parameter values, and return-code values. Consistent support for these will be provided in all SAA environments. This means that a single, consistent communications-programming interface can be used regardless of the environment in which an application is executing.

This, of course, is not the case with other LU 6.2 APIs, which are all different. They differ in the names of the LU 6.2 "calls" used to invoke various LU 6.2 functions, in the calling sequences, parameters, return codes, etc. CPIC clears up the confusion and provides a standard interface across SAA environments.

CPIC CONVERSATIONS

CPIC is used for communications between two programs called partner programs. The partner programs engage in a conversation with one another via the CPIC interface used by each program. As you can see, a conversation is the logical connection between a pair of programs.

Conversations between pairs of programs are actually carried out over an underlying LU-LU session. Each partner program must be represented by an LU that is local to that program's system. The pair of LUs representing the pair of programs (one LU represents one program on one system and another LU represents the other program on another system) provide the program-to-program communications support (using LU 6.2 protocols) for the communications between the programs (the conversations).

For CPIC, the LUs are Type 6.2. Before any communications can take place, the pair of LUs representing the programs must establish an SNA session with one another. The session is the logical connection between a pair of LUs. Remember that the conversation, on the other hand, is the logical connection between the programs.

This session between the pair of LUs is an LU-LU session that makes use of LU 6.2 protocols to carry out communications. It is a standard SNA LU-LU session established using an SNA BIND command and terminated using an SNA UNBIND command. Standard SNA session-level protocols such as chaining and bracketing are also used across the session.

It is important to make a clear distinction between the conversation between the partner programs using CPIC and the underlying session between the pair of LUs over which the conversation is mapped. It is also important to make a distinction between CPIC, which is a programming interface, and the SNA LU 6.2 protocols generated as a result of CPIC usage.

Programs issue CPIC calls in order to carry out a conversation with a partner program. Transparent to the programs, these calls are being serviced by the local LU for each program. The LUs, in turn, translate these CPIC calls into the appropriate SNA LU 6.2 message units and protocols which are used to communicate with the partner LU in order to support the conversation between the programs.

The underlying communications-support software could just as easily translate the CPIC program calls into something other than SNA LU 6.2 protocols. For example, it could translate the calls into OSI protocols for communicating with remote systems connected via an OSI-based network.

The fact that OSI protocols were being used as opposed to SNA LU 6.2 protocols would be transparent to the application programs. The CPIC interface masks the underlying communications and networking support from the applications. IBM does not yet provide CPIC support for any protocols other than LU 6.2, but this may be a future offering.

SIDE INFORMATION

Another difference between CPIC and the LU 6.2 protocol boundary verbs is the concept and usage of "side information." CPIC side information is information needed at initialization time for the conversation to be set up with the partner program. The side information will be system-defined values that typically are set up outside the application program by a systems administrator.

Examples of side information are:

> Partner_LU_name
> Mode_name
> TP_name

This side information is accessed using a symbolic name which identifies the entry in a side-information table containing the appropriate information.

The partner_LU_name identifies the name of the remote LU supporting the partner program to which an attempt will be made to establish a conversation. The mode_name identifies various properties (modes) to be allocated to the conversations. For example, class of service is a property that would define the level and type of service required by this conversation.

The TP_name is the name of the partner program to which connection is desired. This symbolic name is sent to the remote LU which then uses it to start up the corresponding partner program.

Moving this type of initialization information (which is very SNA LU 6.2 oriented and system dependent) out to the side makes CPIC simpler since it only has to refer to this side information rather than build it in-line as part of the program; is less dependent on any environment or system since the rest of the call interface is generic and will be supported in all SAA environments; and is less dependent on LU 6.2 protocols, which holds out the possibility that other protocols such as OSI protocols could be used sometime later, as we discussed.

CPIC CALL INTERFACE

CPIC is a program "call" interface. It consists of a set of program calls that can be issued using high-level programming languages such as C and COBOL. IBM has defined exactly how the CPIC calls are made in each of the languages for which CPIC support is provided. In order to make it easier to use CPIC, IBM has subdivided the calls into two groups: starter-set and advanced-function set. The CPIC calls within these groups are listed below:

Starter-Set:
    Accept_Conversation
    Allocate
    Deallocate
    Initialize_Conversation
    Receive_Data
    Send_Data
Advanced-Function Set:
    Confirm
    Confirmed
    Flush
    Prepare_To_Receive
    Request_To_Send
    Send_Error
    Test_Request_To_Send_Received
    Set_Conversation_Type
    Set_Deallocate_Type
    Set_Error_Detection
    Set_Fill
    Set_Log_Data
    Set_Mode_Name
    Set_Partner_LU_Name
    Set_Prepare_To_Receive_Type
    Set_Receive_Type
    Set_Return_Control
    Set_Send_Type
    Set_Sync_Level
    Set_TP_Name
    Extract_Conversation_Type
    Extract_Mode_Name
    Extract_Partner_LU_Name
    Extract_Sync_Level

Close inspection of these calls would show that they can be subdivided into different categories. Some calls are used for initiating and terminating conversations; for exchanging data with a partner program; for controlling and synchronizing processing between the partner programs; to modify conversation characteristics; and to obtain information about the characteristics of the conversation. The same set of calls can be used for either basic or mapped conversations. Let's look at how they break down into these categories.

INITIALIZATION/TERMINATION

The following CPIC calls are used to establish or terminate a conversation with a partner transaction program:

Initialize_Conversation
Allocate
Accept_Conversation
Deallocate

Initialize_Conversation is issued prior to actually allocating a conversation. It is used to initialize the values of various conversation characteristics which will then be used during the conversation. Allocate is the call used to actually initiate a conversation with a partner program. The conversation-allocation request is accepted via the Accept_Conversation call. Deallocate terminates a conversation.

EXCHANGING DATA

The CPIC calls used to exchange data between the transaction programs engaged in a conversation are Send_Data and Receive_Data. As their names imply, Send_Data is issued to send a data record to the remote program and Receive_Data is issued to get data sent from a program.

SYNCHRONIZATION AND CONTROL

Calls used for synchronization and control purposes include:

Confirm
Confirmed
Flush
Prepare_To_Receive
Send_Error
Request_To_Send
Test_Request_To_Send

Confirm is used to indicate that the local program needs to receive confirmation before it will continue its processing. Typically, the confirmation would be of the receipt of some information and the processing of it to a particular level. The program issuing Confirm waits until a Confirmed reply is sent back from the remote program. The use of Confirm and Confirmed in this manner allows the two programs to synchronize their processing.

Flush is used to force sending of any data still pending in the local LU's send buffers. Prepare_To_Receive is issued in order to change the local program conversation state from send to receive. Send_Error can be used to send an error indication to the remote program. Request_To_Send is a solicitation informing the remote program that the local program wants to send data. Test_Request_To_Send can be used to determine if a request-to-send indicator has been received from the remote program.

MODIFYING CONVERSATION CHARACTERISTICS

A number of CPIC calls can be used to modify conversation characteristics. These include:

> Set_Conversation_Type
> Set_Deallocate_Type
> Set_Error_Direction
> Set_Fill
> Set_Log_Data
> Set_Mode_Name
> Set_Partner_LU_Name
> Set_Prepare_To_Receive_Type
> Set_Receive_Type
> Set_Return_Control
> Set_Send_Type
> Set_Sync_Level
> Set_TP_Name

These calls are self-explanatory. Each is used to modify the corresponding conversation characteristic.

VIEWING CONVERSATION CHARACTERISTICS

There is a set of CPIC calls that can be used to view conversation characteristics, including:

> Extract_Conversation_Type
> Extract_Mode_Name
> Extract_Partner_LU_Name
> Extract_Sync_Level

These, also, are self-explanatory. Each call returns the information on the related conversation characteristic.

CPIC USE OF LU 6.2 APIS

The CPIC call interface is a higher-level interface than the LU 6.2 APIs provided in different systems. CPIC, in effect, sits on top of an LU 6.2 API. While each SAA environment provides consistent support for the CPIC interface, each will still retain its unique LU 6.2 software with its unique LU 6.2 APIs. When an application program issues CPIC calls, these calls will be mapped into the appropriate lower-level LU 6.2 API calls provided by the system on which the application is executing.

NODE SERVICES

In addition to support for the CPIC interface calls, environments that provide CPIC support will also include various node services needed in support of CPIC. These node services are utility-type functions provided by the local operating environment. Services are needed to allow a system administrator to set up and access the side information. Services are also needed to assist in starting up programs. Programs may be started either because of local operator action or because an allocation request has been received from a remote system. Support is also needed for program-termination processing. Any conversations that were not explicitly deallocated by programs must be terminated. This clean-up processing would be handled by node services.

SUMMARY

CPIC is the standard SAA CPI programming interface for communications with other programs. This interface is consistently supported in all SAA environments which will make it easier to write distributed, cooperative processing programs that communicate with one another across SAA environments. CPIC resolves the problems of the incompatibilities of existing LU 6.2 APIs provided in different IBM products.

CPIC is a call-level interface that is supported in high-level languages such as COBOL and C. It is a conversational-level interface. Calls are provided to allow programs to set up logical connections (conversations) with other programs, to exchange data with other programs, to synchronize and control processing between programs, and to initialize, modify, and view conversation characteristics.

CPIC calls are mapped to lower-level LU 6.2 API interfaces and result in SNA LU 6.2 protocols generated in order to support the conversations between partner programs. The conversation is actually carried out across an LU 6.2 session between the pair of LUs supporting the partner programs. The underlying LU 6.2 session is transparent to the CPIC programs.

GLOSSARY

Abstract Syntax Notation One (ASN.1): An ISO standard that describes a set of data type definitions (e.g., defining different data types and the values that can be assigned to them) that are independent of any coding technique used to represent data.

ACSE: *See* Association Control Service Element.

AD/Cycle: IBM's SAA application-development strategy. It provides the framework for developing SAA applications. AD/Cycle tools and services span the life cycle of application program development from initial requirements planning, to program design, to actual development, through maintenance and support.

Advanced Communication Function for the Network Control Progam (ACF/NCP): *See* Network Control Program.

Advanced Communications Function for the Virtual Telecommunications Access Method (ACF/VTAM): *See* Virtual Telecommunications Access Method.

Advanced Function Printing (AFP): A set of printer services implemented in various IBM programs that allows users to intermix different types of data (e.g., text, image, graphics) that can then be sent to IBM's all-points-addressable (APA) page printers.

Advanced Peer-to-Peer Networking (APPN): IBM networking technology that allows networking of multiple Type 2.1 Nodes without requiring a System/

x

370 host in the network. APPN network nodes provide intermediate node network routing and support dynamic networking facilities such as dynamically reconfiguring the network when changes occur and dynamically locating users in the network. APPN software exists on the System/36, 3174, PS/2, and AS/400.

Advanced Program-to-Program Communications (APPC): The marketing term for SNA LU 6.2 program-to-program communications. APPC/LU 6.2 provides a generalized program-to-program communications vehicle that can be used by a wide variety of transaction programs to exchange information. IBM transaction programs such as DIA, SNA/DS, and DDM use LU 6.2 for their program-to-program communications.

AFP: *See* Advanced Function Printing.

AIX: IBM's version of the UNIX operating system. Versions of AIX run on PS/2, RT, RISC System/6000, and System/370/390 processors.

Alert: An unsolicited network management message sent from an entry point or service point product to a focal point when an error has been detected. IBM entry point products such as the 3174 send alert messages to NetView, a focal point product, for processing.

American National Standards Institute (ANSI): An organization made up of representatives from computer users, computer manufacturers, communications carriers, and other companies that addresses various kinds of standards. ANSI is the U.S. representative to the International Standards Organization (ISO) and many ANSI standards parallel ISO standards.

ANSI: *See* American National Standards Institute.

API: *See* Application Programming Interface.

APPC: *See* Advanced Program-to-Program Communications.

Application: A software program that implements some application-level functionality. In SNA networks, application programs are considered end users of the network and are represented by Logical Units (LUs).

Application Development/Cycle: *See* AD/Cycle.

Application Enabler: Software that provides a particular set of services for an application, thus enabling those functions for the application. Examples of application enablers are programming language compilers, database management systems, and dialog managers.

Application Generator: An SAA fourth-generation application development tool specification based on IBM's Cross System Product (CSP). Using an Application Generator such as CSP, users can build applications using fourth-generation tools rather than have to write the application using a third-generation programming language such as COBOL.

Application Programming Interface (API): A set of "calls" that application programs use to get access to services provided by software supporting the application. LU 6.2 Transaction Programs (TPs) interface to the LU supporting them via the application program interface (API) provided by the LU.

Application Services: A Common Communications Support category consisting of a set of architectures that is used to provide a variety of application services that span SAA systems. Examples of Application Services architectures are DIA, SNA/DS, and DDM.

APPN: *See* Advanced Peer-to-Peer Networking.

Architecture: A set of rules and definitions describing the structure and operation of a network. Systems Network Architecture (SNA) is IBM's set of rules and definitions describing how their systems will interconnect and operate in a network.

AS/400: IBM's strategic multi-user, midrange applications-processing system. Supports a wide range of SNA communications including 3270 emulation and peer-to-peer communications using Logical Unit Type 6.2. The AS/400 is the successor to IBM's System/36 and System/38 product lines.

ASN.1: *See* Abstract Syntax Notation One.

Association Control Service Element (ACSE): An ISO standard that defines how logical connections (associations) can be established and terminated between application entities.

C: A high-level programming language developed at Bell Labs. Since the early 1980s, C has become a popular choice for software development. C is one of the programming languages included in the CPI element of SAA.

C/2: The IBM SAA C programming-language compiler for OS/2.

C/370: The IBM SAA C programming-language compiler for MVS and VM.

C/400: The IBM SAA C programming-language compiler for OS/400.

CA: *See* Common Application.

CASE: *See* Computer-Aided Software Engineering.

CCITT: CCITT is an acronym for the Consultative Committee for International Telephony and Telegraphy. It is an international organization that sets communications standards.

CCS: *See* Common Communications Support.

CDRA: *See* Character Data Representation Architecture.

Character Data Representation Architecture (CDRA): CDRA defines the mapping and conversion of character sets between dissimilar computer systems.

CICS: *See* Customer Information Control System.

CLNS: *See* Connectionless Network Services.

COBOL: COBOL is an acronym for Common Business Oriented Language. It is a high-level programming language developed in the 1960s and is popular for business applications. COBOL is one of the programming languages included in the CPI element of SAA.

COBOL/2: The IBM SAA COBOL programming-language compiler for OS/2.

COBOL/400: The IBM SAA COBOL programming-language compiler for OS/400.

Common Application: An application that provides an SAA CUA-compliant user interface, runs in the SAA environments, and supports SAA cooperative processing if appropriate. SAA Common Applications are developed using SAA programming languages or development tools and make use of components included in the SAA CUA, CPI, and/or CCS elements.

Common Communications Support (CCS): An SAA element that consists of components used for communications between SAA systems. The CCS element is subdivided into categories of components including Objects, Data Streams, Application Services, Session Services, Network, and Data Link Controls. The intent of this element is to allow interoperability between SAA systems.

Common Programming Interface (CPI): An SAA element that is subdivided into categories of programming languages and services components. The intent of this element is to standardize on the programming environments to be available on SAA systems. SAA applications are developed using CPI components and interfaces.

Common Programming Interface for Communications (CPIC): The LU 6.2–based application programming interface defined as part of SAA's CPI element. The CPIC interface will be used by application programs for communicating with other application programs.

Common User Access (CUA): An SAA element that contains specifications and guidelines for an application's user interface. The intent of this element is to standardize the user interface provided by SAA application programs. CUA includes support for both nonprogrammable terminals, such as 3270s, and intelligent workstations, such as PS/2s running OS/2.

Communications Controller Node: An SNA network node that acts as a "pure" communications processor to handle functions like network routing and control of physical data links. IBM hardware products like the 3720, 3725, and 3745 act as SNA communications controllers when they are running the Network Control Program (NCP) software. SNA communications controllers are also referred to as Type 4 Nodes.

Communications Interface: The standard CPI application programming interface that application programs use for communicating with other applications. This CPI for communications is also referred to as CPIC. It is based on IBM's LU 6.2 verbs.

Computer-Aided Software Engineering (CASE): Technology consisting of development tools and services used to assist in the development of application programs. Using CASE tools should shorten the development cycle.

Connectionless Network Services (CLNS): An ISO standard that defines a "datagram" type network service in which each piece of user data transmitted through the network is self-contained and can be independently routed by the network.

Connection-oriented Network Services (CONS): An ISO standard that defines network services in support of data transfer across a connection established between network service users.

CONS: *See* Connection-oriented Network Services.

Conversation: The logical connection between two application programs, called Transaction Programs (TPs), using Logical Unit Type 6.2 (LU 6.2). The conversation uses an underlying logical unit–to–logical unit (LU-LU) session for the duration of the conversation.

Conversational Monitor System (CMS): The terminal monitor component of the VM operating system that provides interactive support for VM terminal users.

Cooperative Processing: The ability to access distributed resources in a transparent manner from any system in the network. Systems in the network cooperate with one another in carrying out the distributed access.

CPI: *See* Common Programming Interface.

CPIC: *See* Common Programming Interface for Communications.

CPI Services: A set of common system services and the program interfaces used to access these services. Examples of CPI services are presentation, dialog, query, and communications services.

Cross System Product (CSP): IBM's SAA Application Generator product that includes an application development facility (CSP/AD) and an application execution facility (CSP/AE). Applications developed using CSP/AD facilities can execute in environments that provide CSP/AE support.

CSP: *See* Cross System Product.

CUA: *See* Common User Access.

Customer Information Control System (CICS): A general-purpose System/ 370 mainframe-based transaction management system. CICS is one of IBM's most widely used Data Base/Data Communications (DB/DC) subsystems. It provides a transaction-oriented environment for applications and provides interfaces to file and database systems and provides communications to other systems for these applications.

Database: A collection of information (data) that is collected electronically and typically stored as a set of files. The data can be manipulated by software called a database management system.

Database Interface: The standard CPI programming interface for accessing data in relational databases. The SAA CPI Database Interface is based on Structured Query Language (SQL).

Database Services: The set of services provided by a Database Manager. The services include support for the Database Interface and provide the access to relational databases in each of the SAA environments.

Data Circuit Terminating Equipment (DCE): A communications device, typically a modem, which establishes, maintains, and terminates a session in a network.

Data Link: *See* Link.

Data Link Controls: Protocols used to manage the exchange of information across a single data link connection between two adjacent nodes. Examples of data link control protocols included under SAA are SDLC and Token-Ring.

Data Stream: A contiguous block of data consisting of a mixture of end-user data and format-control codes that is sent from one user to another through the network.

Data Terminal Equipment (DTE): A communications device, such as a terminal or computer, that is the source or destination of signals in a network.

DB2: IBM's mainframe relational database product for the MVS environment that supports the SAA Database Interface.

DCA: *See* Document Content Architecture.

DCE: *See* Data Circuit Terminating Equipment.

DDM: *See* Distributed Data Management.

DIA: *See* Document Interchange Architecture.

Dialog Manager: A set of software within an SAA operating environment that provides dialog services for application programs. Applications request dialog services from the Dialog Manager via Dialog Interface program calls.

Dialog Services: Services provided by a Dialog Manager to application programs when the programs issue Dialog Interface calls. These services make it easier to write interactive text-based applications. Examples of dialog services provided by a Dialog Manager are retrieving and displaying panels of information, accepting user input, managing the dialog between the user and the application, and enforcing conformance to SAA CUA specifications.

Disk Operating System (DOS): IBM's standard operating system for the PC family of systems. DOS is a single tasking operating system that runs on PC and PS/2 systems.

DISOSS: *See* Distributed Office Support System.

Display Station: A CRT terminal or intelligent workstation with a monitor and keyboard allowing information to be entered into the network and with the ability to display information received from the network. Typically associated with 3270 display stations (e.g., 3179).

Distributed Data Management (DDM): An architecture describing a form of remote file access in SNA networks. DDM transaction programs on different systems use LU 6.2 to distribute requests for record and file access.

Distributed Office Support System (DISOSS): An IBM System/370 mainframe-based office application that runs under CICS. DISOSS provides a number of office-oriented services, allowing end users on different systems to exchange mail and documents, to store and retrieve documents from host libraries, and to distribute documents to one or more other users in a network.

Distributed Processing: Processing performed by multiple systems in a network. Part of the processing can be carried out by one system while other parts are carried out by one or more other systems. The processing is distributed among systems.

Distributed Relational Database Architecture (DRDA): The SAA architecture that defines how access to distributed relational data will be supported in SAA environments. Users and applications request access to relational data via SQL commands. If the requested data is on a remote system, DRDA will be used to carry out the distributed request.

Distributed Resource: A resource residing on one system which is being accessed from another system in a network. The resource being accessed is not locally resident on the requesting system. Instead, the resource has been distributed to another system where it physically resides.

Document Content Architecture (DCA): An architecture that defines the format and structure of a particular type of data.

Document Interchange Architecture (DIA): An IBM architecture describing a set of services allowing documents to be exchanged between different systems in an SNA network. DIA services include document library services which allow users to store and retrieve documents to/from host libraries and document distribution services which support distribution of documents to multiple users in the network.

Domain: A portion of an SNA network controlled by a System Services Control Point (SSCP).

DOS: *See* Disk Operating System.

DRDA: *See* Distributed Relational Database Architecture.

DTE: *See* Data Terminal Equipment.

Dumb Terminal: A terminal, such as a 3270 terminal, which has no application-processing capability of its own. It relies on host-based application programs for processing and control. Terminal operators use such terminals to access host applications.

End User: A device, such as a display station or printer, or an application program that is the source or destination of data exchanged in an SNA network. LUs represent end users, serving as their port into and out of the network.

Enterprise Systems Architecture/370 (ESA/370): IBM's level of the System/370-based hardware architecture that is an extension beyond the 370-Extended Architecture (370/XA). ESA/370 features extended hardware-addressing support which allows accessing of virtual storage in multiple address spaces and data spaces. This support significantly extends addressability for applications and systems software.

Entity-Relationship Model: The modeling technique used to define entities and their relationships. The entity-relationship (ER) concept is key to IBM's AD/Cycle strategy and business-modeling information is stored in a repository in ER format.

Entry Model: A CUA user-interface model that is appropriate for data entry, text-based applications used by nonprogrammable terminals. The OS/400 operating system provides Entry Model displays on 5250 terminals attached to AS/400 systems.

Entry Point: An SNA node that provides support for SNA/MS. Entry Points are standard SNA-based products such as 3174 controllers, System/36, System/38, AS/400, Series/1, and PC and PS/2 systems.

ESA/370: *See* Enterprise Systems Architecture/370.

Extended Architecture (XA): The level of the System/370-based architecture that adds extensions to the base System/370 architecture. Extensions in addressability are some of the major enhancements introduced with the 370/XA architecture.

FDOCA: *See* Formatted Data Object Content Architecture.

File: A sequence of related information maintained as a single entity on some file-storage media such as a disk. Files can be organized as record-oriented sequential or indexed files, byte stream files, or others.

File Transfer, Access, and Management (FTAM): An ISO standard that defines remote file access services (e.g., file transfer) similar to many of the services supported by IBM's Distributed Data Management (DDM) architecture.

FOCA: *See* Font Object Content Architecture.

Focal Point: A node in an SNA network where network management services are provided. NetView is IBM's primary host-based focal point product.

Font Object Content Architecture (FOCA): An architecture that describes font type and font characteristics.

Formatted Data Object Content Architecture (FDOCA): FDOCA defines the field-formatted data objects which can be exchanged among SAA systems.

FORTRAN: A high-level programming language developed in the 1950s. It is widely used in the scientific community. FORTRAN is one of the programming languages included in the CPI element of SAA.

FORTRAN/2: The IBM SAA FORTRAN compiler for OS/2.

FORTRAN/400: The IBM SAA FORTRAN compiler for OS/400.

FTAM: *See* File Transfer, Access, and Management.

Functional Layer: One of the major groupings of functions defined by the SNA architecture. Major functions have been isolated into separate layers so changes can be made to one layer without having to change other layers, thereby making it easier to accommodate new technologies in SNA. SNA consists of seven layers—Transaction Services, Presentation Services, Data Flow Control, Transmission Control, Path Control, Data Link Control, and Physical Control.

GDDM: *See* Graphical Data Display Manager.

GOCA: *See* Graphics Object Content Architecture.

Graphical Data Display Manager (GDDM): The product that implements SAA Presentation Services for MVS and VM.

Graphical Model: The SAA CUA user-interface model supported by the OS/2 Presentation Manager. This is a graphical, windows-based user-interface model that is appropriate for decision-intensive, graphical applications running on intelligent workstations such as PS/2s.

Graphics Object Content Architecture (GOCA): The Object Content Architecture that defines primitives and attributes used to define the structure of computer graphics as well as a set of operations for manipulating graphic elements.

Hierarchical: A connection characterized by a master-slave relationship. In SNA terminology, a hierarchical connection involves a Peripheral Node (slave) connection to a host subarea node (master). The Host Node maintains control and is responsible for initiating and terminating the connection.

Host Node: A Type 5 SNA node which contains a System Services Control Point (SSCP). A Host Node is typically a System/370 mainframe computer running VTAM. A Host Node serves as a centralized control point of a network. Host Nodes support application programs and provide network management services. A Host Node is one type of subarea node, the other type being a Communications Controller Node.

Image Object Content Architecture (IOCA): An architecture used to describe the format and structure of image objects that can be transferred between systems.

IMS: *See* Information Management System.

Information Management System (IMS): An IBM System/370 host-based Data Base/Data Communications (DB/DC) subsystem that runs in the MVS environment. IMS supports user-written batch and interactive applications, providing the communications access to remote systems and access to databases maintained by IMS for these applications.

Intelligent Printer Data Stream (IPDS): The data stream used for sending information from a host system to an all-points-addressable page printer, such as a laser or dot matrix printer. IPDS can carry different types of data, including text, image, and graphics.

Intelligent Workstation: A system, such as a personal computer, that has its own processing capability. Local applications can execute on an intelligent workstation so that connection to a host system is not required.

Interactive System Productivity Facility (ISPF): The SAA Dialog Manager for MVS and VM.

Intermediate Node: A node in a network that provides network routing services but is not the source or destination of the data being routed. An intermediate node receives data from one node and, based on addressing information, sends the information to another node. Host Nodes and Communications Controller Nodes can function as intermediate nodes in SNA networks.

International Standards Organization (ISO): An organization that sets international standards in several areas. ISO is particularly active in data communications. Its headquarters is in Geneva.

IOCA: *See* Image Object Content Architecture.

IPDS: *See* Intelligent Printer Data Stream.

ISO: *See* International Standards Organization.

ISPF: *See* Interactive System Productivity Facility.

JES: *See* Job Entry Subsystem.

Job Entry Subsystem (JES): A series of IBM products (JES, JES2, JES3) that allows remote users to submit jobs for execution on System/370 mainframes. The JES subsystems run in the MVS operating system environments.

LAN: *See* Local Area Network.

Layer: *See* Functional Layer.

LEN: *See* Low Entry Networking.

Link: A physical connection between two nodes. Different types of links are supported in SNA networks including System/370 local channel links, Token-Ring LANs, and SDLC links. The Data Link Control (DLC) layer defines different protocols to manage data exchange across the different links.

Local Area Network (LAN): A network connecting devices over a relatively short distance. The Token-Ring is IBM's strategic LAN.

Local Channel: The direct link, via a channel, between an IBM System/370 processor and another System/370 processor, a Communications Controller, or a Peripheral Node. The local channel interface is one of the data links supported in SNA networks.

Logical Unit (LU): A port through which end users of an SNA network communicate with each other. The logical unit (LU) handles and enforces the SNA protocols required for end-user–to–end-user communications.

Logical Unit–To–Logical Unit (LU-LU) Session: A logical connection between the logical units (LUs) representing users of an SNA network. No communications can occur between LUs until they establish an LU-LU session.

Look and Feel: This phrase describes how an application appears to the user and how the user interacts with the application.

Low Entry Networking (LEN): The peer-to-peer connection between a pair of adjacent Type 2.1 Nodes.

LU Type 0: An implementation-defined LU type that is generally used to support program-to-program communications. It is most often used in IBM's industry-specific (e.g., retail POS, banking) systems and is being superceded by LU Type 6.2 in most new applications.

LU Type 1: An LU type designed to support communications between a remote terminal and a host-based application. LU Type 1 is used for sending SNA Character String (SCS) data streams to 3270 printers. It is also used to support 3770 Remote Job Entry (RJE) terminals.

LU Type 2: The LU type that is designed to support communications with display stations using the 3270 data stream format.

LU Type 3: The LU type that is designed to support communications with printers using the 3270 data stream format.

LU Type 4: An early SNA LU type used for peer-to-peer communications between IBM products like the 6670 Information Distributor. LU 4 has now been superceded by LU 6.2 for peer-to-peer communications.

LU Type 6.1: The LU type designed to support program-to-program communications between IBM host-based applications such as CICS and IMS.

LU Type 6.2: The LU type designed to support generalized program-to-program communications. LU 6.2 defines an application program interface which applications use to communicate with each other. Another important feature of LU 6.2 is its ability to support peer-to-peer sessions directly between users on SNA workstations and midrange processors without the intervention of an SNA host.

LU Type 7: The LU type designed to support communications between an application program and a 5250 display station.

Mainframe: A System/370 or System/390 host computer. A mainframe is any model of IBM's System/370, 303X, 308X, 309X, 4300, and 9370 or System/390 ES/9000 series processors. A mainframe functions as a Type 5 Host Node in an SNA network, due to VTAM software which runs in the mainframe. In addition to serving as a network control point, mainframes also support network management facilities and application programs.

Midrange System: One of IBM's nonmainframe, non-PC systems. Typically midrange systems fall between mainframes and PCs in their processing power and capacity. IBM midrange systems include the AS/400, System/36, System/38, Series/1, and 8100.

Mixed Object: Document Content Architecture (MO:DCA): The data stream used to carry compound documents which consist of a mixture of different types of objects, such as graphics text, images, and font objects.

MO:DCA: *See* Mixed Object: Document Content Architecture.

Modem: A device used to interface data communications equipment to analog telecommunications networks. The modem handles the conversion between the digital signals used in computer systems and the analog signals required by many telecommunications networks.

Multidomain SNA Network: An SNA network whose resources (LUs, PUs, and data links) are controlled by more than one SNA host. The System Services Control Point (SSCP) within each of the hosts controls some portion of the network's resources.

Multiple Virtual Storage (MVS): One of IBM's primary operating systems for their System/370 mainframes. Versions of MVS run on System/370, 303X, 308X, 309X, 4300, and 9370 series processors. MVS/SP supports standard System/370 architecture, MVS/XA supports the System/370-Extended Architecture (System/370-XA), and MVS/ESA supports Enterprise Systems Architecture/370 (ESA/370).

MVS: *See* Multiple Virtual Storage.

NCP: *See* Network Control Program.

NetView: IBM's System/370 mainframe-based network management software. NetView provides facilities to allow network operators to monitor and control the network, detect and isolate problems in the network, determine status of network components, and activate and deactivate network resources, among other things.

NetView Distribution Manager: An IBM System/370-based program product used for distributing software and microcode to remote systems in an SNA network.

NetView/PC: An IBM program product that runs on PC or PS/2 systems and is used to provide network management support for non-SNA devices. Applications that interface with NetView/PC are required to support the non-SNA device. These applications can then use the services of NetView/PC to cause alert messages to be sent to NetView on a System/370/390 host.

Network: An SAA CCS category of components related to networking requirements. The only SNA-based component included in this category is Low Entry Networking (LEN) as supported in Type 2.1 Nodes.

Network Addressable Unit (NAU): Logical Units (LUs), Physical Units (PUs), and System Services Control Points (SSCPs) are collectively called Network Addressable Units (NAUs). As the name implies, each NAU is assigned a unique network address. All communications in an SNA network are carried on between NAUs.

Network Control Program (NCP): An IBM program that runs in a 37XX Communications Controller and implements the functions of an SNA Type 4 Node. These functions include network routing and managing physical data links connected to the 37XX.

Network Management: The set of functions and processes used to control a network. Network management functions include activating and deactivating network resources, monitoring status of resources, detecting and isolating problems in the network, distributing software to systems in the network, configuring the network, and other related activities. NetView is IBM's primary System/370/390 host-based network management software.

Network Management Vector Transport (NMVT): An SNA request unit used for sending network management alerts. *See also* Alert.

NMVT: *See* Network Management Vector Transport.

Node: A system that implements SNA functions. The SNA architecture defines different types of nodes, each with a different role in the network. SNA also defines the interactions between nodes that are interconnected in a network.

Node Type: A type of SNA node that has a particular role in an SNA network. SNA defines four different types of nodes—Host (Type 5) Nodes, Communications Controller (Type 4) Nodes, and Type 2.0 and Type 2.1 Peripheral Nodes.

Nonprogrammable Terminal (NPT): A terminal, such as a 3270 dumb terminal, that cannot be user programmed.

NPT: *See* Nonprogrammable Terminal.

Object Content Architecture (OCA): A CCS category that defines the structure and content of objects that may exist in a document, such as text, image, and graphics.

Objects: Within SAA, objects are major data types (e.g., text, image, or graphics) that can be combined to create compound documents.

OCA: *See* Object Content Architecture.

OfficeVision: An IBM family of SAA office applications that provide office services such as word processing, electronic mail, calendar management, decision support, file handling, document distribution, and communications. The OfficeVision family consists of a series of products for each of the SAA environments including the OfficeVision/MVS and OfficeVision/VM series for the System/370 MVS and VM environments, respectively; OfficeVision/400 for the OS/400 environment on AS/400 systems; OfficeVision/2 LAN series for the OS/2 Extended Edition environment on PC and PS/2 systems.

OfficeVision/MVS: IBM's OfficeVision product for MVS. *See also* OfficeVision.

OfficeVision/VM: IBM's OfficeVision product for VM. *See also* OfficeVision.

OfficeVision/2: IBM's OfficeVision product for OS/2. *See also* OfficeVision.

OfficeVision/400: IBM's OfficeVision product for OS/400. *See also* OfficeVision.

Open Software Foundation (OSF): A group of system vendors, including IBM, whose goal is to provide an industry-standard UNIX offering.

Open Systems Interconnection (OSI): A reference model designed by the International Standards Organization (ISO) as a standard for communications. It comprises seven functional layers.

OSF: *See* Open Software Foundation.

OSI: *See* Open Systems Interconnection.

OS/2: A multitasking operating system for IBM's PS/2 family of personal computers. OS/2 will also run on some models of the PC family such as PC AT and PC XT 286 systems.

OS/2 EE: *See* OS/2 Extended Edition.

OS/2 Extended Edition (OS/2 EE): IBM's version of OS/2 that includes an integrated relational database manager and an integrated communications manager. OS/2 EE is the SAA environment for intelligent workstations.

OS/2 Presentation Manager: The software component of OS/2 that provides presentation services supporting the SAA CUA Graphical Model user interface. The OS/2 Presentation Manager supports the SAA CPI Presentation Interface.

OS/2 Query Manager: The set of code integrated within OS/2 that provides query services allowing users and application programs to access relational databases. The OS/2 Query Manager supports the SAA CPI Query Interface.

OS/400: The native operating system for IBM's AS/400 family of systems. OS/400 is one of the major SAA operating environments.

Panel Interface Models: CUA defines different panel (screen) models for different users, devices, and applications. The four basic CUA models are Entry, Graphical, Text Subset, and Workplace.

PC: IBM's original family of personal computer systems. PCs are based on Intel microprocessors including the 8088, 8086, and 80286 chips. DOS is the primary operating system running on most PCs. The original PC line was enhanced to include PC XT and PC AT models. The PC family has been superceded by the PS/2 family.

Peer-to-Peer Communications: Communications between two adjacent Type 2.1 Nodes. This type of peer connectivity is called Low Entry Networking (LEN). Such communications do not require a System/370 mainframe to be involved. This is contrasted with hierarchical communications in which a Type 2.0 or Type 2.1 Peripheral Node must be connected to a host system. Only LU 6.2 sessions are supported across peer-to-peer connections between Type 2.1 Nodes.

Peripheral Node: A Type 2.0 or Type 2.1 SNA node. Peripheral Nodes support the attachment of end users to the network. End users may be devices such as displays and printers or they may be application programs. Type 2.0 Nodes are restricted to connecting to Host Nodes or Communications Controller Nodes while Type 2.1 Nodes can also directly connect to other Type 2.1 Nodes without host involvement.

Personal Computer: *See* PC.

Personal System/2: *See* PS/2.

Physical Unit (PU): An SNA Network Addressable Unit (NAU) responsible for managing a node's resources such as data links attached to the node. Each SNA node contains a PU except a Type 2.1 Node which contains a Control Point.

PL/I: A high-level programming language developed by IBM. PL/I is one of the programming languages included in the CPI element of SAA.

Portability: The ability to move a program from one environment to another.

Presentation Manager: Software in an SAA environment that provides presentation services and support for the SAA CPI Presentation Interface. The OS/2 Presentation Manager is an example of a Presentation Manager.

Presentation Services: Services to allow application programs to display or print information and to accept input from users. Presentation Services are provided by a Presentation Manager. Applications request services from the Presentation Manager via the Presentation Interface.

Presentation Text Object Content Architecture (PTOCA): The Object Content Architecture that describes a document that is in presentation form; that is, it is ready to be displayed or printed.

PrintManager Interface: The SAA CPI standard application programming interface for print services.

Procedures Language: An SAA third-generation, procedures-oriented programming language. Procedures Language is one of the programming languages included in the CPI element of SAA.

Procedures Language 2/REXX: The IBM SAA Procedures Language product for OS/2.

Procedures Language 400/REXX: The IBM SAA Procedures Language product for OS/400.

Programmable Workstation (PWS): An intelligent workstation that can be user-programmed. For example, the PS/2 is IBM's primary PWS for SAA applications.

Program-to-Program Communications: Communications between a pair of programs. LU 6.2 provides program-to-program communications protocols. Two Transaction Programs (TPs) can communicate with one another using LU 6.2 protocols. IBM refers to this as Advanced Program-to-Program Communications (APPC).

Protocol: A set of rules of interaction between communicating components. Each layer of the SNA architecture defines different protocols to support the various types of communications supported at each of the layers. For example, data link control protocols, such as SDLC, define the rules of interaction between two nodes connected by a single data link.

Protocol Boundary: The architected interface between a Transaction Program (TP) and a Type 6.2 LU. The protocol boundary consists of a set of "verbs" describing the functions provided by the LU which are available to the TP.

PS/2: IBM's family of personal computer systems that is the next generation beyond the original PC family. The PS/2 family consists of a number of models differing in processing power and capacity. Like the PC family, PS/2 models are based on Intel microprocessors. Lower-end PS/2 models are bus-compatible with IBM's PC models while higher-end PS/2 models have a MicroChannel Architecture (MCA) bus. OS/2 is the primary operating system for the PS/2 although DOS is widely used as well.

PTOCA: *See* Presentation Text Object Content Architecture.

PU: *See* Physical Unit.

PWS: *See* Programmable Workstation.

QMF: *See* OS/2 Query Manager.

Query Interface: The standard SAA CPI query programming interface. Application programs can issue Query Interface calls to request query services from a Query Manager. Query services allow users and applications to access data in a relational database (query the database).

Query Services: The services provided by a Query Manager that allow users to access information from a relational database. Both query-by-example and menu-driven query services are provided by various IBM Query Manager products. Applications request Query Services by issuing SAA Query Interface calls.

Repository: A central storage location containing data that can be shared and accessed by users, applications, and systems throughout an enterprise.

Repository Interface: The SAA CPI programming interface for accessing information stored in a repository. A Repository Manager provides repository services such as defining entities and their relationships and storing this information in a repository. Repository services are requested via the Repository Interface.

Repository Manager/MVS: The IBM product that implements the SAA CPI Repository Interface and provides repository services for MVS.

Resource Recovery Interface (RRI): The SAA CPI application programming interface that provides two-phase commit support needed when multiple resources are to be updated simultaneously.

Revisable Form Text: Document Content Architecture (RFT:DCA): The data stream used to carry documents that are in revisable format.

REXX: *See* Procedures Language.

RFT:DCA: *See* Revisable Form Text: Document Content Architecture.

RISC System/6000 (RS/6000): A family of RISC-based computers introduced by IBM in 1990.

RPG (Report Program Generator): A programming language for business applications. RPG is one of the programming languages included in the CPI element of SAA.

RPG/400: The SAA RPG compiler for OS/400.

RRI: *See* Resource Recovery Interface.

RS/6000: *See* RISC System/6000.

SAA: *See* Systems Application Architecture.

SCS: *See* SNA Character String.

SDLC: *See* Synchronous Data Link Control.

Series/1: A family of midrange computers from IBM used for business applications and as communications processors. Series/1 was introduced in the mid 1970s.

Service Point: A node in an SNA network that provides network management support for a non-SNA product. NetView/PC is an example of a service point product.

Session: The logical connection between a pair of SNA Network Addressable Units (e.g., SSCPs, PUs, LUs). Before any communications are possible between a pair of NAUs, a session must be established that logically connects the pair. SNA supports SSCP-SSCP, SSCP-PU, SSCP-LU, and LU-LU sessions. SNA session-level protocols are used to manage the exchange of information across the session between the pair of NAUs.

Single Domain Network: An SNA network with only one System/370 or System/390 host and, therefore, only a single System Services Control Point (SSCP) (which is implemented in VTAM in the System/370 host). All resources in the network are controlled by the single host.

SNA: *See* Systems Network Architecture.

SNA Character String (SCS): A data stream consisting of intermixed end-user data, single-byte control codes, and/or multibyte control sequences. The control codes and sequences are used to direct the presentation of the end-user data on display stations or printers. SCS is the type of data stream used with LU Type 1 processing.

SNA/Distribution Services (SNA/DS): An architecture that describes a generalized, asynchronous delivery facility based on store-and-forward techniques. SNA/DS is used to distribute different types of objects (e.g., mail, documents, programs) through an SNA network. SNA/DS is used in conjunction with Document Interchange Architecture (DIA) to provide electronic mail services. SNA/DS uses LU 6.2 for its program-to-program communications.

SNA/DS: *See* SNA/Distribution Services.

SNA/Management Services: IBM's architected set of network management services that is used for managing systems in an SNA network. NetView is IBM's major host-based product that supports SNA/Management Services.

SNA/MS: *See* SNA Management Services.

SNA Network: Multiple interconnected systems using SNA protocols between systems to provide support for end-to-end information exchange. Typically, an SNA network consists of one or more System/370 mainframes that act as central control points, multiple communications controllers that act as intermediate routing nodes, and many terminals, PCs, and multiuser systems that support end users of the network.

SQL: *See* Structured Query Language.

SQL/DS: *See* Structured Query Language/Data System.

Structured Query Language (SQL): A set of commands used to access relational databases. The SAA CPI Database Interface is based on SQL.

Structured Query Language/Data System (SQL/DS): The IBM SAA relational database product for VM.

Synchronous Data Link Control (SDLC): The primary IBM data link protocol used for wide-area network connections. SDLC protocols are used to manage information exchange across a single physical data link between two nodes. These data links may be switched lines, leased lines, T1 links, satellite links, or other communications facilities.

System Services Control Point (SSCP): A Network Addressable Unit (NAU) that serves as a network control point. SSCP functions are implemented in VTAM on System/370/390 mainframes. The SSCP is responsible for managing other network resources (e.g., PUs, LUs) under its control.

SystemView: IBM's SAA strategy for enterprise-wide information systems management.

System/36: An IBM multi-user, midrange applications-processing system. Supports a wide range of SNA communications including 3270 emulation and peer-to-peer communications using Logical Unit Type 6.2. The System/36 is being replaced by IBM's AS/400 system.

System/38: An IBM multi-user, midrange applications-processing system. Supports a wide range of SNA communications including 3270 emulation and peer-to-peer communications using Logical Unit Type 6.2. The System/38 is being replaced by IBM's AS/400 system.

System/88: A fault-tolerant midrange IBM system typically used where high availability is a requirement.

System/370: IBM's family of mainframe processors that are based on the System/370 architecture. Included in this family are 308X, 3090, 4300, and 9300 processors.

System/390: IBM's newest family of mainframe processors that are based on the System/390 architecture. Included in this family are ES/9000 series of processors.

System/370/390: A generic designation for any of IBM's mainframe processors including those which implement the System/370 architecture or the System/390 architecture.

Systems Application Architecture (SAA): IBM's umbrella architecture that consists of components used to bring greater consistency to IBM mainframe, midrange, and workstation products. SAA covers user interface, programming languages and services, and communications issues.

Systems Network Architecture (SNA): IBM's primary architecture describing how communications and networking are supported between interconnected IBM systems. SNA defines a set of logical components, each with a particular role in the network. It describes sets of protocols used for communications between logical components. SNA also defines a set of layers that describe different levels of functionality needed to support end-user–to–end-user communications across a network.

Text Subset: An SAA CUA model that provides a text-based subset of the user interface defined by the CUA Graphical Model. The Text Subset includes support for action bars, pull-down windows, and pop-up menus. It can be used with nonprogrammable terminals to approximate the windows-based Graphical Model interface supported on programmable workstations.

3174 Enterprise Controller: A communications processor used to attach display stations, printers, and PCs to IBM mainframes. These devices are attached to the 3174 controller via coaxial cables or Token-Ring LANs.

3270: A family of IBM products which includes cluster controllers and devices like display stations and printers which are attached to IBM mainframes via cluster controllers.

3270 Data Stream: A data stream containing end-user data and control codes that are sent between application programs and 3270 display stations and printers, or systems providing 3270 emulation.

3720 Communications Controller: An intelligent communications processor which, when running IBM's Network Control Program (NCP), functions as an SNA Communications Controller Node (Type 4 Node).

3725 Communications Controller: An intelligent communications processor which, when running IBM's Network Control Program (NCP), functions as an SNA Communications Controller Node (Type 4 Node).

3745 Communications Controller: An intelligent communications processor which, when running IBM's Network Control Program (NCP), functions as an SNA Communications Controller Node (Type 4 Node).

Time Sharing Option (TSO)/Extended: A System/370-based MVS subsystem that allows multiple terminal users to use System/370 facilities and services concurrently (time share the use of these facilities) in an interactive manner. TSO is bundled with the MVS operating system.

Token-Ring: IBM's strategic local area network (LAN) based on a token-passing scheme that is compatible with the IEEE 802.2 and 802.5 Token-Ring standards. A Token-Ring LAN interface is one of the data link types supported in SNA networks.

Transaction Program (TP): An IBM-supplied or user-written application program that directly interfaces to a Type 6.2 LU via the LU 6.2 application programming interface (API) provided by the LU. A logical connection, called a conversation, must be set up between the Transaction Programs (TPs) before any communication can take place. The conversation and exchange of information between the TPs is carried out over an underlying SNA LU 6.2 session managed by the pair of LUs supporting the TPs. Examples of IBM-supplied TPs are DIA, SNA/DS, and DDM.

TSO/E: *See* Time Sharing Option/Extended.

Type 2.0 Node: An SNA Peripheral Node that is capable of only hierarchical connections with a host system. Examples of Type 2.0 Node products are 3270 cluster controllers and other systems emulating 3270 operation.

Type 2.1 Node: An SNA Peripheral Node that supports both hierarchical connections to Host Nodes as well as peer-to-peer connections to other Type 2.1 Nodes with no host involvement. Examples of Type 2.1 Nodes are AS/400s, System/36s, System/38s, and PCs. APPC software in these systems supports the Type 2.1 Node facilities.

Type 4 Node: An SNA Communications Controller Node that serves as an intermediate routing node in an SNA network. Type 4 Node functions are implemented by Network Control Program (NCP) software running in a 37XX Communications Controller. The primary functions of a Type 4 Node are network routing and managing physical data links connected to the node.

Type 5 Node: An SNA Host Node characterized by the fact that it includes a System Services Control Point (SSCP). A Type 5 Host Node is typically a System/370 or System/390 mainframe running VTAM. It supports application program end users and provides network management services.

UNIX: An operating system originally developed by AT&T that is widely supported on different hardware platforms. IBM's implementation of UNIX is called AIX.

User: *See* End User.

Verbs: The LU functions available to Transaction Programs (TPs) that are formally architected as part of the LU 6.2 Protocol Boundary.

Virtual Machine (VM): One of IBM's primary System/370/390 operating systems. VM presents a virtual machine interface to users so that to each user it appears that the entire machine is dedicated to their use.

Virtual Storage Extended (VSE): One of IBM's primary System/370/390 operating systems. VSE is used primarily on such low-end System/370 systems as the 4300 and 9370. Many of the same applications are available under MVS memory and system resources, making it more desirable for smaller installations.

Virtual Telecommunications Access Method (VTAM): The SNA software that runs in the System/370/390 mainframes and implements the functions of a Type 5 SNA Host Node. Commonly referred to as VTAM, this software implements the functions of an SSCP, provides the interface to network operators, and provides SNA support for host-based application programs.

VM: *See* Virtual Machine.

VSE: *See* Virtual Storage Extended.

VS FORTRAN: The IBM SAA FORTRAN compiler for MVS and VM.

VTAM: *See* Virtual Telecommunications Access Method.

Workplace: An SAA CUA user interface model that is an extension to the Graphical Model. The Workplace Model includes standard icons representing common items found in the workplace (e.g., telephone, printer, in and out baskets, etc.). The Workplace Model supports integration of applications through direct icon manipulation. This model is designed to work on intelligent graphical workstations.

XA: *See* Extended Architecture.

X.25: A CCITT standard that defines the interface between Data Terminal Equipment (DTE) and Data Circuit Terminating Equipment (DCE) using packet-switched protocols. This is the interface between a user system and a network, which is typically an X.25-based packet-switched network. The X.25 standard defines three interface levels—Physical, Data Link, and Packet.

X.400: A CCITT message-handling standard that defines electronic mail services similar to many of the services provided by the IBM DIA and SNA/DS architectures.

INDEX